The Birth of the Academic Article

The Birth of the Academic Article

Le Journal des Sçavans and the *Philosophical Transactions*, 1665–1700

David Banks

SHEFFIELD UK BRISTOL CT

Published by Equinox Publishing Ltd
UK: Office 415, The Workstation, 15 Paternoster Row, Sheffield, South Yorkshire, S1 2BX
USA: ISD, 70 Enterprise Drive, Bristol, CT 06010

www.equinoxpub.com

First published 2017. First printing in paperback 2019

British Library Cataloguing-in-Publication Data
A catalogue record for this book is available from the British Library.
ISBN 978-1-78179-232-2 (hardback)
ISBN 978-1-78179-830-0 (paperback)
ISBN 978-1-78179-379-4 (eBook)

Library of Congress Cataloging-in-Publication Data
Names: Banks, David, 1943– author.
Title: The Birth of the Academic Article : *Le Journal des Sçavans* and the *Philosophical Transactions*, 1665–1700 / David Banks.
Description: Sheffield, UK; Bristol, CT : Equinox Publishing Ltd, [2016] |
Includes bibliographical references and index.
Identifiers: LCCN 2015031046 | ISBN 9781781792322 (hb)
Subjects: LCSH: Systemic grammar–History. | Functionalism (Linguistics)–History. | Academic writing–History–16th century. | Academic writing–History–17th century. | Scholarly periodicals–France–History–16th century. | Scholarly periodicals–France–History–17th century. | Scholarly periodicals–England–History–16th century. | Scholarly periodicals–England–History–17th century. | France–Intellectual life–History. | England–Intellectual life–History. |
Philosophical Transactions of the Royal Society of London. Series A, Mathematical and physical sciences. | *Journal des sçavans* (Paris, France)
Classification: LCC P149 .B36 2016 | DDC 415–dc23
LC record available at http://lccn.loc.gov/2015031046

Typeset by S.J.I. Services, New Delhi

Contents

1 Getting things started: by way of introduction

When I first stumbled on the historical fact (I am tempted to say coincidence) that the first two academic periodicals appeared within two months of each other in 1665, the first in Paris, the second in London, I found this intriguing and fascinating, all the more so since the two journals concerned, the *Journal des Sçavans* and the *Philosophical Transactions*, both still exist in some form and have thus been in existence, with only very minor interruptions, for three and a half centuries. Of course, it probably wasn't so much of a coincidence as all that, since general newspapers had been around for some time, so it was on the cards that periodical publications of a more specialized type should come into being; but the fact is fascinating nonetheless since the historical and social situations of the two countries are in stark contrast. Since texts are an emanation of the society within which they are produced, the very different situations in the two countries have produced quite different types of documents. This provides a demonstration of the importance of context in the creation of text and a brilliant case study of the interplay between context and text.

Science, and hence scientific writing, is at the heart of contemporary life. Daily life now depends on technical achievements, based ultimately on scientific research; it is hard to think of a single activity in contemporary life which does not depend to some extent on the application of scientific research. Thus, the writing up of this research is fundamental, but because of that very fact, it has become more and more specialized over the years. Hence, the scientific research article has become one of the most widely studied types of text, not only because of its intrinsic interest, but also because of the more prosaic fact that, since English has become the lingua franca of the international scientific community, non-anglophone scientists are faced with the problem of mastering a specialized variety of a second language, in order to get their work published.

For many years I was interested in this kind of study into the linguistic features of contemporary scientific language. After a time, however, I gradually became interested in the question of how scientific language comes to be the way it is. Just as in general linguistics diachronic study can shed light on contemporary linguistic conundrums, so, surely, a historical study of scientific text should give us a better understanding of scientific text as it is today. This interest culminated in my book, *The Development of Scientific Writing* (Banks 2008a), which paints a broad picture of scientific writing from Chaucer to the end of the twentieth century. The present book focuses on a short period, and on a single type of text. The type of text, probably the most prestigious, is that of the academic journal article and the period covered is from 1665 to 1695. Our study starts in 1665 because, as pointed out above, that is the date of the very first scientific periodicals; our period ends in 1700 because the previous year, in 1699, the French Académie Royale des Sciences decided to distribute its publications on a much wider basis than had been the case before. This constituted a radical change in the situation on the ground, and thus the end of the century provides a suitable cut-off point.

I shall begin by giving the linguistic background, explaining the general approach which I shall adopt, and some of the linguistic phenomena that I intend to analyse, which may be less familiar to some readers. This will be followed by the historical background, covering the general history of France and England in the seventeenth century, with points relating to the *Journal des Sçavans* and the *Philosophical Transactions* in more detail. I shall then describe the selection of texts which I have made from the issues for the period covered, with information about the genres to be found and the subjects covered. The main part of the book gives the results of analyses of four major linguistic phenomena: first, thematic structure, which shows what the authors consider to be their starting point, and, from that point of view, their centre of interest, and how they use that in the construction of their text; second, process types, which show what types of actions, events and states the authors primarily deal with; third, modality, which shows how the authors enter into their texts, modulating and qualifying them; and finally, nominalization of processes, which shows how the authors manipulate their text by reifying certain types of process.

All of the linguistic phenomena discussed will be extensively illustrated with examples from the corpus. The book also contains quite a lot of numbers. However, I make no claims to being a statistician, and these are simply the numbers as I found them. No statistical tests have been applied. Hence, I prefer to think of these as quantified results rather than statistics properly so-called.

The analyses I have carried out have all been done by hand. There are several reasons for this. The texts are available on the Internet, but only in image form, so they are not, in their present form, amenable to digital treatment by computer. In addition, the linguistic phenomena I am considering cannot, in the main, be recognized automatically; they require human judgement, and, to the best of my knowledge, no programs (yet) exist to carry out these types of analysis. In the course of working, certain aspects of the text emerge, and it is much easier to modify a method of analysis to take account of this when working manually than in the case of automatic analysis, which would require modification of a computer program. This provides an additional justification for manual analysis.

2 Linguistic background

Language is one of the most intriguing aspects of the human condition. It is inherent in human existence and it would be impossible to conceive of human existence without it. It is so inherent that, without thinking about it, we tend to take it for granted, and have the impression that we understand it. But when we look in more detail at the way it functions it becomes fascinatingly elusive. Part of this elusiveness is due to the fact that it is in constant evolution. It is easy to see this when we read texts that were written some time ago. Even texts that were created only a few decades ago are written in a way that no longer corresponds to how we write today. Seeing the way language has changed gives us important insights into the development of human civilization. As language develops, it does not do so in a simple uniform fashion: there are periods when it is fairly stable and change is slow and steady, but at other times it undergoes short bursts of sudden acceleration that alter language patterns rapidly and sometimes radically. Moreover, language change may take place differently in different domains, so that rapid change in, say, legal language may not necessarily be matched in other domains.

The type of language that we will study in this book is academic, that is, the sort of language that intellectuals and savants use in communicating with each other. We are interested in the late seventeenth century, because it was at this point in history that academic writing, which had previously been mainly in Latin, began to be produced in the vernacular languages of western Europe. Until the middle of the seventeenth century, little academic work had been written in languages other than Latin. By the end of the century, the use of Latin was on the way out: Gross *et al.* describe the decline of Latin in the late seventeenth century as 'precipitous' (2002: 33). This was then the period when the basic ground rules of academic writing in the vernacular were laid down, and although the style has developed considerably in the intervening centuries, the style of contemporary academic writing can be traced back to its beginnings in the second half of the seventeenth century.

The beginning of the academic article can be dated quite precisely, for the first two academic periodicals both appeared in 1665; the *Journal des Sçavans* on 5 January in Paris, and the *Philosophical Transactions* on 6 March in London. Curiously, these two periodicals both still exist and have been published continuously, with only very minor interruptions, ever since. They thus provide an amazing store of textual information, witnessing to the evolution of academic writing over a period of three and a half centuries. In this book I intend to concentrate on that early period from 1665 to the end of the century during which the basis was established from which academic style was to develop.

Looking at specialized text from a historical point of view is a fairly recent development in linguistics. Moreover, until very recently, such works were mainly of a sociolinguistic orientation and dealt mainly with scientific English. The book usually considered as the groundbreaking work in this field is Bazerman (1988). This, like some of the other early works in this field, was developed from an earlier series of articles. One of the chapters deals with the *Philosophical Transactions* in the period 1665 to 1800, and another with the controversy round Newton's theory of light. The main thrust of the book is on the relationship between the texts and the social situations which produced them. There had been a few earlier books on the development of scientific language, but these tended to treat scientific language as purely a question of vocabulary (e.g. Savory 1953). Several works can be seen as being in the wake of Bazerman (1988). Gross (1996), the first edition of which appeared in 1990, is based, like Bazerman, on earlier articles. It has chapters on Newton and on Darwin, and one wide-ranging chapter which covers Bacon, Sprat, Newton and Leibniz. But the interest of the author is in the rhetoric of the texts, rather different to the linguistic analytical approach, which I wish to use and which deals with the detail of the language as encoded. Atkinson (1999) deals with the *Philosophical Transactions* over the extensive period of 1675 to 1975. He too treats the texts from a sociological and rhetorical point of view. Valle (1999) is fairly similar, in that it deals with the *Philosophical Transactions* for the period 1665 to 1966, but only with texts in the life sciences, and, once again, basically from a sociolinguistic viewpoint. The book of this type which is perhaps closest to my own preoccupations is Gross *et al.* (2002). This covers a wide period from the seventeenth to the twentieth century, it is partly rhetorical but does discuss some linguistic features, and it includes languages other than English. The languages for the seventeenth century are English and French; German is added for the eighteenth and nineteenth centuries, but the authors revert to English only for the twentieth century, presumably because of the increasing dominance of English in the scientific field in the course of that century. However, although consideration is given to texts in French and German, quotations from these languages are given in English translation only, showing that the specific way in which the linguistic features are encoded and function is not of prime interest to them. More recently, some collections of articles devoted to specific specialized fields have been published, notably Taavitsainen and Pahta (2011), and Moskowich and Crespo (2012). The first of these deals with medical texts in the sixteenth to eighteenth centuries, and the second with texts in the field of astronomy from 1700 to 1900. Both of these books are devoted exclusively to English texts.

A suitable framework

It is not possible to talk about language without having some sort of standpoint. That means having a theory. I feel that all linguistic theories fall into three broad groups. There are those that are formalist, that is, which treat language as if it were no more than its form, a sort of linguistic algebra, with independent existence. Probably the best known of this type of approach is generative grammar and its various offshoots derived from the work of Chomsky (e.g. Chomsky 1957, 1965). There are those which are cognitive in intent, in that they attempt to discern the mental processes which are at play in communication. Such approaches have not only been particularly popular in the United States, but have also achieved a great deal of success in France, based on the work of Culioli (1990, 1999a, 1999b) and Adamczewski (Adamczewski, 1996, 2002; Adamczewski and Delmas 1982). The third type are those that attempt to discover how language functions internally, and how it functions externally in society. It is this type of approach which is best adapted to my purposes. There have been numerous attempts to develop theories of this type, including Martinet in France (e.g. Martinet 1985), Dik in Holland, and van Valin in the United States (e.g. van Valin 2001). Butler has studied and compared several of these approaches (Butler 2003a, 2003b). However, the version of functionalism which suits my purposes best is that based on the work of Michael Halliday and commonly known as Systemic Functional Linguistics (see, e.g. Halliday 1978, 2014; Halliday and Matthiessen 1999; Banks 2005). This approach insists on the fact that language is produced in and through society, and thus underlines the importance of context in the production and interpretation of communication.

This is not the place to give a full outline of systemic functional theory, but it does seem appropriate to give a brief account of those elements of the theory which I shall be using in the analytical sections of this book for those readers who may be less familiar with them. There are three in particular which I feel require some comment: they are thematic structure, process types, and grammatical metaphor.

Thematic structure

The systemic functional account of language provides for three types of meaning at the level of the clause. These types of meanings, called metafunctions, are: ideational, that part of meaning relating to actions, events and states in the external world and the participants in and circumstances of them; interpersonal, that part of meaning concerning the relationship between the speaker and his addressees, and between the speaker and his message; and textual, that part of meaning relating to the way the message is structured.

Thematic structure fits into the textual metafunction. Each clause has a theme and a rheme. The theme is the speaker's starting point, and in both English and French is placed in initial position. The remainder of the clause constitutes the rheme. These ideas derive from ideas developed within the Prague School (Firbas 1992), but differ in distinguishing thematic structure from information structure, which provides for a given element and a new or focalized (Banks 2005) element. In the Prague School approach, thematic structure and information structure are conflated.

The theme has one obligatory element, the topical theme, which functions as a major component of the clause, that is, as subject, predicator, complement or circumstantial adjunct. Thus, in the following quotation, the subject, *The Mines of Mercury in Friuli, a Territory belonging to the Venetians*, functions as topical theme.[1]

> **The Mines of *Mercury* in *Friuli*, a Territory belonging to the *Venetians*,** are about a days Journey and a half distant from *Goritia* Northwards, at a place call'd *Idria*, scituated in a Valley of the *Julian Alps*. (*Philosophical Transactions*, 3 April 1665)

1 In all examples and quotations the original spelling and typography have been preserved as far as possible, with the exception of 'long s', which has been replaced by a modern 's'.
The relevant parts of examples are printed in bold. Where appropriate, different clauses are printed on separate lines.

In the following, the circumstantial adjunct, *At Derby (which differs from London in Longitude 5. min.)*, functions as topical theme.

> **At Derby (which differs from London in Longitude 5. min.)** Mr. *Flamstead* observ'd the beginning of the entrance of the True Shadow B. 5. & 19′. (*Philosophical Transactions*, 22 February 1675)

In the following, the subject, the pronoun *Il*, functions as topical theme.

> **Il** auoit encore dessein de mettre à la fin vn tres ample Vocabulaire, pour expliquer tous les mots obscurs qui se trouuent dans ces regles. (*Journal des Sçavans*, 9 mars 1665)
> [He still had the intention of placing an extensive vocabulary at the end to explain all the obscure words found in these rules.][2]

In the following, the circumstantial adjunct, *Dans la 2^e^*, functions as topical theme.

> **Dans la 2^e^**, il traite amplement de la guerre de Candie, dont il tire les particularitez de l'Histoire de Nani. (*Journal des Sçavans*, 5 mars 1685)
> [In the second, he deals at length with the Candian war, from which derives the specific characteristics of the history of Nani.]

The topical theme may be preceded by one or more optional themes. These are interpersonal themes or textual themes. The former indicate the speaker's relationship with the clause; the latter link the clause to the surrounding discourse. The following are examples of interpersonal theme.

> **Doubtless**, as Old Sea-men have their prognosticks of Storms at Sea, so may the like be had on Land, to prepare us to secure our Houses and Lives. (*Philosophical Transactions*, 26 July 1675)

> **Peut-estre** qu'ils seront plus retenus en France quand ils sçauront que la Jurisprudence du Royaume ne leur est pas plus favorable que la disposition du Droit Canonique. (*Journal des Sçavans*, 20 juin 1695)
> [Perhaps they will be more restrained in France when they learn that the jurisprudence of the Kingdom is not more favourable to them than the disposition of canon law.]

The following are examples of textual theme.

> **And** men have made such works, as have produced changes great enough to be perceived. (*Philosophical Transactions*, 4 December 1665)

> **Ensuite** il passé aux végetaux ... (*Journal des Sçavans*, 6 mai 1675)
> [Then he goes on to plants ...]

---

2 All glosses of French examples and quotations are my own, and are intended as indications of meaning and structure, and not as polished translations.

One of the most important aspects of thematic structure is the role it plays in the argument structure of a text. This is known as thematic progression (Halliday 1988, 1998; Banks 2008a, 2008b). Where a theme is derived from a previous rheme, this is termed linear progression; where a theme is derived from a previous theme, this is termed constant progression. The following are examples of linear progression.

> We preserve our Fish from putrefaction by **burying them in the Snow**. **Bodies frozen** do swell, and are changed in taste and colour. (*Philosophical Transactions*, 22 February 1675)

> Ce liure est composé **en Dialogue**.
> **La scene** est aux Iacobins d'Auignon, où vn Aragonois entrant vn iour de la Conception, querela vn Iacobin de ce qu'il ne chantoit pas les Vespres de cette Feste ... (*Journal des Sçavans*, 23 février 1665)
> [This book is written as a dialogue.
> The scene takes place at the Jacobins of Avignon, where an Aragonais, arriving on the feast of the Conception, argues with a Jacobin because he was not singing the Vespers of the feastday ...]

In the first of these examples, the theme, *Bodies frozen*, follows on from the previous clause where fish are said to be buried in snow; in the second, the scene is that of the dialogue which constitutes the book.

The following are examples of constant progression.

> **I** opened the *Cornu* towards the end as at L, and saw there likewise a good quantity of the *Semen*, which was very lively.
> **I** opened the *Cornu* on the right side, and found a like number of the living animals. (*Philosophical Transactions*, 22 August 1685)

> **Mademoiselle Le Fevre** a reparé heureusement ces deux defaults:
> **elle** y a ajoûté quelques fragments qui avoient esté ômis dans toutes les autres editions ... (*Journal des Sçavans*, 11 mars 1675)
> [Fortunately, Mademoiselle Le Fevre has corrected these two errors:
> she has added some fragments that had been omitted in all the other editions ...]

The first of these has the simplest form of constant progression, where the theme of the first clause, in this case the first person pronoun *I*, is repeated as the theme of the second clause. In the second example, the theme of the second clause, *elle*, refers back to the theme of the first clause, *Mademoiselle Le Fevre*.

Process types

The ideational component of the systemic model concerns the representation of the external world in terms of processes, participants and circumstances. Processes are the actions, events and states which take place in the external world, and which are most usually encoded in verbal form. I shall use a system which has five different process types: material, mental, relational, verbal and existential.

Material processes are actions and events of a physical nature.

> This I **put** into a Glass pipe, and **wrapt** it up in soft leather, because the nights were something cold. (*Philosophical Transactions*, 22 August 1685)

> ... lors que le feu y **reduisit** en cendres dans le siècle dernier cent quarante mille maisons ... (*Journal des Sçavans*, 15 janvier 1685)
> [... when, in the last century, fire reduced forty thousand houses to ashes ...]

Mental processes are events of a cerebral nature. It is possible to distinguish three subtypes, cognitive, perception, and affective. Cognitive mental processes are mental events of the thinking type.

> Of all which **'tis hoped**, that shortly a fuller and more particular accompt will be given. (*Philosophical Transactions*, 4 December 1665)

> Tout le monde **connoist** assez le merite de la famille dont M. Arnaud d'Andilly avoit l'avantage d'estre sorty. (*Journal des Sçavans*, 9 septembre 1675)
> [Everyone knows fairly well the merits of the family from which M. Arnaud d'Andilly comes.]

Perception mental processes are processes involving the senses. In our documents, these are mainly processes of seeing, though the other senses, such as hearing, do occasionally occur.

> I never **observed**, that the smell of *Tobacco*, or smels that are rank, did any waies annoy the worm. (*Philosophical Transactions*, 3 April 1665)

> On en **voit** des exemples parmi les vegetaux, particuliérement dans les arbres les plus fertiles chargez des plus beaux fruits, qui produisent des avortons, lesquels restent dans leur petitesse sans se corrompre. (*Journal des Sçavans*, 20 juin 1695)
> [One can see examples among the plants, notably the most fertile trees, loaded with the most beautiful fruit, which produce stunted specimens, which remain tiny but do not rot.]

Affective mental processes are expressions of liking and disliking.

Next Morning I went from one Ship to another, till at length it **pleased** God that I met with my Wife and two of my negroes. (*Philosophical Transactions*, March–April 1694)

... & il rapport une action bien plus Chrestienne que politique ; qui est qu'ayant à livrer ou à soutenir un combat dans lequel il y alloit de la vie & de la Couronne, il **aima** mieux s'exposer à perdre comme il fit, l'une & l'autre, que de se servir pour augmenter ses troupes, d'un plus grand nombre de soldats qui avoitent refusé de se faire Chrestiens. (*Journal des Sçavans*, 16 avril 1685)
[... and he recounts an action which is more Christian than political, which is that when he had to take part in or support a combat where he risked his life and the crown, he preferred to risk losing both, as he did, rather then use the occasion to increase his troops with a large number of soldiers who had refused to become Christians.]

Relational processes express a link between two items or between an item and one of its properties. These too can be divided into three subtypes, attributive, identifying, and possessive. Attributive relational processes link an item with one of its properties.

We can hardly imagine, that at *Farnham*, and other places, where many hundreds of Acres of strong-sented *Hopps* **are** fully ripe, be given no peculiar indication besides odour in the Air ... (*Philosophical Transactions*, 26 July 1675)

Il veut que la violence en **soit** quelquefois si grande, que la seule cheûte d'une nuée **soit** capable de causer les plus grand vens, & d'exciter les plus furieuses tempestes ... (*Journal des Sçavans*, 11 mars 1675)
[He claims that the violence of it is so great that the falling of a cloud is by itself sufficient to produce the strongest winds and to arouse the most furious storms ...]

Identifying relational processes link two expressions which name the same item.

To joyn all these circumstances together, 'Tis notorious, that at least six years since (a good while before it was heard off, that any one did pretend to have so much as thought of it) the Learned and Ingenious Dr. *Christopher Wren* did propose in the *University* of *Oxford* (where he now **is** the worthy Savilian Professor of *Astronomy*, and where very many curious persons are ready to attest this relation) ... (*Philosophical Transactions*, 4 December 1665)

Mr. Barrow appuye son sentiment par des conjectures tres fortes; & sur ce principle que Pappus **est** l'inventeur de la mesure de cette derniere figure, il pretend que les Lunes d'Hippocrate de Chio ont au contraire donné occasion à la découverte de *l'Arbelon*. (*Journal des Sçavans*, 9 septembre 1675) [Mr. Barrow supports his belief with strong suppositions, and on the principle that Pappus is the inventor of the method of measuring this figure, he claims that the moons of Hippocrates of Chios were, on the contrary, the occasion of the discovery of the arbelon.]

Possessive relational processes include possession as such, and relationships that can be assimilated to it, such as inclusion, and to these are added spatial relationships.

But he proceeds to speak of the *Inclination*, which the *Mandril* **must have** upon the *Plain* of the *Ring*, when the *Ring* **should have** 10. or 12 Inches; and finds, that it would make but 6 or. 7. minutes of inclination, and that a Glass **would have** less *convexity*, and consequently, less difference from a Glass perfectly plain, than the 7. or 8. part of a Line. (*Philosophical Transactions*, 5 June 1665)

Il ne nous reste plus rien de ce qu'il a fait sur les fleuves, les vents, les poissons, les oiseaux &c. & de huit cent volumes, qu'on asseure qu'il a composez, nous **n'avons** plus que quelques hymnes, quelques epigrammes & quelques fragments. (*Journal des Sçavans*, 11 mars 1675)
[Nothing now remains of what he did on rivers, winds, fish, birds, etc., and of the eight hundred volumes he is said to have written, we now have only a few hymns, epigrams, and fragments.]

Verbal processes are processes of communication. This includes both spoken and written communication.

And long before that time, *viz. A* 1664 the 15*th*. of *March*, (witness the same *Journal*) Mr. *Boyle* **mention'd** to the *R. Society*, that Corals or Oyster shells pounded, and put into distilled Vinegar, might prove fit Substances or produce Air Wholsom for Inspiration. (*Philosophical Transactions*, 22 November 1675)

Nostre auteur **donne** au dernier le titre & la qualité de Saint & de Martyr; & il en **rapporte** une action bien plus Chrestienne que politique ... (*Journal des Sçavans*, 16 avril 1685)
[Our author gives to the last of them the title and quality of saint and martyr, and he reports an action which is Christian rather than political ...]

Existential processes simply state the existence of an entity.

Our people settled a Town at *Leguanea* side, and there **is** about 500 Graves already, and People every day a dying still. (*Philosophical Transactions*, March–April 1694)

> Pour les lettres il y en **a** desia **eu** deux editions : la premiere de Masson, qui est rempli d'vne infinite de fautes : & vne autre de Duchesne, qui est beaucoup meilleure ; mais dans laquelle on ne laisse pas de trouuer quelque chose à redire. (*Journal des Sçavans*, 12 janvier 1665)
> [For the letters, there have already been two editions: the first by Masson, which is full of innumerable errors, and another by Duchesne, which is much better, but in which we continue to find things to criticize.]

Grammatical metaphor

Grammatical metaphor is the use of a non-congruent grammatical form (Halliday 2014; Ravelli 1988; Taverniers 2003; Banks 2005). The form of grammatical metaphor which has received most comment, the one which will be analysed here, is that of nominalized processes. Processes are congruently encoded as verbs; this is their non-metaphorical form. Where they are encoded in some other grammatical form, such as nouns (or adjectives, etc.), this constitutes a grammatical metaphor.

The difference between traditional or semantic metaphor and grammatical metaphor lies in the fact that in the former the grammatical form is the same (noun for noun, verb for verb, etc.), but the meaning is different (*the rosy fingers of the dawn* doesn't literally mean the same thing as *the rays of the sun at sunrise*), whereas in the latter the grammatical form is different but the meaning is the same (apart from that which can be directly attributed to the change of form itself).

Using grammatical metaphor has both grammatical and semantic effects. Grammatically, the use of a nominalized process means that it is no longer necessary to express the putative subject or, if the process is bivalent, the object, although these may be made available by other grammatical means. The fact that the metaphor is nominal in form means that it can itself be used with any nominal function, subject, object, or prepositional completive. This also means that the nominalized process can be modified and qualified (or postmodified). From a more semantic point of view, the fact that the metaphor is now nominal means that it takes on some of the qualities of an entity. Thus it is presented as having a certain permanence and objectivity; it is presented as an incontrovertible reality. In scientific language nominalized processes can be used as a way of repackaging previous non-metaphorical material (Halliday 1988, 1998). In some other types of text, such as political tracts, it can be used as a way of presenting material as being absolute fact, and thus stifling possible argument (Banks 2013b).

> See Mr. *Boyles* **Experiments** at the end of his *Effluviums*, and *Hist. R.S. p*.228; and since Gold it self is by **mixture** volatilized in your *N*.87; and since our Old Philosophers do allow the Sun to give a potent **assistance** in the **generation** of all things that are generated. (*Philosophical Transactions*, 26 July 1675)

This short extract has four nominalized material processes: *Experiments*, with its subject expressed in the possessive modifier, *Mr. Boyles*; *mixture*, whose supposed subject is a very general 'anyone', and whose object is *Gold*; *assistance*, whose subject is *the Sun*, and whose object is *the generation*; and finally *generation* itself, with *all things that are generated* as its object.

> 2. Que pour croire les veritez de la Religion qui nous sont confirmées par le **témoignage** & l'autorité des Peres, il n'est pas necessaire qu'ils soient infaillibles ny qu'ils ayent toûjours esté exempts d'erreur. (*Journal des Sçavans*, 14 janvier 1675)
> [2. That in order to believe the truths of religion that have been confirmed by the testimony and authority of the Fathers, it is not necessary that they be infallible nor that they have always been free of error.]

In this example, *témoignage* is a nominalized form of the verbal process of witnessing. The putative subject of this process can be found in the qualifying group, *des Peres*.

Context

On a more general level, I feel that Systemic Functional Linguistics provides a suitable framework because I firmly believe that language is produced in and by a social situation, and cannot be fully understood without reference to that situation. This has been described by Halliday as a social semiotic (Halliday 1978). The context generates language, but the language produced is then part of the context, which is thus itself changed, so there is a constant process of generation and change between language and its context. This context has sometimes been termed register, and sometimes genre, with some authors distinguishing between the two (Halliday 1978; Martin 1992; Martin and Rose 2008; Eggins 1994; Thompson 2004). Register has usually been analysed in terms of field (the ongoing activity of which the language is a part), tenor (the relationship between the speaker and his addressees), and mode (the type of communication, usually written or spoken or some combination of these). However, for the purposes of this book it will not be necessary to make such distinctions and we will simply treat the context in a more general way.

Of course, Halliday was not the only thinker to produce such ideas in the second half of the twentieth century. For example, in 1969 Foucault described the task he had set himself as follows.

> Tâche qui consiste à ne pas – à ne plus – traiter les discours comme des ensembles de signes (d'éléments signifiants renvoyant à des contenus ou à des représentations) mais comme des pratiques qui forment systématiquement les objets dont ils parlent. (Foucault 1969: 66–67).
> [A task which consists in not – in no longer – treating discourse as a set of signs (of signifying elements referring to a content or representations) but as a practice which systematically forms the objects about which it speaks.]

However, where with thinkers like Foucault this remained a philosophical viewpoint, Systemic Functional Linguistics developed a framework for analysis. It is this framework which I shall use as a basis for my analyses.

3 Historical background

The year 1665 is a key one in the history of academic writing. On 5 January of that year the first issue of the *Journal des Sçavans* appeared in Paris. It thus has the distinction of being the first-ever academic periodical. Just two months later, on 3 March, the *Philosophical Transactions* appeared in London. For reasons which will later become clear, this publication can in some senses be considered the first scientific periodical. Both of these publications still exist, and have been considered major journals in the intervening centuries. Study of these two journals is obviously of great significance for the study of academic writing and its history, for they laid down the basis for the initial conventions and later development of the academic article. When I talk about study of the journals, I obviously mean study of the texts which were published in them. However, texts cannot be fully understood in isolation. Any text forms part of a context, and derives from the context which produces it and of which it subsequently becomes a part. The histories of France and England in the seventeenth century were diametrically different, and so they produced very differing political and social contexts. We will look in general at the histories of these two countries, and then in detail at the ways in which the two journals came to be founded and how they subsequently developed. Moreover, the history of the *Journal de Sçavans* is closely linked to that of the Académie Royale des Sciences, and that of the *Philosophical Transactions* to that of the Royal Society of London. This also will need to be considered.

France in the seventeenth century

The beginning of the seventeenth century saw Henri IV on the throne of France. He had come to the throne in 1589, in a disturbed period following civil wars between Protestant and Catholic factions. By force of character and an autocratic rule, Henri IV was able to reunite the country and establish himself as a popular ruler. Nevertheless religious disputes continued throughout his reign, and it was this that led ultimately to his assassination by a Catholic fanatic in 1610. He was succeeded by his nine-year-old son, who became Louis XIII. His mother, Marie de Médicis, was named Regent. Louis XIII was married at the age of fourteen to Anne of Austria, and two years later, in 1617, he took over the reins of power by force. However, a poor choice of counsellors, first by Marie de Médicis as Regent, and subsequently by Louis XIII himself, meant that the country was poorly governed, until in 1624 Cardinal Richelieu was appointed as counsellor. Under Richelieu, the Protestant opposition was finally vanquished, and numerous plots were put down; gradually an autocratic government was established, under the centralized authority of the monarch. In 1638, after twenty-three years of childless marriage, Anne of Austria gave birth to a son. By the time Louis XIII died in 1643, the year after Richelieu himself, France had a stable, centralized regime.

Thus, in 1643 Louis XIV came to the throne. He was only five years old at the time, and so his reign, like his father's, began with a period of regency by his mother, Anne of Austria, aided by Cardinal Mazarin, who had succeeded Richelieu. This was the beginning of the longest reign in French history: Louis XIV reigned until his death in 1715. France was virtually governed by Mazarin from the accession of Louis XIV, until Mazarin's own death in 1661, at which point the king took over sole control of the affairs of state. His education had given him a deep conviction of the Divine Right of Kings. His notion of his kingly role gave him a semi-divine status; his will and his decisions were absolute, and could not be contradicted, or even discussed. Parliament was excluded from the decision-making system, and he governed with a small group of ministers of his own choosing. The most important of these was Jean-Baptiste Colbert (Gignoux 1941). Louis XIII had bequeathed to his son, Louis XIV, a relatively stable and centralized country, but under him this was reinforced and concentrated. His belief in his own divine mission meant that he had to prove himself the greatest monarch of the age, and this manifested itself in making France the economic and cultural centre of Europe, as an expression of the glory of its monarch. France did indeed prosper under the governance of Colbert, and it experienced a period of stability under a highly centralized and autocratic government, while becoming the most powerful state in Europe and its financial and cultural centre. It was to maintain this position well into the eighteenth century. Thus seventeenth-century France is characterized by increasing stability, and an increasingly centralized state power, which are both well established by the 1660s, and would only be reinforced in the following decades.

England in the seventeenth century

The history of England in the seventeenth century could hardly be more different from that of France (Hill 1969). In 1603, Elizabeth I died. The 'Virgin Queen' had, by definition, no direct descendants, and the next in line for the throne was James VI of Scotland, the son of Elizabeth's stepsister, Mary Queen of Scots. He thus became, also, James I of England. James was a Protestant, and religious disputes bedevilled his reign. The best-known of these events was the Gunpowder Plot in 1605, the unsuccessful attempt to blow up Parliament by a group of Catholic conspirators who included Guy Fawkes. This is still celebrated in England on 5 November on Bonfire Night, with bonfires, fireworks, and the burning of an effigy of Guy Fawkes. Originally an anti-Catholic celebration, it has over the years lost all religious connotations. James I also had difficulties with Parliament, which was determined to preserve its rights. He himself believed in the Divine Right of Kings, but this was at odds with the conviction of the parliamentarians, who thought they had a right to curb royal actions. When James died in 1625, he was succeeded by his son, who became Charles I. Like his father he was involved in constant disputes with Parliament. Most of these concerned either religion or finance. Charles had Catholic sympathies. His queen was Henrietta, a sister of Louis XIII of France (Dupuy 1994). She was a Catholic, and there were numerous Catholics at court. Parliament, on the other hand, was fiercely Protestant. In addition, Charles had to find sources of revenue, but Parliament frequently disagreed with the ways in which he wanted to raise taxes. Things went from bad to worse, including war with the Scots in 1638 and a rebellion in Ireland in 1641. This all came to a head in 1642, when civil war eventually broke out, with the royalist Cavaliers facing the anti-royalist Roundheads in a series of battles that was to last almost a decade. Charles was captured in 1646, and there were some attempts at negotiation, but in 1648 he escaped to the Isle of Wight, from where he organized an unsuccessful invasion via Scotland. He was recaptured, tried, and executed in 1649.

The monarchy and the House of Lords were abolished, but the anti-royalist camp was far from unified and squabbling continued between its many factions, particularly between Parliament and the army. The person who had come to the fore during the Civil War was Oliver Cromwell, and it was he who took control in the period which followed, known as the Interregnum. This situation was formalized in 1653, when Parliament named Cromwell Lord Protector. Although Parliament continued to exist, in the years that followed the regime resembled in many ways a military dictatorship. Puritan values and principles dominated a way of life that was imposed by force of law. So the abolition of the monarchy did not usher in a period of freedom; on the contrary, the Interregnum was no less repressive than the monarchy which had preceded it. Cromwell died in 1658 and, since the constitution which had been set up allowed him to appoint his successor, he named his son Richard to succeed him. However, Richard had none of his father's taste for power, and in 1659, less than a year after his father's death, he resigned. This left the way open for the restoration of the monarchy.

So it was that in 1660 Charles II, the son of Charles I, was invited back as king. However, the situation was no longer that left by his father eleven years earlier. The terms on which the Restoration of the monarchy was to be based were, in the words set down by Parliament, government by 'King, Lords and Commons'; while pre-Interregnum monarchs had always clung to the notion of their divine right, from the Restoration on this was no longer possible. From 1660 onwards there were three elements in the government equation.

The early years of the reign of Charles II were beset by natural catastrophes. In 1665 an outbreak of bubonic plague reached London, causing the death of 15 per cent of the population. This was followed, the next year, by the Great Fire of London. Although the initial fire, which started in a bakery, was fairly small, it spread rapidly because of the meteorological conditions, in particular the wind. The fire raged for several days, and by the time it finally died down, 80 per cent of the city had been destroyed, including 13,000 houses and 89 churches. However, it is possible that the Great Fire put paid to the last traces of the plague.

Although the balance of power had changed radically, one aspect of Charles's reign was similar to the pre-Civil War period; that was his constant disputes with Parliament, particularly on questions of a religious nature. He died in 1685, leaving no legitimate heir, and was succeeded by his brother James, who became James II. In his reign the religious disputes continued, and indeed intensified. Both Charles II and James II had wives who were Catholics, and Charles even made a deathbed claim to be a Catholic; James II was himself a Catholic. There were numerous Catholics at court, Catholics were appointed to high positions in the administrative and military spheres, and in general anti-Catholic laws were relaxed. In 1688, a group of exasperated, but influential, Anglicans invited William of Orange to come and take over the monarchy in England. James attempted to backtrack, but it was too late. Seeing his support dwindling, he fled to exile in France.

William of Orange was a grandson of Charles I, and his wife, Mary, was James II's daughter, so William was James's son-in-law. His arrival was known as the Glorious Revolution, and it was achieved without bloodshed. But the fact that William had been invited by Parliament was significant. The power of Parliament was reinforced and it decided to name William and Mary as joint sovereigns. The terms by which this was done established the first constitutional monarchy. Mary died in 1694, and William continued to reign, as William III, until his death in 1702.

Thus it can be seen that the histories of France and England in the seventeenth century present a stark contrast. France, after some early turbulence particularly during the Wars of Religion, became relatively stable, and under Louis XIV established a highly centralized and powerful state, where the Divine Right of Kings was the undisputed political theory. England, on the other hand, went through one of the most turbulent periods in her history, with revolution, the Civil War, the execution of Charles I, the repression during the Interregnum under Cromwell, the Restoration of the monarchy, and the Glorious Revolution which placed William and Mary on the throne. In the course of the century, England moved from the Divine Right of Kings to a constitutional monarchy, thus totally changing the status of the monarchy and its relationship with Parliament (Clark 1956; Kishlansky 1996).

The *Journal des Sçavans*

The *Journal des Sçavans* first appeared in 1665, and its first issue is dated 5 January. Thus it was created when Louis XIV had been on the throne for twenty-two years, and the centralized state of the Sun King was well established. France was powerful, stable, and in many ways the cultural centre of Europe. There have been a number of histories of the *Journal des Sçavans*, the first being that by Denis François Camusat, published in 1734 (reprinted 2011). To this can be added those of Cocheris in 1860 and Morgan in 1928, as well as a number of shorter works, such as Daremberg (1859), Paris (1903), Longnon (1965) and Birn (1965), and the more recent work of Vittu (2001, 2002a, 2002b, 2005).

The *Journal des Sçavans* was founded by Denis de Sallo. He was born in 1626 in Paris, but his family originally came from the Poitou region. He was the eldest of five sons of Jacques de Sallo, who was a counsellor in the Grande Chambre du Parlement in Paris. He studied law, and in 1652 became himself a counsellor in the Parlement. In 1665 he married Gabrielle Ménardeau, and they had one son and four daughters, all of whom became nuns. He died in Paris in 1669, at the relatively early age, even for those days, of forty-four.

The notion of a periodical was not totally new. Newspapers of some sort had been in existence for over forty years. In France, probably the most famous, though not actually the first, of these was the *Gazette de France*, founded by Théophraste Renaudot in 1631. It was in about 1663 that Colbert, Louis XIV's first minister, had the idea of forming a small group of intellectuals who would advise him and provide information on the arts, literature, and science. This group came to be known as the '*petite académie*'. Colbert's objective, in this as in many of his other initiatives, was state control.

> ... les lettres et les sciences ne sont, aux yeux de Colbert, qu'un domaine de plus où il importe que le Roi affirme comme ailleurs la splendeur et l'authorité de l'Etat. (Gignoux 1941: 157)
> [... in the eyes of Colbert, literature and the sciences were just another domain where it was essential that the King assert the splendor and authority of the State.]

There had even been a previous plan to produce a journal of the type which Denis de Sallo would eventually bring out. This project had been elaborated by Eudes de Mézeray, who, in 1663, had gone as far as obtaining a royal licence, necessary for any publication in those days of state control, for a journal to be entitled the *Journal Littéraire Générale*. However, this project was never carried through. De Sallo had begun to attend the *petite académie*, and at the instigation of Colbert, he decided to take up the idea that had been hatched by Mézeray.

The first issue of 5 January was 12 pages long, in quarto (a little smaller than contemporary A4), and the intention was that it should appear weekly. The notice to the reader begins with the following description of the project:

> Le dessein de ce Journal estant de faire sçavoir ce qui se passe de nouveau dans la Republique des lettres, il sera composé,
>
> Premièrement d'vn Catalogue exact des principaux liures qui s'imprimeront dans l'Europe. Et on ne se contentera pas de donner les simples titres, comme ont fait iusques à présent la pluspart des Bibliographes : mais de plus on dira dequoy ils traitent, & à quoy ils peuuent estre vtiles.
>
> Secondement, quand il viendra à mourir quelque personne celebre par sa doctrine & par ces ouvrages, on en fera l'Eloge, & on donnera vn Catalogue de ce qu'il aura mis au jour, avec les principales circonstances de sa vie.
>
> En troisiesme lieu on fera sçavoir les experiences de Physiques & de Chymie, qui peuuent servir à expliquer les effets de la Nature : les nouuelles descouuertes qui se font dans les Arts & dans les Sciences, comme les machines & les inventions vtiles ou curieuses que peuuent fournir les Mathematiques : les obseruations du Ciel, celles des Meteores, & ce que l'Anatomie pourra trouuer de nouueau dans les animaux.

> En quatriesme lieu, les principales decisions des Tribunaux Seculiers & Ecclesiastiques, les censures de Sorbonne & des autres Vniuersitez, tant de ce Royaume que des Pays estrangers.
>
> Enfin, on taschera de faire en sorte qu'il ne se passe rien dans l'Europe digne de la curiosité des Gens de lettres, qu'on ne puisse apprendre par ce Iournal.
>
> [Since the purpose of this Journal is to make known whatever new happens in the Republic of Letters, it will contain,
>
> Firstly, an exact catalogue of the main books which are published in Europe. It will not simply give a list of titles, as most bibliographers have done so far, but it will also say what subjects they deal with and why they might be useful.
>
> Secondly, when someone who is famous for his teaching or his books dies, we will give his obituary and a list of what he has discovered, with the main events of his life.
>
> Thirdly, we will make known the experiments in physics and chemistry which can be used to explain natural phenomena; new discoveries that are made in the arts and sciences, like useful or curious machines and inventions that mathematics can provide; celestial observations, those of meteors; and whatever anatomy can discover that is new in animals.
>
> Fourthly, the main decisions of secular and ecclesiastical courts, the decisions of the Sorbonne and other universities, in this kingdom and abroad.
>
> Finally, we will try to act in such a way that there is nothing which happens in Europe worthy of the attention of men of letters that cannot be learnt in this Journal.]

Despite this wide-ranging declaration, the first issue contained seven book reviews and an extract from a letter, and in the event the *Journal des Sçavans* would turn out to be essentially a journal devoted to book reviews.

The strange spelling 'Sçavans' was based on the mistaken belief that the word was derived from the Latin word 'scire', rather than 'sapere', which is the correct derivation. This spelling was used until 1697, when the 'ç' was dropped to produce 'Savans'. In 1701, the journal reverted to the spelling 'Sçavans', which again remained in use until 1791, when the spelling 'Savans' was brought back. In 1833, this was replaced by the spelling 'Savants', which remains in use today.

The name of Denis de Sallo did not appear on the first issue; instead, it carried the pseudonym of '*Sieur* de Hédovville'. Some claim that he had some land at a place called Hédouville in Normandy, but it is more likely that it derives from his valet, Germain Roussel, who was a native of Hédouville, near Pontoise. According to Paris (1903: 7), his use of a pseudonym was simply a common practice of the time ['un usage très répandu de son temps']. Cocheris (1860) puts it down to his modesty. However, the most widespread explanation (Camusat 1734; Morgan 1928; Birn 1965) is that it would be easier to get frank criticism of the Journal if it was not known that he was the editor. According to Morgan:

> Il est peu probable qu'il n'adopta pas de pseudonyme par simple crainte de persécutions, mais parce qu'il croyait, par ce moyen, être plus à même de juger de l'impression que produirait son ouvrage, et de profiter des critiques lancées contre lui. (Morgan 1928: 65)
> [It is unlikely that he adopted a pseudonym simply for fear of persecution, but because he believed that in this way he would be in a better position to evaluate the impression made by his publication, and to benefit from the criticisms made of him.]

If this is true it would seem to have been rather naïve, for his editorship appears to have been an open secret. And although Morgan discounts the possibility of fear of reprisals, future events would show such a fear to have been fully justified.

De Sallo was moving into uncharted territory. The book review was a genre which did not yet exist, and so he had to create it. His reviews, which he may well have thought of as being written with total frankness, were, in fact, hard-hitting and contained biting criticism. This inevitably antagonized the writers concerned, who were unused to this sort of attack. Several disputes arose, the most important of which concerned a book by Charles Patin on the history of medals. De Sallo's review appeared in the issue of 23 February, following which Charles Patin's father Guy Patin published an open letter, to which de Sallo replied in the issue of 9 March. Colbert entered the fray to defend the *Journal des Sçavans*. De Sallo might have been able to ride out this storm, but more serious difficulties lay ahead. De Sallo was a supporter of the Gallican Church, which was Jansenist in orientation and opposed to the Church of Rome. In several of his reviews he openly took the side of the Gallicans, and even mocked the bigotry of the Roman church. This inevitably attracted the ire of the Church of Rome, and in particular of the Jesuits, who persuaded the papal nuncio to use his power to have the journal suppressed. Thus after only 13 issues the *Journal des Sçavans* disappeared. Nevertheless, the short-lived editorship of Denis de Sallo had produced a radical change in intellectual life. Morgan sums this up by saying:

> En l'espace de trois mois, il avait lancé une entreprise qui, malgré toutes les difficultés attachées à cette expérience, et toute l'opposition de puissants ennemis, avait bouleversé l'ancien système de la critique et indiqué à l'Europe entière un moyen pratique et efficace de répandre la science et de distinguer le vrai du faux. (Morgan 1928: 125)

> [In the space of three months, he had launched a project which, in spite of the difficulties linked to such an experiment, and all the opposition from powerful enemies, had shaken up the previous system of criticism, and shown the whole of Europe a practical and efficient way of disseminating knowledge and distinguishing truth from falsehood.]

Colbert, however, was not to be outdone; he still believed in his project, and called on the Abbé Gallois to take over editorship of the journal. He had been born in Paris in 1632, and was a true intellectual, mastering several disciplines. He had been the tutor of de Sallo's children, and was himself a member of the *petite académie.* Thus he was already well known to Colbert, and would later become a close friend, living in his house and giving him Latin lessons. Strangely, in view of what had happened, the royal licence to publish remained in de Sallo's name until his death, and was only then transferred to Gallois, and de Sallo continued to work for the journal behind the scenes. The first issue produced by the Abbé Gallois appeared on 4 January 1666. He declared his intention to be less critical than de Sallo:

> Aussi est-on résolu de s'en abstenir à l'avenir, et au lieu d'exercer la critique, de s'attacher à bien lire les livres pour en pouvoir rendre un compte plus exact qu'on a fait jusqu'à présent.
> [And we have decided not to do this in future, and instead of being critical, to concentrate on reading the books carefully, in order to give a more exact account of them than has been done so far.]

In practice Gallois would find it difficult to stick to his non-critical plan. Unfortunately for the journal the Abbé Gallois had numerous other occupations, including, later, being secretary of the Académie Royal des Sciences. Gallois maintained the weekly regularity of the publication throughout 1666, but thereafter, due to his many other activities, it became increasingly irregular. In 1667, there were 16 issues, 13 in 1668, and a total of only 17 in the period 1669 to 1674: four in 1669, one in 1670, three in 1671, eight in 1672, none at all in 1673, and one in 1674. Thus, the *Journal des Sçavans* had become an occasional publication. In 1674 the Abbé Gallois resigned. Despite the irregularity of the journal its reputation did not suffer, and indeed seems to have increased, almost because of its increased rarity:

> La rareté des livraisons du Journal, qui serait aujourd'hui une cause de ruine, produisit un effet tout à fait contraire au dix-septième siècle. Elle ne servait qu'à augmenter l'avidité et le nombre des lecteurs, de telle sorte que Gallois laissa le Journal en 1674 plus prospère qu'il ne l'avait jamais été. (Morgan 1928: 174)
> [The irregular appearance of the Journal, which today would cause its ruin, produced the completely opposite effect in the seventeenth century. It only

> served to increase the enthusiasm and the number of its readers, so that Gallois left the Journal more prosperous in 1674 than it had ever been.]

On the Abbé Gallois's resignation, Colbert called on the Abbé de la Roque to take over as editor. If de Sallo and Gallois could be described as genuine intellectuals, this was not the case of de la Roque. He was more of a hard-working journalist, who lacked the intellectual spark of his predecessors. According to Camusat, writing some sixty years later:

> ... il n'avoit ni le discernement nécessaire pour bien choisir ce qui méritoit l'attention de ses lecteurs, ni l'érudition suffisante pour relever des bagatelles par des observations instructive. Il a bien fait pis : ses Journaux sont farcis d'erreurs ... (Camusat 1734: Vol. 2, p.11)
> [He had neither the discrimination necessary to choose that which was worthy of his readers' attention, nor sufficient erudition to point out insignificant details by instructive observations. He did even worse: his Journals are full of errors.]

Paris points out that he carried out the task competently and methodically, but 'mediocre, il l'accomplit médiocrement' (1903: 13) [being mediocre, he did it in mediocre fashion]. Despite his hard work, and the fact that the journal was much more regular than it had been under Gallois, as now it appeared every fortnight, and sometimes weekly, it lost prestige, and its readership fell. His attempts at popularization lost him even more readers:

> La Roque en essayant de plaire à deux publics si incompatibles, perdit l'un et autre. Son Journal devint trop banal pour les savants, tout en restant trop élevé pour les gens du peuple. (Morgan 1928: 191)
> [La Roque, in trying to please two highly incompatible readerships, lost both of them. His Journal became too banal for intellectuals, while remaining too highbrow for the general public.]

At the end of 1686, de la Roque resigned. Colbert had died in 1683, but the new Chancellor, Louis Boucherat, wanted to revive the fortunes of the *Journal des Sçavans,* and after some hesitation appointed Louis Cousin as editor. He had been born in Paris in 1627, was a lawyer by profession and had risen to become President of the Cours des Monnaies. His first issue appeared on 17 November 1687. Six issues appeared that year, 46 the following year, and 42 in each of the years from 1689 to 1701, when he resigned. Under his editorship the *Journal des Sçavans* was re-established as a major influential publication. In 1701, on Cousin's resignation, the then Chancellor, Pontchartrain, decided to make the journal an official government publication, which it had in fact been, unofficially, from the start:

> Pontchartrain résolut de faire du journal, qui dès son origine avait été patronné et sans doute subventionné par le Gouvernement, une véritable institution d'Etat. (Paris 1903: 15)
> [Pontchartrain decided to make the journal, which since its creation had been supported and probably subsidized by the government, a state institution.]

It is also possible that editors of the *Journal des Sçavans* received an unofficial state stipend (Barnes 1936). The production of the *Journal des Sçavans* was consigned by Pontchartrain, not to a single editor, but to an editorial committee, under the chairmanship of the Abbé Bignon.

The *Journal des Sçavans* had a series of editors over the next decade, but it became increasingly dominated by medical concerns, with a large number of articles devoted to the plague. It ceased publication in 1723, but was revived the following year, again under the editorship of the Abbé Bignon, with the Abbé Desfontaines as his deputy. The journal continued publication until in 1792 it disappeared, a victim of the French Revolution. There was an attempt to revive it in 1796, but on this occasion it lasted a mere few months. It was only twenty years later, in 1816, that it was resurrected on a more permanent basis. From this point on it was linked, at least unofficially, to the Institut de France. In the course of the nineteenth century the scope of the journal was reduced until scientific subjects disappeared altogether. In 1900, the state ceased funding the publication. After several difficult financial years, responsibility for the journal was taken over, in 1909, by the Académie des Inscriptions et Belles-Lettres, who continue to publish it today. In 1903 Gaston Paris described its scope as follows:

> Notre domaine reste encore assez vaste : histoire politique, géographique, économique et sociale, histoire de la civilisation, histoire des religions et des philosophies, histoires des lettres, des arts et des sciences, histoire des langues, rien de ce qui a été humain ne nous sera étranger. (Paris 1903: 30)
> [Our domain still remains fairly wide: political, geographic, economic and social history, history of civilization, religious and philosophical history, history of literature, of the arts and science, and history of languages; nothing that is human is outside our scope.]

Thus it can be seen that from the early twentieth century on, the *Journal des Savants* (to give it its modern spelling) has become virtually a journal of history, in the wide sense of the term, and so it remains today.

The Académie Royale des Sciences

The history of the *Journal des Sçavans* is complicated by the arrival on the scene of the Académie Royale des Sciences, which was founded in 1666, the year after the first publication of the *Journal des Sçavans*. Although a number of privately sponsored groups had preceded the Académie Royale des Sciences, it was different in many ways to any of the groupings which had gone before it. Like the *Journal des Sçavans*, it formed part of Colbert's control strategy; hence it was conceived of as a way of making science subservient to the state, and using it for the glorification of the monarchy.

> Even more crucial for him and for Louis XIV was the opportunity to fulfill the dream of centralizing all the cultural activities of the realm around the monarch. Science, as much as literature and the arts, was meant to bring brilliance to the Crown as well as to bask in the dazzling glory of the Roi Soleil. (Hahn 1971: 9)

For some time there had been a number of informal groups which met to discuss topics of intellectual interest. Some of these had literary or political interests, such as that founded by de Thou, or the group which met under the aegis of the journalist Renaudot at the Bureau d'Adresse. Others had a more scientific leaning, such as the group sponsored by Thévenot, or the Académie Montmor. In 1663, Sorbière, who was acting secretary of the Académie Montmor, sent Colbert a copy of a pamphlet he had written which outlined plans for the reform of the Académie. He was disturbed by disorder in their meetings, but also by the expense of their activities. His fears were justified when the group collapsed the following year. Auzout, the well-known astronomer, also called for royal sponsorship of astronomical research in his *Ephéméride du comète*. And in 1665 Thévenot's group disbanded after he had appealed to Colbert for state subsidy because of the increasing cost of experimentation. Thus, the need for some sort of state intervention, particularly in the form of financial help, was widely felt. By this time an anonymous plan for some sort of academy was circulating fairly widely.

Finally, in 1666, Colbert did set up an *Académie*, with a wide-ranging brief, including the humanities. This was done on an informal basis, and the group had no charter or letters patent. This initial attempt was to prove abortive: The Académie Française, the Sorbonne, the Paris medical faculty, and the Parlement all had vested interests in maintaining the status quo, and were opposed to the creation of this new institution, which they saw as poaching on their territory. As a result the Académie was whittled down to a group with purely scientific interests. This group held its first meeting on 22 December 1666 in the king's library, and thus the Académie Royale des Sciences was born (Hahn 1962; Hirschfield 1981[3]).

The original members of the Académie Royale des Sciences were all French, with the exception of the Dutchman, Christiaan Huygens, who was drafted in as head. They received a stipend or *pension,* thus making them the first scientific civil servants in history. Its status was rather curious, for although it was a royal institution, financed by the state, and with premises supplied by the monarchy, it was technically unofficial, for it had no charter or letters patent, and indeed it would not receive these until 1713 (Hahn 1962; Hirschfield 1981; Biagioli 1996). Nevertheless, it was 'the largest, best supported, and most renowned scientific institution of the age' (McClellan 2001: 7). The nature of the Académie's work was collective or collegial, and thus anonymous. The work produced was presented as the work of the whole group. According to Hirschfield:

> Anonymity was assumed by the members of the Academy because they considered it of less importance for the public to know to whom to render honor for a piece of scientific work than to recognize and know the work's value. By limiting personal glory, the group hoped to gain in stature in the public eye as a whole and at the same time bind the members of the Academy together and promote an atmosphere of expectation where competition for personal laurels would be minimized. (Hirschfield 1981: 69)

However, this is probably giving a highly idealized picture of human nature, even that of scientists inspired by intellectual ideals. While no doubt entering into the collegial spirit of the Académie, they still sought for recognition of their personal contributions, and for the establishment of priority, particularly when commercial or financial interests might be at stake. As Hahn points out:

> Seventeenth-century scientists were no less concerned with the establishment of priority than their modern counterparts, for their personal reputations were also at stake. Thus after announcing a new discovery or idea in the Academy's closed meeting, an individual often sent his findings to the one periodical that could guarantee quick publication, the *Journal des Savants.* (Hahn 1971: 27)

This does not mean that the Académie Royale des Sciences did not produce publications. They did, but the object of these publications was not the dissemination of knowledge, but, as was Colbert's original purpose in setting

---

[3] Although published in book form for the first time in 1981, this is his doctoral thesis originally written in 1957.

up the Académie, the glorification of Louis XIV, the Sun King. The fact of having been commissioned by the king and being subsequently offered back to him, was considered sufficient *raison d'être* for the work of the Académie, and so further diffusion beyond that necessary for his glorification was unnecessary and unwarranted. When publications of the Académie were produced, they were luxurious, elegant folio editions, printed on fine paper and often lavishly illustrated. They were elegantly bound in red morocco. These luxury items were printed in small numbers, and distributed only to members of the Académie themselves, and to friends of the king. Their object was to add to the glory of Louis XIV (Licoppe 1994, 1996; Biagioli 1996; Hirschfield 1981). It was only when the Académie was reorganized in 1699 that a more regular publication with wider distribution was decided upon, and the volume for the year 1699 did not in fact appear until 1702 (McClellan 2001). Hence, from 1665 until the end of the century the *Journal des Sçavans* in France and the *Philosophical Transactions* in England were the major outlets for new scientific writing.

The Royal Society

Like the Académie Royale des Sciences, the Royal Society had its origins in earlier groupings. The earliest account of the Royal Society is that of Thomas Sprat, who published his *History of the Royal Society* in 1667, just a few years after its creation. The word *history* is to be taken here in its seventeenth-century sense, closer to our idea of an account, and, in fact, it is a defence of, and virtually a manifesto for, the Society (Morgan 2009). More recent studies include Lyons (1944), Stimson (1948), McKie (1960) and the more popular account by Gribbin (2005). Ideas about a possible society were circulating as early as the 1640s, and, in 1645 this crystallized in a group which met at Gresham College in London. Gresham College had been founded in 1596, and provided for seven professors in divinity, law, physic (i.e. anatomy and medicine), geometry, astronomy, rhetoric and music. The lectures were public and given in English and Latin. McKie describes Gresham College as 'the matrix in which the Royal Society originated and in which it was formed and moulded' (1960: 8). From 1648 on some of the members migrated to Oxford, where they had been given university appointments, and they continued to meet in their new environment, first in William Petty's rooms, then in those of John Wilkins in Wadham College, and finally in Robert Boyle's lodgings. The members of the Oxford group continued to attend the meetings at Gresham College when they were in London.

It was at a Gresham College meeting on 28 November 1660 that a formal decision to create a society was formulated. Following a lecture on astronomy by Christopher Wren, the twelve members present agreed to meet on a weekly basis to discuss matters of a 'philosophical' nature. They also laid down an initial fee of ten shillings, plus a weekly payment of one shilling.[4] That this was fairly costly for the period can be judged from the fact that a shilling corresponds to the daily wage of a skilled worker like a thatcher, mason, or carpenter, while unskilled labourers would have earned less (Ashley 1964). A university professor might expect to earn £1 (one pound) a week (Gribbin 2005), so the weekly payment would have corresponded to about 5% of his salary (although he would also get free board and lodging).

Although the group which had met in the 1640s had Parliamentary leanings, by 1660 the group was distinctly Royalist. Of those present at the meeting five were distinct Royalists, and the others were moderates, or generally in favour of the Restoration. They drew up a list of forty-one potential members, only one of whom did not ultimately join the group, and of these at least thirty-one were Royalists. In founding the society they were no doubt to some extent looking over their shoulders to other groups in continental Europe such as the Accademia dei Lincei, which had been founded in Rome at the beginning of the seventeenth century, and the various groups which had been formed in France. They may also have been influenced by the description of the fictitious Salomon's House, which was a society of natural philosophers described by Francis Bacon in his *New Atlantis* of 1627 (Bacon 1905).

On 5 December, Robert Moray reported to the Society that the king approved of their undertaking. On 3 May members of the Society showed the king the rings of Saturn and other astronomical phenomena through his own telescope. This event is described by John Evelyn in his diary.

> This evening I was with my Lord Brouncker, Sir Robert Moray, Sir Paul Neile, Monsieur Zulichem, and Bull (all of them of our Society, and excellent mathematicians), to show his Majesty, who was present, Saturn's annulus, as some thought, but as Zulichem affirmed with his Balteus (as that learned gentleman had published), very near eclipsed by the moon, near the Mons Porphrytis; also, Jupiter and satellites, through his majesty's great telescope, drawing thirty-five feet; on which were divers discourses. (Evelyn 1906: 168)

---

4 In pre-decimal currency, there were 20 shillings in a pound (sterling), and the shilling was divided into 12 pence. This system prevailed until Great Britain changed to a decimal system in 1971.

A Royal Charter was granted on 15 July the following year, and thus the society officially became the 'Royal Society'. Robert Hooke, who had been working as Boyle's assistant, was appointed curator, that is, his job was to prepare experiments to be carried out before the assembled members. However, any hopes the members of the Royal Society might have had of benefiting from more than moral support from the monarchy proved to be unfounded. The crown never subsidized the Royal Society on a regular basis, although it did in the years to come occasionally help to finance specific projects. This was to be a determining fact for the Royal Society, since the result was that it had to rely on members' subscriptions for its financial survival. The original entrance fee of 10 shillings was doubled to £1 in 1661, and doubled again to £2 in 1662, with a fee of £5 for peers. It was therefore in the Society's financial interest to recruit members who had the financial means to pay, whether or not they had any real interest in science. This had the additional advantage of giving the Society greater respectability, and the aristocracy were positively encouraged to become members: those above the rank of baron were allowed in on request, unlike those lower down the social scale, who had to be nominated and elected. Hunter (1982) calculates that the 479 British Fellows elected in the period 1660–1700 were socially distributed as follows:

16% courtiers, politicians and diplomats
16% medical practitioners
15% gentlemen of independent means
14% aristocracy
12% scholars, writers
8% divines
7% merchants and tradesmen
4% lawyers
4% civil servants and armed forces
3% uncertain

From this it can be seen that the membership was highly weighted towards the top end of the social (and financial) scale. According to Hunter, about 70% took some interest in the Society's activities, but this still leaves 30% who took no interest, and the interest of many of the 70% tended to be short-lived.

> Thus it came about that in the early days of the Society about one-third of the Fellows consisted of scientific men of eminence and merit, the remainder being made up of those who might be interested in the new philosophy and its aims, but who did not devote themselves seriously to the advancement of natural knowledge. The Society therefore started with

> a membership which was composed in part of scientific men, and in part of those who may be taken as representing the ordinary intellectual and cultivated life of the day, but who for the most part were but little interested in scientific investigation. (Lyons 1944: 52)

This is probably putting the best possible gloss on a situation where some non-scientific members treated the Royal Society, if they treated it at all, as a gentlemen's club. This situation was to perdure, and would not be finally eliminated until the middle of the nineteenth century.

> For two centuries two-thirds of the Fellows were men who had no scientific knowledge or any real interest in the advancement of science, so that for many years, in fact until after 1830, more than half the members of the Councils belonged to that category. (Lyons 1944: 46)

The upshot of this situation was that non-payment of subscriptions became a constant problem for the Royal Society. Arrears in 1663 amounted to £158. 4s. 6d. (one hundred and fifty-eight pounds, four shillings and sixpence), but by 1673 this had risen to £2114. 1s. 6d., and by 1680 to £3259. 5s. 6d. (Bluhm 1958).

Some felt that there were shortcomings in the terms of the original Royal Charter, and on 22 April 1663 a second Royal Charter was issued. This gave the Royal Society the official title of the Royal Society of London for Improving Natural Knowledge. John Wilkins and Henry Oldenburg were appointed as secretaries, and the motto, suggested by John Evelyn, *Nullius in verba*, was adopted. This is frequently glossed as 'Take nobody's word for it.'

Thus the Royal Society was set on its way. It was shortly to be followed by the Académie Royale des Sciences in France. While they recognized each other as the leading scientific societies of the day (Crosland 2005), there were significant differences between them. The French body was made up of appointed members, and restricted to eminent scientists. It was state-funded, its members were paid retainers, and it operated in premises supplied by the state. It thus had no financial problems but on the other hand it was subject to state control, the state being its paymaster. The Royal Society was totally independent, but had to finance itself and find its own premises. It was therefore open to anyone with a nominal interest (or even none) in science, as long as they were able and willing to pay the subscription, on which the Society relied for financial survival (Bluhm 1958; McKie 1960; Crosland 2005).

The *Philosophical Transactions*

The *Philosophical Transactions* was the brainchild of Henry Oldenburg. He was born in Bremen, in present-day Germany, probably in 1615, though the exact date is uncertain. After obtaining the degree of Master of Theology at the local gymnasium, he came to England, where he earned his living as tutor in a number of wealthy families. In 1648 he left to travel in continental Europe, returning to Bremen in 1652. The following year he was appointed as a diplomatic agent to the government of Cromwell, with the brief of assuring the neutrality of Bremen in the context of the first Anglo-Dutch war. When the war ended in 1655, he became tutor to Richard Jones, the son of Lady Ranelagh and nephew of Robert Boyle. In 1656 he accompanied Jones to Oxford, where he met Boyle and was introduced to the group then meeting in Wilkins's rooms at Wadham College. The following year Jones and Oldenburg left for a tour in continental Europe, where they remained until 1660, spending the final year in Paris. During this tour and particularly during their period in Paris, Oldenburg cultivated the taste for natural philosophy which he had acquired at Oxford, and built up a network of scientific acquaintances. Oldenburg was not present at the inaugural meeting of the Royal Society, but his name was on the list of potential members then drawn up. When the Society received its charter, Oldenburg was one of the two secretaries appointed. The fact that, in addition to his native language, German, he was competent in English, French, Italian and Latin may have influenced this decision (Bluhm 1960; Hall 2002; Avramov 1999).

Although most members of the early Royal Society were *virtuosi*, or gentlemen amateurs, who were financially independent, and could thus personally finance their scientific activities, this was not the case for Henry Oldenburg. He had to earn his living, and did so mainly through teaching and translating. However, he had become the centre of a network of correspondence. Such networks were not uncommon. The one which had centred on Mersenne in Paris is probably the most well-known, but also in France was that of Fabri de Peirsec, and in England those of Haak, Hartlib, and Collins (Moessner 2007; Hall 1994). Up to this point the main ways in which scientific information was disseminated was either through books or through letters. Books, however, were expensive, took a great deal of time to produce, and it was not particularly easy to find out what was available (Hall 1975); letters were more immediate and contained up-to-date information. It was thus that these letters took on a communal aspect. It was understood that they should be copied, passed on, read at meetings, and in general disseminated as widely as possible. This was generally accepted to such an extent that having written something in a letter of this type could be used as an official claim in a priority dispute (Gotti 2006; Banks 2013c).

Oldenburg read an extract from the *Journal des Sçavans* to the members of the Royal Society on 11 January 1665, only six days after it had been published in Paris. This not only shows that scientists in London and Paris were in fairly close contact, but also that communications in the late seventeenth century were relatively rapid. Sir Robert Moray, in a letter to Christiaan Huygens, dated 3 February, said the following:

> Quant a la Gazette des Scauants, Nous en auons veu un essay ; mais on y trouue desia a redire. Vous dites bien que la chose pourra estre utile pourueu qu'on ne las gaste point. Monsieur Oldenburg nous a fait un eschantillon d'un semblable dessein bien plus philosophique, et nous faisons estat de l'y engager, sil se peut faire. Jl ne se meslera pas des choses Juridiques ny Theologiques, mais outre les choses philosophiques qui nous viennent de delà la mer il publiera les experiences, au moins les chefs, qui se sont icy. Mais de ne sera quune fois le mois, en Anglois, et une fois en trois mois, en latin. (quoted in Bluhm 1960; 190)
> [As for the Gazette des Sçavans, we have seen a trial issue; but there is much to criticize in it. As you rightly say, the thing could be useful, as long as it isn't spoilt. Mr. Oldenburg has shown us a sample of a similar but much more philosophical project, and we are encouraging him to do it, if he can. He will not meddle with Legal or Theological affairs, but in addition to philosophical information which comes to us from abroad, he will publish the experiments, at least the most important, that take place here. But it will only be once a month in English, and once every three months in Latin.]

Thus it was that, on 1 March, the Royal Society officially decided

> That the Philosophical Transactions, to be composed by Mr Oldenburg, be printed on the first Monday of every month, if he have sufficient matter for it, and that the tract be licensed under the Charter by the Council of the Society, being first reviewed by some members of the same; and that the President be now desired to license the first papers thereof, being written in four sheets in folio, to be printed by John Martyn and James Allestree. (quoted in Lyons 1944: 56)

Although some might claim that Oldenburg got his idea from the *Journal des Sçavans* (Bluhm 1960), in view of the time scales involved, this seems unlikely. Oldenburg could hardly have prepared and had printed the first issue in the period between 11 January and 6 March. His plans were probably already in an advanced stage at that point, though such ideas may have been generally in the air at the time. The publication thus had the imprimatur of the Royal Society, but Oldenburg accepted full financial and editorial responsibility (Kronick 1962). The first issue of the *Philosophical Transactions* appeared on 6 March. Unlike the *Journal des Sçavans*, which concentrated on book reviews, the *Philosophical Transactions* was basically a newsletter of scientific information.

Events beyond Oldenburg's control meant that the *Philosophical Transactions* had a difficult start. In the course of its first year of publication, its production was interrupted by the plague. At the end of the issue dated 3 July, Oldenburg printed the following ominous warning:

> *The* Reader *is hereby advertised, that by reason of the present Contagion in* London, *which may unhappily cause an interruption aswel of* Correspondencies, *as of* Publick Meetings, *the Printing of these* Philosophical Transactions *may possibly for a while be intermitted; though endeavour shall be used to continue them, if it may be.* (*Philosophical Transactions*, 5 July 1665)

This did indeed prove to be the case, but Oldenburg, unlike most others in his position, stayed on in London. However, the printers were among those who had fled the city, and the next issue did not appear until 6 November, Oldenburg having arranged for it to be printed in Oxford (Lyons 1944).

On 20 June 1667, at the height of the Second Dutch War and anti-foreigner paranoia, a warrant was issued for the arrest of Henry Oldenburg. It would seem that in one of his letters some of his remarks had been interpreted as being a slight on the king, who had taken umbrage. Oldenburg was imprisoned in the Tower. On 8 August, he was visited by Evelyn, who records his visit in his diary.

> Visited Mr. Oldenburg, a close prisoner in the Tower, being suspected of writing intelligence. I had an order from Lord Arlington, Secretary of State, which caused me to be admitted. This gentleman was secretary to our Society, and I am confident will prove an innocent person. (Evelyn 1906: 278)

Rather than imprisonment, it was more a case of the internment of an alien in time of war, for no charges were brought, and his release, on 26 August, followed swiftly on the end of the war and the signing of the treaty of Breda, on 31 July (McKie 1948).

After this interruption, Oldenburg continued to publish the *Philosophical Transactions* regularly until his death in 1677. Nehemiah Grew continued for a further five issues, which appeared in the course of 1678. The task then fell to Robert Hooke. Unfortunately, Hooke had had a bitter dispute with Oldenburg, and it would seem that the idea of continuing Oldenburg's work rankled; at all events, Hooke discontinued the *Philosophical Transactions*, and replaced it with a journal of his own making, the *Philosophical Collections.* Seven issues appeared between February 1679 and January 1683 (Kronick 1991), but it never enjoyed the success of the *Philosophical Transactions.* In 1683, the *Philosophical Transactions* was revived under the editorship of Robert Plot until 1687, when it again ceased publication. It was again revived in 1690, with Richard Waller as editor. He was succeeded by Sir Hans Sloane in 1695, who edited the journal until 1713 and was followed by Edmund Halley, who held the post until 1721. In 1752, the editor was replaced by an editorial committee, and the Royal Society took over financial responsibility for the publication, so from this date the *Philosophical Transactions* became an official publication of the Royal Society. In 1887, the *Philosophical Transactions* was divided into a Series A, dealing with mathematics and physics, and a Series B, dealing with biology. In 1832, the Royal Society had introduced a new publication, the *Proceedings of the Royal Society.* Initially, this published Society news and abstracts of papers published in the *Philosophical Transactions,* but it developed into a scientific journal in its own right. In 1905, it was decided that the *Proceedings* should be split into an A Series and a B Series on the same lines as the *Philosophical Transactions.* Moreover, it was decided that the *Proceedings* would publish shorter papers, up to 24 pages, while the *Philosophical Transactions* would publish longer and more elaborate papers. In 1997, a further change was introduced whereby primary research was to be published in the *Proceedings,* while the *Philosophical Transactions* would publish theme-based series of review articles and monographs on single topics. Hence the *Philosophical Transactions* continues to be published as a high-ranking scientific publication, though it is no longer the organ of primary research which it was for over 330 years (Atkinson 1999).

Moray's letter to Huygens mentioned a Latin edition of the *Philosophical Transactions* to be published quarterly. It may even be that Oldenburg considered this Latin edition to be potentially more important than the English edition.

> From the very start of the enterprise, Oldenburg had envisaged that there would be a three-monthly Latin version. And since it would reach a far wider audience than the English, this Latin work could properly be considered its more important branch.
>
> At first it seemed likely to appear. Oldenburg repeatedly told friends that their authorship of discoveries could only be protected from continental 'usurpation' by such an edition. (Johns 2000: 171)

At all events, this Latin edition never appeared. Oldenburg interrupted his preparation of the Latin edition when he discovered that a Latin translation was being prepared by a certain John Sterpin. A first volume of this translation was printed in Frankfurt am Main in 1671. However, when Oldenburg saw this translation he found it so poor and riddled with faults that he forbade Sterpin to continue with it. A further attempt at a Latin translation was made by Christopher Sand, who even asked Oldenburg for advice on several occasions; this was printed in Amsterdam in 1672. This too turned out to be a poor translation, and was severely criticized in a *Philosophical Transactions* review (Kronick 1990). So efforts to produce a Latin edition fizzled out, and the fame of the *Philosophical Transactions* spread as an English journal.

From the outset, the members of the Royal Society were aware that it was necessary for them to create a new style in writing. This search is clearly typified in the work of Robert Boyle, who gradually developed the experimental essay for his purely scientific work, whereas he found the Socratic dialogue appropriate to his more philosophical work, such as *The Sceptical Chymist* (Boyle 2003 [1661]). He also reserved a distinct style for his religious writings (Gotti 1996; Hunter 2009). The need for new modes of expression is expounded at length in Sprat's *History*.

> But lastly, in these, and all other businesses, that have come under their care; there is one thing more, about which the *Society* has been most solicitous; and that is, the manner of their *Discourse*: which, unless they had been very watchful to keep in due temper, the whole spirit and vigour of their *Design*, had been soon eaten out, by the luxury and redundance of *speech*. The ill effects of this superfluity of talking, have already overwhelm'd most other *Arts* and *Professions*; insomuch, that when I consider the means of *happy living*, and the causes of their corruption, I can hardly forbear recanting what I said before; and concluding, that eloquence ought to be banish'd out of all *civil Societies*, as a thing fatal to Peace and good Manners. (Sprat 2003 [1667]: 111)

A little later he launches into a diatribe against obscure ways of speaking.

> Who can behold, without indignation, how many mists and uncertainties, these specious *Tropes* and *Figures* have brought on our Knowledg? How many rewards, which are due to more profitable, and difficult *Arts*, have been still snatch'd away by the easie vanity of *fine speaking?* For now I am warm'd with this just Anger, I cannot with-hold my self, from betraying the shallowness of all these seeming Mysteries; upon which, *we Writers*, and *Speakers*, look so big. And, in few words, I dare say; that of all the Studies of men, nothing may be sooner obtain'd, than this vicious abundance of *Phrase*, this trick of *Metaphors*, this volubility of *Tongue*, which makes so great a noise in the World. (Sprat 2003 [1667]: 112)

And a little later still he describes the efforts of the Royal Society to find a new rhetoric.

> They have therefore been most rigorous in putting in execution, the only Remedy, that can be found for this *extravagance*: and that has been, a constant Resolution, to reject all the amplifications, digressions, and swellings of style: to return back to the primitive purity, and shortness, when men deliver'd so many *things*, almost in an equal number of *words*. They have exacted from all their members, a close naked, natural way of speaking; positive expressions; clear senses; a native easiness: bringing all things as near the mathematical plainness, as they can: and preferring the language of Artizans, Countrymen, and Merchants, before that, of Wits, or Scholars. (Sprat 2003 [1667]: 113)

Sprat has frequently been taken to be referring to the use of so-called 'inkhorn terms'. Barber points out that

> [t]his coining of words for fine effect, for the achieving of magniloquence, sometimes led to abuse and excess. The 'bravery' of new words could easily degenerate into obscurity, affectation, and pomposity. (Barber 1997: 56)

While it is true that Sprat may have had a florid obscure style in mind, he may also have been thinking of the writings of scholastics, alchemists, and Paracelsians, whose writings were esoteric and intended to be understood only by the initiated.

> The alchemists, even when honest, wrote on the principle that if the reader had not been admitted to the secrets he would fail to understand, and if he had would scarcely need further guidance. (Hall 1962: 223)

And although the Paracelsians rejected the ancient authority of classical authors and praised experiment and observation,

> Much of what they write is pure jargon, obscure and imposing terms being used to impress people, while such an air of mystery is thrown about their theories, so much is said and so little revealed – if indeed known – that we can understand their being branded as quacks by the outraged Galenists. (Jones 1982: 7)

The academic situation

University education at this time was dominated by the study of the Ancients. The works of Aristotle were considered the pinnacle of achievement in physics, Galen was the touchstone in medicine, and Ptolemy rode high in the study of astronomy. Of course, these were not the only authors studied and cited, but this trio constituted the high points of attainment in these areas. In order to understand why this was the case, it is necessary to understand the mindset of seventeenth-century man. His world view was that the history of the universe was akin to that of an individual human being, with a youthful period of vigour, gradually ageing and ultimately reaching senility. It was thus thought that the zenith of human achievement had been reached during the classical period of ancient Greece and Rome. By the seventeenth century humanity had reached its old age, if not its dotage, and so could no longer hope to equal the attainments of its youth. Since it was believed that Aristotle and the other 'Ancients' had already said everything that was relevant about the sciences, experiment was pointless, since it was impossible to add to the store of knowledge that the ancient Greeks and Romans had left us. All that could be done was to explain their texts in terms of the seventeenth-century context; discovering new facts, which potentially could show the ancients to be mistaken, was not considered feasible (Jones 1982).

> Aristotle's writings were still generally accepted as authoritatively marking the limits that man could reach in pursuit of a knowledge of his world, while the power of the human mind was regarded as having steadily and inevitably declined during the centuries that had passed ... (McKie 1960: 3)

Even when difficulties with this model were perceived, the tendency was not to reject it, but simply to patch it up (Henry 2002a).

In many ways it was not so much the Ancients as such that the 'Moderns' rejected, but the way in which the writings of the classical thinkers were used in seventeenth-century university practice. And if many universities maintained a hard line in upholding the authority of the Ancients as the basis of instruction (Debus 1970), it was because these texts were used as the unquestioned bases of the discussion and argument that made up the major part of university education. In this framework there was no place for practical experiment.

> It was this subordination of experiential statements to the structure of argument, without subjecting them to much investigation, which prompted the seventeenth-century charges of slavish adherence to ancient authority, rather than any widespread and genuinely uncritical acceptance of Aristotelian texts. (Dear 1985: 149)

Consequently, research was outside the generally perceived scope of the universities.

> Research was not then reckoned to be a function of the universities at all and far more intellectual progress was achieved in the Royal Society once it was established in London in 1660 than either at Oxford or Cambridge. (Ashley 1964: 130)

This goes some way to explaining why those who espoused the experimental method were, in general, outside the university system. In particular, it is noticeable that relatively few of the early members of the Royal Society held university posts. Newton, of course, did have a university appointment, but his chair was in mathematics, not in experimental science. It is also true that some future members of the Royal Society obtained university posts when Cromwell came to power, but these were political appointments, replacing Royalists with Parliamentarians, and because of this they tended to be replaced in their turn when the political tide turned at the Restoration.

In addition to this, it has been suggested by Merton (1938) that the rise of Puritanism in England provided a particularly fertile soil for the new experimental science. While disputed by some (Mulligan 1973; Hunter 1982), it is a hypothesis that merits attention. For the Puritans, the purpose of human life was seen as the glorification of God. This had been true for Catholicism too, but the consequences were different; whereas for the Catholic the glorification of God meant retreat from the world to monastic seclusion, for the Puritan it involved immersing himself in the world as God's creation.

> For both medieval Catholicism and Calvinism, this world was evil, but, whereas the prescribed solution for the one was retirement from the world into the spiritual calm of the monastery, it was incumbent on the other to conquer the temptations of this world by *remaking it* through ceaseless, unflinching toil. (Merton 1938: 417)

Moreover, this involvement with the physical world was to produce results which were useful to society in general. These ideas had ultimately been derived from Calvin, and were the foundation of the Protestant work ethic (Weber 1930). Activity which was socially useful was the prime way of glorifying God. This was what the Puritans conceived of as good 'works.' For those who believed in the fully fledged Calvinistic doctrine of predestination, good works were the outward sign of having been chosen by God, and being a member of God's elect; for those who no longer believed in predestination, probably the case of most English Puritans at this time, good works were the means of achieving a state of grace, and hence becoming a member of God's elect. So whereas Catholicism had tolerated scientific activity, Puritanism positively encouraged, indeed virtually required, it as a means of improving the human social situation, seen as a way of glorifying God. Of course, good works had a place in the Catholic scheme of things, but there again it differed from the Puritan viewpoint.

> In the Puritan case it involved the notion of a transcendental god and an orientation to the 'other world,' it is true, but it also demanded a mastery over this world through a study of its processes; while in the Catholic instance,

> it demanded complete absorption, save for an unbanishable minimum, in the supersensuous, in an intuitive love of God. (Merton 1938: 467)

Thus the entwining of God's glorification and the improvement of the human condition in the Puritan conception of man's role in the world created a situation conducive to the scientific endeavour.

To this might be added the point that scholastic philosophy was the underpinning of Catholic theology. But scholastic philosophy, particularly in the Thomist form which informed Catholic dogma, was basically Aristotelian. So, by espousing an empirical experimental approach, and rejecting the Aristotelian stance of the universities, the new scientists were also rejecting the foundations of Catholic theology. This would also inevitably be conducive to the Puritan mind.

Philosophical stance

A further difference between science as practised in England, particularly by the members of the Royal Society and those who gravitated around it, and science as practised in France and embodied in the work of the Académie Royale des Sciences was the philosophical bases of their respective approaches. Francis Bacon, who had lived from 1561 to 1626, was in many ways the father figure of the Royal Society. Although he was not an experimental scientist himself, he had built up a philosophy which espoused experimental science, a revolutionary position for the time. His position can be summarized as a three-pronged attack on the prevailing situation (Henry 2002b). First, he argued for practical observation and experiment, a genuine hands-on approach, as opposed to the purely logical and argumentative methods used by other intellectuals of the day. Secondly, he believed that new knowledge should have practical applications directed towards the improvement of the human situation. It is from this point of view that Farrington (1951) describes him as the philosopher of industrial science, and Dear (2005) claims that it was Bacon who added the notion of practicality to natural philosophy, which had previously been purely theoretical. Thirdly, he was in favour of an inductive form of reasoning, that is one in which the facts supplied by practical observation and experiment form the basis of the reasoning process. This contrasted with the prevailing preference for deductive reasoning, where it was not a requirement that the ideas which formed the premises of an argument be tested beforehand against experience. Bacon's position as the *maître à penser* of the Royal Society is enshrined in Sprat's *History*:

> The *Third* sort of *new Philosophers*, have been those, who have not onely disagreed from the *Antients*, but have also propos'd to themselves the right course of slow, and sure *Experimenting*: and have prosecuted it as far, as the shortness of their own Lives, or the multiplicity of their other affairs, or the narrowness of their Fortunes, have given them leave. Such as these, we are to expect to be but few: for they must devest themselves of many vain conceptions, and overcome a thousand false Images, which lye like Monsters in their way, before they can get as far as this. And of these, I shall onely mention one great Man, who had the true Imagination of the whole extent of this Enterprize, as it is now set on foot; and that is, the *Lord Bacon*. In whose Books there are every where scattered the best arguments, that can be produc'd for the defence of Experimental Philosophy; and the best directions, that are needful to promote it. (Sprat 2003 [1667]: 35)

Although Bacon has sometimes been presented as a pure encyclopaedist, advocating the collecting of everything and anything, in fact he was not in favour of haphazard collecting, and believed that experimentation should be guided and organized.

> Bacon by no means understood his experimental way to be pure empiricism. He had no use for random experimentation, undertaken without aim or guiding principle, however much he might at various times fall into the error of collecting diverse experiments ... (Hall 1994: 254)

Whereas the empirical method and inductive reasoning advocated by Bacon became the cornerstone of the work of the Royal Society, in France intellectual endeavour was still very much under the influence of Descartes. Descartes, too, had done away with reliance on the Ancients, but in his case it was to replace this with a purely deductive method, starting from scratch after operating a *tabula rasa* of accumulated knowledge.

> The French philosopher started with the simple principle, *Cogito, ergo sum*, upon which, by means of reasoning and clear ideas, he sought to construct a sound edifice. The English philosopher, on the other hand, though insisting just as emphatically upon the necessity of purging the mind of all notions, proposed a sensuous and material basis for man to build his ideas of nature upon. (Jones 1982: 49)

The Académie Royale was also, of course, in the business of experimental science, but the influence of Descartes meant that emphases were different. For them the creation of theory was of major importance, so that the details that they gleaned from experimentation were seen as being of value not in themselves, but insofar as they were useful in constructing a theory (Gross *et al.* 2002). This meant that where the English scientists would provide profuse detail, their French counterparts did not consider this necessary (Licoppe 1994, 1996).

> One specific feature of the experimental narrative in the Boyle manner … is his obsessive concern with recounting all the particulars attending the experiment … This profusion of detail … is without an equivalent in their French contemporaries. (Licoppe 1994: 211)

Thus the Royal Society advocated an inductive method, and the Académie Royale favoured a deductive method (Salomon-Bayet 2008). In simple terms, induction uses data to construct a theory, while deduction suggests a theory and then attempts to test it against data. While simplistic, this does give some idea of the different tendencies. Moreover, it is probably true that neither exists in its pure form: the inductive scientist has some idea of the theory that he is working towards, and the deductive thinker is aware of the available data that he can use. Nevertheless, the difference in general direction is significant. When Newton, at the beginning of his book *Opticks*, said, 'My design in this Book is not to explain the Properties of Light by Hypotheses, but to propose and prove them by Reason and Experiments' (Newton 1952 [1730]: 1), he was explicitly rejecting the Cartesian method of establishing theory (hypotheses) before moving on to look at the data (Brading 2012). Although probably written before 1690, this was not first published until 1704, running to a fourth edition by 1730. Fara describes it as a 'manifesto', in which Newton set out a 'mathematical, experimental style of research' (2002: 10). French scientists were to adopt the Newtonian point of view, and hence an inductive Baconian stance, in the course of the eighteenth century, particularly following the influence of Voltaire (Le Ru 2005). However, the influence of Descartes has persisted in the humanities, and the Cartesian–Baconian distinction is still frequently perceptible in some areas of thought, and is often the factor that divides francophone and anglophone academics (Banks 2002, 2004).

4 The documents to be used: a corpus

The main object of this study is to analyse and compare a number of linguistic features in the *Philosophical Transactions* and the *Journal des Sçavans*, from the date of their creation in 1665 to the end of the seventeenth century. It was in 1699 that the Académie Royale des Sciences decided to alter its policy of not publishing widely its activities and results, and from that time on they were published as the *Histoire de l'Académie Royale des Sciences. Avec les Memoires de Mathématique et de Physique.* The volume for 1699 actually appeared in 1702 (McClellan 2001). Since the Académie was interested in specifically scientific matters, in terms of scope at least, the *Mémoires* were much closer to the *Philosophical Transactions* than was the *Journal des Sçavans*. Thus, the appearance of the *Mémoires* produced a radical change in terms of scientific publishing in France. This leaves the period of 1665 to 1700 as a peculiar window, during which the *Philosophical Transactions* and the *Journal des Sçavans* were the two main outlets for academic writing in English and French. Although there were many fairly short-lived periodicals that appeared in the wake of these two, probably the only serious rival was the *Acta Eruditorum*, which was published in Germany from 1682 to 1731, but it published in Latin, not in a vernacular language.

In an ideal world, one would choose to analyse the total production of the two journals for the whole of this period. However, such an undertaking implies the availability of the texts in a form suitable for computerized analysis. This is not the case. Although the texts can be found on various Internet sites,[5] they are available only in image form, which renders them unsuitable for computerized linguistic analysis. Moreover, even if they were available in a suitable form, computerized analysis depends on the features under study being recognizable from their form, since ultimately a computer can only recognize forms. As will be seen, not all of the features

[5] I have used those available on Gallica, the site of the French Bibliothèque Nationale: http://gallica.bnf.fr

which I wish to consider in this book can be reduced to a simple question of form. All this points to manual analysis as the only solution in the present circumstances. However, manual analysis requires a corpus of a manageable size, and previous experience (and not only my own) has shown that something of the order of 120,000 words is close to the limit of what is feasible in terms of manual analysis. In my study of the *Philosophical Transactions* from 1700 to 1980 (Banks 2008a), I used a corpus with a number of words estimated at 126,555.

For the present study, I have decided to take examples at ten-year intervals – 1665, 1675, 1685 and 1695. For each of these years I chose a number of issues at random (at least, haphazardly, if not randomly in the mathematical sense). In the case of the *Philosophical Transactions* the issues chosen were as follows:

1665	April 3 June 5 December 4	1685	March 23 August 22
1675	February 22 July 26 November 22		

At the time of carrying out the study the issues for 1695 were not available, so these have been replaced by issues for the year 1694. The issues selected were:

1694	March/April July/August

In the case of the *Journal des Sçavans*, the issues selected were:

1665	January 12 January 26 February 9 February 23 March 9	1685	January 21 March 5 April 16 June 4 July 30
1675	January 14 March 11 May 6 July 1 September 9	1695	January 3 February 21 April 25 June 20 August 8

The number of words was estimated by counting the number of words in three or four lines on a page, and multiplying the average by the number of lines. This was done for three or four pages in each issue, and the average was then multiplied by the number of pages in the issue. In a small number of cases where two different sizes of type face were used within a single issue, the two sections were estimated separately. This gave the following results for each of the years and journals concerned:

Philosophical Transactions
1665: 20,595
1675: 23,877
1685: 15,573
1694: 17,250

Journal des Sçavans
1665: 15,031
1675: 14,085
1685: 15,549
1695: 21,782

This gives a total of 77,295 words for the *Philosophical Transactions*, and 66,447 words for the *Journal des Sçavans*. The grand total for the whole corpus is 143,742, or, in round terms, a little more than 140,000 words, which is a perfectly reasonable size for manual analysis. If it errs, it is on the large side. Full details of the estimated number of words for each issue in the corpus are given in Appendix 1. The number of pages in different issues of the *Journal des Sçavans* is stable over time, but the *Philosophical Transactions* grows considerably over the period. Moreover, some issues, notably of the *Philosophical Transactions*, include items which are simply tables of measurements of observations; these are not included in the word count since they are not amenable to the type of linguistic analysis with which this book is concerned. A small number of items printed in Latin are also excluded from the word count, although they will be included in the discussions of genre and field of study.

Although there are slightly more words in the *Philosophical Transactions* component, the *Journal des Sçavans* component has more items than the other component. For the *Philosophical Transactions* we have 64 items (discounting four which are in Latin) for 77,295 words, an average of 1208 words per item, whereas for the *Journal des Sçavans* there are 115 items for 66,447 words, an average of 578 words per item. Hence, the entries in the *Philosophical Transactions* are on average longer than those in the *Journal des Sçavans*. This, however, masks the fact that there may be great variation between individual entries, particularly in the case of the *Philosophical Transactions*. The size of issues of the *Journal des Sçavans* remains stable at a steady 12 pages per issue over the period studied. The size of issues of the *Philosophical Transactions* varies, probably depending on the availability of material for publication, but in general the size rises over time from 16 to 40 pages. The average number of words per item in the *Journal des Sçavans* falls from 518 in 1665 to 420 in 1685, but rises to 1037 in 1695. In the *Philosophical Transactions* the average length of items rises steadily from 936 words in 1665 to 1438 in 1694.

Genre

We have seen that Denis de Sallo took the editorial decision to make his periodical basically a journal of book reviews. In fact, many of the entries are relatively short, and perhaps 'book notice' might be a more correct term for these shorter items; however, they have all been subsumed under the general term of 'book review'. Consequently, the issues in the corpus are all of this type, that is, mainly book reviews with the addition of usually just one other item, which can take the form of a report, scientific or legal, an obituary, an article or an extract from an article or letter, a book summary, an editorial note. The issues for 1685 frequently end with a list of new publications (other than those reviewed). Table 1 shows the genres which occur in the *Journal des Sçavans* for each of the years under consideration.

Full details can be found in Appendix 2, which gives the title or heading of each entry as it appears in the original and its classification in terms of

Table 1. Genre types in the *Journal des Sçavans.*

Genre	*1665*	*1675*	*1685*	*1695*	*Total*	*%*[a]
Book review	25	22	26	18	91	79
Legal report	1	–	–	–	1	1
Scientific report	1	–	–	–	1	1
Obituary notice	1	1	–	–	2	2
Letter extract	1	–	1	2	4	3
Article	–	–	2	–	2	2
Article extract	–	3	4	–	7	6
Book summary	–	1	–	–	1	1
List	–	–	4	1	5	4
Editorial	–	1	–	–	1	1
Total	29	28	37	21	115	

[a] Percentages are rounded to the nearest integer. Any discrepancies are due to rounding.

genre and subject matter. As can be seen, the classification of the *Journal des Sçavans* as a journal of book reviews is fully justified, 79% of the 115 items in the corpus being of this type. The headings for these items give the title and usually, but not always, the author of the book under review, and frequently the size (folio, quarto, octavo, etc.) and where the book can be obtained. Thus the issue for 1 September 1675 has the entry:

> *HISTOIRE DE L'ANCIEN TESTAMENT tirée de l'Ecriture Sainte par Mr. Arnauld d'Andilly.* In 4. A Paris chez Pierre le Petit, ruë saint Jacques.

Since subtitles in books of this period can on occasion be long, headings can also be relatively long. For example, the issue for 20 June 1695 has the following heading:

> BIBLIOTHECA LATINO-HEBRAICA, SIVE DE *Scriptoribus Latinis qui ex diversis nationibus contra Judeos, vel de re Hebraïca, utcunque scripsere : additis observationibus criticis & philologico-historicis, quibus quæ circa pairiam, æternem, vitæ institutum, mortemque Auctorum consideranda veniunt, exponuntur. Cum quadruplici indice, nominum, cognominum, heterodoxorum, & materium. Loco Coronidis adventus Messiæ ad Judæorum blasphemiis ac Hæreticorum calumniis vindicates, sacrarum Scripturarum, sanctorum Patrum, conciliorum, Rabbinorumque suffragiis obsignatus, &c. Auctore & vindice D. Carolo Josepho Imbonato Mediolanensi, Cong. S. Bern. Ord. Cist. Monacho, &c. In fol. Romæ.* & se trouve à Paris chez Jean Anisson. 1695.

The other genre types occur rarely and spasmodically, many of them only once in the whole corpus. There are seven article extracts, accounting for 6% of the corpus. From our point of view it is interesting that five of these items are taken from the *Philosophical Transactions*, which the *Journal des Sçavans* calls the 'Journal d'Angleterre'. Thus the issue for 6 May 1675 has an item headed:

> *EXTRAIT DV IOVRNAL D'ANGLETERRE contenant un extrait d'un mémoire de Paulus Biornonus qui est en Islande, où il répond à quelques questions qu'on luy avoit faites touchant cette Isle.*
> [Extract from the English Journal containing an extract from a treatise by Paulus Biornonus who is in Iceland, where he replies to some questions that he had been asked about this island.]

The significance of the distribution of genre types in the *Journal des Sçavans*, with its overwhelming percentage of book reviews, becomes clear when this is compared with the genre types found in the *Philosophical Transactions*. The distribution in the *Philosophical Transactions* is given in Table 2.

Table 2. Genre types in the *Philosophical Transactions*.

Genre	*1665*	*1675*	*1685*	*1694*	*Total*	*%*
Letter	1	3	2	2	8	12
Letter extract	8	3	3	1	15	22
Article	1	4	5	7	17	25
Paper	–	–	1	–	1	1
Book extract	6	1	–	–	7	10
Book review	3	7	3	2	15	22
Book summary	–	1	–	–	1	1
News item	2	–	–	–	2	3
List	–	1	–	–	1	1
Editorial	1	–	–	–	1	1
Total	22	20	14	12	68	

Full details are given in Appendix 3. It can be seen that four of these types were regular features: letters, letter extracts, articles, and book reviews. Letters and letter extracts together count for more than a third (34%) of the items. Letters are those that are printed with a salutation and some also have a valediction. They are frequently labelled as letters in the heading, such as this entry from the 1694 March/April issue:

> I. *A LETTER from* Hans Sloane, *M.D. and S.R.S with several Accounts of the Earthquakes in* Peru October *the* 20*th*. 1687. *And at* Jamaica, February 19*th*. 168$^7/_8$ *and* June *the* 7*th*.1692.

This item begins with the salutation 'SIR', and ends with the valediction 'Your most Obedient Servant, HANS SLOANE'. The following item is a letter extract; it lacks the formal marks of a letter and is labelled as an extract in the heading:

> *An Extract of a Letter of Father* Alvarez de Toledo *a* Franciscan *Friar, Dated* 29 Oct. 1687. *from* Lima, *giving some Particulars of an Earthquake which happened there the* 20th *of that Month.*

Two of the letter extracts are printed in Latin rather than English. Articles are free-standing items, which may well have been accompanied by a covering letter (Gotti 2006). These frequently have simply a title and author, but are sometimes labelled as an 'account' or a 'relation', though these terms, particularly 'account', can be used for other genre types too. The following is an example from the June 1665 issue:

> *A Relation of some extraordinary Tydes in the West-Isles of* Scotland, *as it was communicated by Sr.* Robert Moray.

Of the 17 articles in the corpus, three are printed in Latin. Book reviews were a regular feature; of the issues in the corpus, only that for July/August 1694 has none at all. However, overall they account for only 22% of the items, compared with 79% in the *Journal des Sçavans*. Papers occur only irregularly. The one that appears in the corpus had been presented to the Dublin Society:

> *A Discourse on the* Dissection *of a* Monstrous Double Catt; *read before the* Dublin Society *by* Dr. Mullen.

However, in other issues of the *Philosophical Transactions*, the papers that turn up tend to have been presented to the Royal Society. Book extracts are probably over-represented in the corpus, due to the fact that five of the seven that occur in the corpus do so in a single issue, that for 5 June 1665, in which Oldenburg gives particular prominence to a new book by Adrien Auzout. The first of these has the heading:

> Monsieur Auzout's *Judgement touching the Apertures of* Object-Glasses, *and their* Proportions, *in respect of the several* Lengths *of* Telescopes.

The news item is an item of news which Oldenburg had heard about, usually in his correspondence, but which he wrote up, briefly, himself. Although not prominent in the corpus, the news item was significant in the way the *Philosophical Transactions* developed in its early period. The very first issue, 6 March 1665, was basically made up of news items; there were nine of these, plus an editorial introduction and an obituary notice for Fermat. Thus the whole issue was written by Oldenburg himself. However, from the second issue (3 April 1665) on, he began using verbatim material. Letter extracts appear, with introductions, and occasionally a short closing section, by Oldenburg himself (Bluhm 1960; Kronick 1962). By the end of the first year of publication, Oldenburg had established a norm whereby he used verbatim material whenever possible. There are two types of instance where this was not possible. The first is where items were too long, and he had to summarize; this is particularly the case with book extracts. The second is where the item was not in English, and he had to translate (Banks 2009b).

Thus we see that editorial decisions impinge greatly on the genre types included. The *Journal des Sçavans* is dominated by book reviews, whereas the *Philosophical Transactions* has a wider range of regular features, within which book reviews have their place, but nothing like the predominant role they play in the French journal. The contents of the *Philosophical Transactions* are largely based initially on Oldenburg's correspondence, and following him, that of later editors. Not only the letters, and letter extracts, but also the articles and books came to him with the correspondence. Even the news items were based on information gleaned mainly from his postbag.

Subject matter

Denis de Sallo, in the *Journal des Sçavans,* set out to cover the whole field of human knowledge. We would therefore expect to find a wide range of subjects treated in the pages of his journal, and this is indeed the case. Gascoigne (1985) claims that one should not use present-day categories to classify texts from earlier periods, since these do not correspond to the categories of the period in question. While this is to some extant true, a classification in

Table 3. Subject matter in the *Journal des Sçavans.*

Subject	*1665*	*1675*	*1685*	*1695*	*Total*	*%*
Theology	4	6	8	2	20	17%
History	5	3	5	2	15	13%
Law	6	–	–	3	9	8%
Philosophy	1	–	1	–	2	2%
Sociology	1	–	–	–	1	1%
Classics	1	2	1	1	5	4%
Literature	2	1	–	–	3	3%
Language	1	–	1	–	2	2%
Biography	–	2	–	2	4	3%
Bibliography	–	1	–	1	2	2%
Numismatics	2	–	–	–	2	2%
Architecture	–	–	1	–	1	1%
Art	–	–	–	1	1	1%
Mathematics	1	2	2	–	5	4%
Technology	–	2	2	1	5	4%
Agriculture	–	1	–	–	1	1%
Geography	1	2	–	2	5	4%
Geology	–	–	1	–	1	1%
Medicine	2	2	8	1	13	11%
Biology	–	–	–	1	1	1%
Chemistry	–	1	1	–	2	2%
Physics	1	–	–	–	1	1%
Astronomy	1	2	1	–	4	3%
Editorial	–	1	–	–	1	1%
General	–	–	5	4	9	8%
Total	29	28	37	21	115	

terms of the categories of the late seventeenth century would pose problems for the modern reader, and would require extensive knowledge of the conventions of the time. I find it more useful to use contemporary categories, even though some of these would not have been recognized by the writers of these texts. Admittedly, the boundaries of these categories may be fuzzy when applied to the late seventeenth century, but this makes them more easily understandable to the modern reader, while still giving a good general picture of the situation. Table 3 gives the distribution of items in the *Journal des Sçavans* corpus in terms of their subject matter.

The table has been organized with humanities subjects towards the top of the table and more scientific subjects towards the bottom, with the exception of Editorial and General, which come at the end. Items dealing with human physiology have been classed with Medicine. It is immediately noticeable that Theology and History are the two major components, accounting together for 30% of the sample. Theology accounts for 17% of this sample but this underestimates the influence of religion insofar as it frequently appears in other guises. History is sometimes church history; this is clearly the case for three of the 15 examples in the corpus, such as the following item from the issue for 3 January 1695:

> MEMOIRES POUR SERVIR A *L'HISTOIRE Ecclesiastique des six premiers siecles, justifiez par les citations des Auteurs Originaux ; avec une Chronologie, &c. Tome Second. Par le Sieur D.T. In 4. à* Paris chez Ch. Robustel. 1694.

Law might sometimes be considered canon law rather than civil law, such as this entry from the 9 March 1665 issue which concerns monastic rules:

> *CODEX REGVLARVM, QVAS SANCTI Patres Monachis a Virginibus Sanctimonialibus præscripsere. Collectus olim à S. Benedicto Anianiensi Abbate. Lucas Holstenius, Vaticanæ Bibliothecæ Præfectus editit. A Paris, chez L. Billaine, au Palais.*

Three of the nine items categorized as law could be considered to be of this type. Of the four items labelled Biography, two might be considered hagiography, such as this biography of Thomas Becket, which appeared in the 14 January 1675 issue:

> *LA VIE DE S. THOMAS ARCHEVESQVE DE Cantorbery & martyr.* A Paris chez P. le Petit.

After Theology, the most common subject area is History, with 13% of the entries. If we consider that the humanities include those subjects from Theology down to Art, there are no other subject areas which account for more than 10%. Law, the next most important, accounts for 8% of the items. The whole of this humanities area accounts for 58% of the sample. If we consider that the entries from Mathematics down to Astronomy cover the scientific area, then only Medicine, with 11%, accounts for more than 10% of the items. No other subject in the scientific area accounts for more than 4%, and the whole of this area accounts for 33% of the items. Thus the importance accorded to the humanities is considerably more than that accorded to the sciences. The only items not included in either humanities or science are one editorial note and those items labelled General. These latter are items which cover more than one subject area, and so could not be classified under one specific area. They include three book reviews and one letter extract, the other five being the lists of new publications that appeared in most issues in 1685. Thus the list printed at the end of the 15 January 1685 issue, under the heading

> NOUVEAUTEZ DE LA HUITAINE, tant pour les Artts que pour les Sciences.

includes the mention of eight works covering the areas of theology, medicine, geography and numismatics.

The significance of the range of subject areas covered by the *Journal des Sçavans* becomes clear when this is compared with the subject areas covered by the *Philosophical Transactions,* given in Table 4. Here, in comparison with 33% for the whole of the scientific area in the *Journal des Sçavans,* Astronomy

Table 4. Subject matter in the *Philosophical Transactions.*

Subject	*1665*	*1675*	*1685*	*1694*	*Total*	*%*
Astronomy	5	4	1	1	11	16%
Medicine	2	–	6	3	11	16%
Physics	3	3	2	1	9	13%
Biology	3	1	3	–	7	10%
Geology	–	2	2	4	8	12%
Geography	–	2	–	–	2	3%
Mathematics	–	1	–	1	2	3%
Technology	8	–	–	1	9	13%
Agriculture	–	5	–	–	5	7%
Economics	–	1	–	–	1	2%
History	–	–	–	1	1	2%
General	1	1	–	–	2	3%
Total	22	20	14	12	68	

and Medicine account for 16% each, Technology for 13%, Physics a further 13%, with Biology and Geology representing 10% each. If we consider that the scientific area is covered by everything from Astronomy down to Agriculture, this accounts for 64 of the 68 items, or 94%. This can be pushed even further, since the two items labelled General are, first of all, a review of Robert Hooke's *Micrographia*, which appeared in the 3 April 1665 issue:

> *An Account of* Micrographia, *or the* Physiological Descriptions *of* Minute Bodies, *made by* Magnifying Glasses.

In this work Hooke describes his microscope observations of many types of body, both organic and inorganic, so that the subject areas might include biology, botany, geology, etc., and he also describes the construction of a number of instruments which might fall into the area of technology. However, all of these are in the scientific area. The second item classed as General is a letter extract which refers back to the previous issue and touches on technology, astronomy and physics, but again remains within the scientific area. If we add these two items to the scientific sector, we find that 66 of the 68 items (97%) are in the scientific area. Only the two items labelled Economics and History are outside the scientific area, and it is perhaps significant that both of these are book reviews, rather than items of correspondence.

The results given here coincide fairly well with previous results carried out on smaller samples (Banks 2009a, 2012a). Those studies found that, for example, book reviews represented 86% of the *Journal des Sçavans* items, and 18% to 21% of the *Philosophical Transactions* items; this compares with the 79% for the *Journal des Sçavans* and 22% for the *Philosophical Transactions* found here. They also found that 20% to 33% of the *Journal des Sçavans* items and 75% to 85% of the *Philosophical Transactions* items were scientific, compared to the 33% for the *Journal des Sçavans* and 94% to 97% for the *Philosophical Transactions* found here. Since this study has been carried out on a rather larger corpus, the results can be taken to be a fine-tuning of those of the previous studies.

Possible distortion

No corpus will ever produce exactly the same results as the sum total of the texts it is intended to represent. It is therefore useful to attempt to see the extent to which the corpus differs from the total texts. In order to do this, the genre and subject area results in the *Philosophical Transactions* corpus for 1665 and 1675 have been compared with the results for the whole of those years. Table 5 gives the percentage distribution of genre types for the

Table 5. Percentage distribution of genres in the *Philosophical Transactions* of 1665.

Genre	*Corpus*	*Whole year*
Letter	5%	2%
Letter extract	36%	27%
Article	5%	5%
Paper	–	7%
Paper report	–	9%
Book extract	27%	14%
Book review	14%	7%
Book summary	–	2%
Book announcement	–	4%
Obituary notice	–	2%
News item	9%	16%
List	–	2%
Editorial	5%	4%

Table 6. Percentage distribution of genres in the *Philosophical Transactions* of 1675.

Genre	*Corpus*	*Whole year*
Letter	15%	15%
Letter extract	15%	21%
Article	20%	16%
Book extract	5%	5%
Book review	35%	36%
Book summary	5%	1%
Book announcement	–	1%
News item	–	1%
List	5%	1%
Editorial	–	1%

corpus and whole year for the 1665 issues of the *Philosophical Transactions*. Table 6 gives the results for 1675.

The results for 1675 seem to be more coherent than those for 1665, probably due to the fact that, in the course of 1665, Oldenburg was settling into the task and working out, by trial and error, a system of editorial strategy, giving greater differences between individual issues in that first year. For 1675, there are 75 items in the whole year, of which 20 are included in

Table 7. Percentage distribution of genres in the *Philosophical Transactions* of 1665 and 1675.

Genre	*Corpus*	*Whole years*
Letter	10%	9%
Letter extract	26%	24%
Article	12%	11%
Paper	–	3%
Paper report	–	4%
Book extract	17%	9%
Book review	24%	24%
Book summary	2%	2%
Book announcement	–	2%
Obituary notice	–	1%
News item	5%	8%
List	2%	2%
Editorial	2%	2%

the corpus. The distribution is similar, the four major items – book reviews, letters, letter extracts and articles – being the same in each. In the corpus, letter extracts are slightly under-represented, and articles slightly over-represented, to about the same degree.

If the results for these two years are combined, the results given in Table 7 are obtained. It can be seen that the corpus results compare well with those of the texts as a whole, and probably better than either of the years individually. Of the five items which account for 10% or more in the corpus, four (letters, letter extracts, book reviews and articles) are all within one or two percentage points of the results for the texts as a whole. Book extracts is the only item seriously overestimated; this is due to the inclusion in the corpus of the issue for 5 June 1665, which has five of the 12 book extracts which appeared in the course of these two years. Although this might be considered a slight distortion, it does not seem sufficient to warrant altering what appeared by chance in the corpus. It is sufficient to be aware that this slight bias exists.

The equivalent exercise carried out for subject areas produces similar results. Those for 1665 are given in Table 8. The major categories are well represented, with some over-representation of Technology and Astronomy, and some under-representation of Biology.

Table 8. Percentage distribution of subject areas in the *Philosophical Transactions* of 1665.

Subject area	*Corpus*	*Whole year*
Astronomy	23%	18%
Medicine	9%	9%
Physics	14%	14%
Chemistry	–	2%
Biology	14%	20%
Geology	–	5%
Mathematics	–	2%
Technology	36%	27%
Agriculture	–	2%
General	5%	4%

The results for 1675 are given in Table 9. For 1675, with the exception of Agriculture, which is over-represented, the general distribution corresponds fairly well. When the results for the two years are conflated, the results given in Table 10 emerge. Here the fit between the two distributions is fairly

Table 9. Percentage distribution of subject areas in the *Philosophical Transactions* of 1675.

Subject area	*Corpus*	*Whole year*
Astronomy	20%	17%
Medicine	–	7%
Physics	15%	16%
Chemistry	–	3%
Biology	5%	7%
Botany	–	7%
Geology	10%	5%
Geography	10%	7%
Mathematics	5%	4%
Technology	–	5%
Agriculture	25%	9%
Architecture	–	1%
Language	–	1%
Economics	5%	1%
General	5%	9%

Table 10. Percentage distribution of subject areas in the *Philosophical Transactions* of 1665 and 1675.

Subject area	*Corpus*	*Whole years*
Astronomy	21%	18%
Medicine	5%	8%
Physics	14%	15%
Chemistry	–	2%
Biology	10%	12%
Botany	–	4%
Geology	5%	5%
Geography	5%	4%
Mathematics	2%	3%
Technology	19%	15%
Agriculture	12%	6%
Architecture	–	1%
Language	–	1%
Economics	2%	1%
General	5%	7%

good. Astronomy is within three percentage points, and Technology within four, as are the other major areas, Physics and Biology. Even in the case of Agriculture the difference is reduced to six percentage points.

Hence, on the basis of these tests, it seems reasonable to accept that the results given by the corpus will be a fair representation of what is to be found in the texts as a whole.

5 Thematic structure: a starting point

Thematic structure relates to the way in which a speaker or writer organizes his discourse. As we have seen, at the level of the clause, it distinguishes between a theme and a rheme, the theme being the component which the speaker takes as his starting point. It is from this starting point that he constructs the message contained in the clause. The theme is particularly important because it is a way of highlighting the speaker's centre of interest. The thematic material of a clause has one obligatory element, known as the topical theme; this may optionally be preceded by one or more textual or interpersonal themes. In what follows, 'theme' refers to topical theme unless otherwise specifically stated. Study of the themes chosen by a speaker shows where his main interest lies. These are the items on which he wishes to lay emphasis, and to which the rest of the clause relates. Moreover, the themes chosen play an important role in the construction of the argumentation of a text. The origin of a theme in the previous discourse and the introduction of new themes organize the text as it moves forward, creating its argument structure. It is factors like these which have been used to show that the thematic structure of scientific writing is the driving force of the text (Halliday 1988, 1994, 1998; Banks 2008a, 2008b). This is what is behind certain features promoted as being typical of scientific text, such as the use of passive forms (e.g. Barber 1962; Turner 1972; Tarone *et al.* 1981, 1998). It used to be thought that scientific writers chose the passive as a means of avoiding agentive subjects and of maintaining an objective and impersonal stance. It is now evident that this is not the case, but that the scientific writer chooses his themes in terms of his interest; one of the outcomes of this is the use of the passive. For example, an interest in an object of study leads to that object of study appearing in theme position; one way of doing this is to construct the clause in passive form. The thematic structure of the corpus has been analysed for both of the journals concerned. Since the *Journal des Sçavans* was first in the field, we will deal with that journal first.

The *Journal des Sçavans*

Any of the four main grammatical functions can serve as theme, though some are much more frequent than others. The unmarked grammatical function of a theme is that of subject. This type of text is no exception to this tendency, and the vast majority of themes in the *Journal des Sçavans* component of the corpus are grammatical subjects:

> **Ces Vies** sont escrites d'vne maniere tres-agreable. **Elles** ont esté d'autant mieux recuës qu'il n'y auoit rien sur ce sujet dans nostre langue. **L'Autheur** dit dans la Preface de cét ouvrage, qu'il ne l'a entrepris, que pour seruir d'instruction à vn jeune seigneur. (*Journal des Sçavans*, 12 janvier 1665)
> [These Lives are written in a pleasant manner. They have been all the more well received in that there was nothing on the subject in our language. The author says, in the Preface of the work, that he only undertook it, so that it could serve in the education of a young lord.]

The predicator, on the other hand, is relatively rare. Even the small number found here is to some extent enhanced by the admittedly arguable decision to count the impersonal radical modal phrase *il faut* with the predicators:

> **Il faloit** examiner si la multiplication de ces sieges episcopaux au lieu d'estre utile à la religion, n'y seroit point prejudiciable, & si les peuples estoient disposez à recevoir avec respect ces nouveaux Prelats. (*Journal des Sçavans*, 25 avril 1695)
> [It was necessary to study whether the multiplication of these episcopal sees, rather than being useful to religion, was not detrimental and whether the people were ready to receive these new prelates with respect.]

Otherwise, cases of predicators functioning as theme occur as imperatives, in cases of grammatical inversion, or where a non-finite predicator is preceded by grammatical metaphor functioning as an interpersonal theme; the following are examples of the first type:

> Maintenant **voyons** s'il est possible que le globe de l'œil ou le Chrystallin change de conformation pour voir des objets differemment éloignez ; & **supposons** par exemple qu'un œil puisse changer de forme autant qu'il est necessaire pour voir avec la mesme distinction un objet à un pied de distance, & un autre à six pieds. (*Journal des Sçavans*, 30 juillet 1685)
> [Now let us see if it is possible for the globe of the eye or the chrystalline lens to change shape in order to see objects at different distances; and let us suppose for example that an eye can change shape as often as is necessary to see with the same clarity an object one foot away, and another six feet away.]

If predicators are rare as theme, complements are even rarer. In the following case the thematization of the complement results from the (grammatically) obligatory position of the pronoun complement before the verb:

> Aussi **les** traite-t-il de digressions Physiques pour la plus-part; parce qu'elles sont en effet des questions de Physique plustost que de mathematique. (*Journal des Sçavans*, 14 janvier 1675)
> [Moreover he treats them as physical digressions for the most part, since they are questions of physics rather than mathematics.]

The major form of marked theme is that of the (circumstantial) adjunct, by far the most common after the unmarked subject theme. These can occur as words, groups, or clauses:

> **Dans la 2^e^**, il traite amplement de la guerre de Candie, dont il tire les particularitez de l'Histoire de Nani. (*Journal des Sçavans*, 5 mars 1685)
> [In the second, he deals at length with the Candian war, from which derives the specific characteristics of the history of Nani.]

> Ainsi **ayant fait apporter en sa presence un petit enfant du Comte qui n'avoit encore que trois ans**, il le menaça de le faire mourir à ses yeux & de devenir son ennemy, s'il ne se faisoit baptizer avec son fils ; ce que le Comte executa avec encore tout le people qu'il gouvernoit. (*Journal des Sçavans*, 16 avril 1685)
> [Thus, having had one of the Count's small children, who was just three years old, brought before him, he threatened to have him killed before his eyes, and to become his enemy, if he wasn't baptized with his son, and this the Count did, with all the people he governed.]

There are two exceptional forms which can function as theme in addition to the four major grammatical functions. These occur in cleft structures, which Halliday calls theme predication (Halliday 2014), and in extraposition, which Thompson calls thematized comment (Thompson 2004). In cleft structures it is the cleft item which functions as theme:

> **C'est à ces reflexions pleines de detours, de peu de bonne foy & de chicane**, que M. de Tournai répond dans ce livre. (*Journal des Sçavans*, 4 juin 1685)
> [It is to these reflections, full of digressions, little good faith, and petty quibbles, that M. de Tournai replies in this book.]

In the case of extraposition, it is the extraposition matrix which functions as theme:

> **Ce n'est plus une chose rare** que d'en voir qui entendent le latin, & qui écrivent avec une pureté digne de l'ancienne Rome : mais Mademoiselle Le Fevre a peu de compagnes de son application à la langue Grecque. (*Journal des Sçavans*, 11 mars 1685)
> [It is no longer a rare thing to see ladies who understand Latin and write it with a purity worthy of ancient Rome, but Mademoiselle Le Fevre has few equals in her mastery of Greek.]

Table 11. Grammatical functions of themes in the *Journal des Sçavans.*

Function	*1665*	*1675*	*1685*	*1695*	*Total*	*%*
Subject	338	331	308	444	1421	73%
Predicator	6	4	6	8	24	1%
Complement	1	1	2	–	4	*[6]
Adjunct	96	102	95	140	433	22%
Cleft	4	12	6	10	32	2%
Extraposition	10	9	9	8	36	2%
Total	455	459	426	610	1950	

Table 12. Percentages of grammatical function as themes.

Function	*1665*	*1675*	*1685*	*1695*
Subject	74%	72%	72%	73%
Predicator	1%	1%	1%	1%
Complement	*	*	*	–
Adjunct	21%	22%	22%	23%
Cleft	1%	3%	1%	2%
Extraposition	2%	2%	2%	1%

Table 11 gives the numbers of themes according to their grammatical function found in the *Journal des Sçavans* component of the corpus.

Clauses which are susceptible to thematic structure analysis are known as ranking clauses. The *Journal des Sçavans* component has 1950 such clauses. There are over 400 in each of the first three years, with an increase of about a third in 1695. As expected, subjects account for the vast majority of themes. The only thing about these figures which might cause some surprise is the relatively healthy 22% for adjuncts. Although one would expect adjuncts to be the main category after subjects, this is rather more than some might expect. In order that the figures for different years may be more easily compared, Table 12 gives the percentage distribution for each year.

Table 12 shows the remarkable stability of this distribution over the period. Despite the increase in the number of ranking clauses in 1695, the percentage distribution of functions is virtually the same as in the previous years. Subjects account for between 72% and 74% of the themes; adjuncts account for between 21% and 23%. The other functions never account for more than 3%.

6 Percentages of less than 0.5% are indicated by an asterisk in all tables.

Table 13. Numbers of clausal adjuncts as theme.

Adjunct type	*1665*	*1675*	*1685*	*1695*	*Total*	*% of adjuncts*
Finite clause	32	30	38	33	133	31%
Non-finite clause	16	23	14	41	94	22%
Total	48	53	52	74	227	52%

The fact that the percentage of adjuncts seems relatively high is due not only to the clausal complexity of the writing of this period (Banks 2015), but to the fact that adjuncts that have clausal form, that is finite clauses, and non-finite clauses (including for these purposes gerundive phrases) are common. These clausal adjuncts account for over half of the total number of adjunct themes, and hence 12% of all themes are of this type. Table 13 shows the numbers of clausal adjuncts. As can be seen, 31% of adjunct themes are in the form of a finite clause.

> **Avant que le Roy Aufrede eut fondé cette Université sur le fin du neuviéme siècle, l'an huit cens soixante-dix-neuf,** les lettres y avoient fleury pendant long-temps. (*Journal des Sçavans*, 9 septembre 1675)
> [Before King Alfred founded this University towards the end of the ninth century, in the year eight hundred and sixty-nine, the study of Letters had flourished for a long time.]

A further 22% of the adjuncts are in the form of a non-finite clause or gerundive phrase:

> ... mais **les irruptions des Goths, des Huns & des Lombards, les ayant constraint de les abandonner**, plusieurs familles se retirerent dans les Isles, où ils bastirent des maisons dont la ville de Venise & les autres Citez maritimes qui en sont voisines furent insensiblement formées. (*Journal des Sçavans*, 5 mars 1685)
> [... but the incursions of the Goths, Huns and Lombards having forced them to abandon them, several families withdrew to the islands, where they built houses from which the town of Venice and other neighbouring cities were imperceptibly formed.]

> **En se congelant à mesure qu'elle entroit dans la mer** (ce qui forçoit la matiére qui survenoit de nouveau à couler par dessus ce qui estoit congelé) elle avoit fait encore retirer ses eaux plus loin en arriere que la portée d'un mousquet & environ deux fois autant d'espace en largeur. (*Journal des Sçavans*, 4 juin 1685)
> [In hardening as it entered the sea (which forced the matter which still arrived to flow over what was hardened), it made the water withdraw as far as the range of a musket, and over an area about twice as wide.]

Table 14. Clausal adjuncts as percentages of adjunct themes.

Adjunct type	*1665*	*1675*	*1685*	*1695*
Finite clause	33%	29%	40%	24%
Non-finite clause	17%	23%	15%	29%
All clause types	50%	52%	55%	53%

Table 14 shows percentages of clausal adjuncts for each year. The percentage of adjunct themes which have a clausal form is fairly stable, ranging from 50% to 55%. However, the way this figure is distributed between finite and non-finite forms is variable, finite types accounting for between 24% and 40% depending on the year, and non-finite types varying from 15% to 29%. One might note that it is only in 1695 that non-finite types are more common than finite types.

Textual and interpersonal themes

The function of textual themes is to link the text, and thus help form a coherent discourse. The function of interpersonal themes is to thematize the writer's attitude to the discourse. Table 15 shows the incidence of textual and interpersonal themes in the *Journal des Sçavans* component of the corpus. Textual themes occur in less than a third of the clauses:

> **D'ailleurs** il parloit beaucoup, & aimoit à dire ce qu'il sçavoit. (*Journal des Sçavans*, 21 février 1695)
> [Moreover he talked a lot, and liked telling what he knew.]

Table 15. Numbers of textual and interpersonal themes in the *Journal des Sçavans*.

	1665	*1675*	*1685*	*1695*	*Total*	*% of ranking clauses*
Textual	186	166	114	101	568	29%
Interpersonal	23	14	16	9	62	3%

There are occasional occurrences of two adjacent textual themes in the same clause but this is extremely rare:

> ... **& ainsi** i'ai franchy le pas. (*Journal des Sçavans*, 23 février 1665)
> [... and so I took the step]

Interpersonal themes are relatively rare, occurring in only 3% of ranking clauses overall. Where they occur, these frequently take the grammatical form of extraposition, but where the extraposed matrix functions as a grammatical metaphor of modality:

Table 16. Percentages of textual and interpersonal themes in the *Journal des Sçavans.*

	1665	*1675*	*1685*	*1695*
Textual	41%	36%	27%	17%
Interpersonal	5%	3%	4%	1%

> **Il est vray qu**'on a laissé glisser une infinité d'erreurs dans l'art des *Talismans*, & qu'on en a dit des choses si peu croyables, que cet art ne passe plus que pour une superstition, & on ne regard à present ces medailles que comme autant d'enchantement & de sortileges. (*Journal des Sçavans*, 11 mars 1675)
>
> [It is true that we have let a multitude of errors slip into the art of the talisman, and things that are unbelievable have been said about them, so that this art no longer passes for anything more than a superstition, and these medals are thought of as so much spells and magic.]

Table 16 gives the percentage distribution of textual themes for each year. Here it can be seen that textual themes, while relatively common in 1665, being present in 41% of the ranking clauses, fall steadily over the years to only 17% in 1695. Although the percentage of interpersonal themes seems to fall, the numbers involved are fairly minimal in any case.

Thematic progression

The relationship between a theme and the preceding discourse is significant in terms of the type of text which is being constructed. Where a theme is derived from a preceding theme, this is called constant progression, and the link between the two is called a constant link; where a theme is derived from a preceding rheme, we talk of linear progression and a linear link. Only very short texts will be made up of only one type of progression; most texts will have a mixture of both, but one type may dominate. Texts that are descriptive and simple narratives will tend to have a majority of constant links; texts that are more argumentative in nature will tend to have more linear links. Although not all themes can be clearly characterized as being derived from a prior theme or rheme, this will be the case for most. In the *Journal des Sçavans* component, almost three-quarters of the themes can be clearly analysed as constant or linear. The details are given in Table 17.

Table 17. Thematic progression in the *Journal des Sçavans.*

	1665	*1675*	*1685*	*1695*	*Total*	*% of ranking clauses*
Constant	135	144	125	186	590	30%
Linear	175	183	176	274	808	41%

Table 18. Percentage distribution of thematic progression in the *Journal des Sçavans.*

	1665	*1675*	*1685*	*1695*
Constant	30%	31%	29%	30%
Linear	38%	40%	41%	45%

The incidence of linear progression is more frequent than that of constant progression. While constant progression accounts for 30% of the themes, linear progression accounts for just over 40%. The percentage distributions for each year are given in Table 18.

It can be seen that the incidence of constant progression remains stable over the period, at roughly 30%, with a range of 29% to 31%. On the other hand, the incidence of linear progression increases as the century moves on. From 38% of the themes in 1665 it gradually increases to 45% in 1695. This might be taken to indicate an increasingly more closely structured form of argumentation in these texts as time goes on.

Semantic categorization of themes

In my previous work (Banks 2008a, 2008b) I developed a series of semantic categories for themes in early scientific writing. This categorization was subsequently used in a series of publications (Banks 2008c, 2009b, 2010a, 2010b, 2011, 2012a, 2012b, 2012c). The categorization was originally developed for a study of the *Philosophical Transactions.* Had one started with the *Journal des Sçavans,* it is not impossible that a slightly different categorization might have resulted. However, the categories work reasonably well for the *Journal des Sçavans* too, with a few minor adaptations or extensions. It is therefore useful to retain the same categories, as this permits comparison between the *Journal des Sçavans* and the *Philosophical Transactions,* as well as with the earlier work. There are 15 categories in all. They are as follows:

Obj. The object of study. This may be the object being observed, or experimented on. In the case of the *Journal des Sçavans* it may be the subject of discussion, and hence abstract or at least non-physical, rather than the sort of physical object found more commonly in the *Philosophical Transactions.*

> **Ce bateau** n'est pas different des autres. (*Journal des Sçavans,* 14 janvier 1675)
> [This boat is no different to the others.]

Exp. Terms relating to experiment or the experimental process. In its simplest form this may be no more than doing something with an object of study.

Cette experience commune dans la Chirurgie a fait naître à M. Guide habile Medecin Anglois, la premiere pensée de se servir de ce mesme vin pour guerir la retention d'urine. (*Journal des Sçavans*, 5 mars 1685)
[This practice, common in surgery, first suggested to Mr. Guide, an able English doctor, the idea of using this same wine to cure urine retention.]

Equip. Equipment or objects used as such in experiment.

Mais **puisque celles-là ont déjà seruy auec tant de succés**, & que ces autres sont encore plus iustes : I'ay d'autant plus de suiet de croire que l'inuention des longitudes sera dans sa perfection derniere. (*Journal des Sçavans*, 23 février 1665)
[But since those have already been used with so much success, and these others are even more accurate, I have all the more reason to believe that the solution of longitude will be in its final perfection.]

Obs. The observation (as opposed to experiment) of an object of study.

Ces observations furent faites en compagnie du R. P. Fontaney Regent de Mathem, dans le Coll. de Loüis le Grand, & des PP. Visdelou, Bouvet, & Tachard, quatre de ceux qui ont esté choisis en qualité de mathematiciens de S.M. pour aller à la Chine avec toutes sortes d'instruments propres pour faire des observations Astronomiques, Geographiques & Physiques ... (*Journal des Sçavans*, 5 mars 1685)
[These observations were made in the presence of the Rev. Fontaney, Regent of Mathem, in the College of Louis le Grand, and the Revs. Visdelou, Bouvet & Tachard, four of those who were chosen as mathematicians of H.M. to go to China with all sorts of instruments designed to make astronomical, geographical and physical observations ...]

Auth. References to the author, or a group to which the author belongs. In the case of the *Journal des Sçavans*, this is the person writing for the journal, i.e. usually the editor or, when he had one, one of his team of reviewers. In some cases, this can be very general, as in the use of the French impersonal pronoun *on*, where it can mean everyone, the writer included.

... mais **on** se contentera de remarquer de quoy il est traité dans les premiers & les derniers ; parce qu'on pourra par là facilement iuger du reste. (*Journal des Sçavans*, 9 février 1665)
[... but we will simply note what is dealt with in the first and the last, because from that it is easy to judge the rest.]

Oth. Human beings other than the author or groups to which he belongs. In the case of the *Journal des Sçavans*, since it is made up chiefly of book reviews, the human beings in question will frequently be the author of the book under review, or in appropriate cases the translator or editor. In some cases it may also be persons discussed in the book under review, particularly in works of history or biography.

> **L'Empereur Heraclius** l'honoroit de sa confidence. (*Journal des Sçavans*, 6 mai 1675)
> [The Emperor Heraclius honoured him with his confidence.]

Meta. References to other parts of the same text, that is, to the journal or parts within the *Journal des Sçavans* itself, or previous issues of the journal.

> ... mais **la brieveté de ce Iournal** ne permet pas de la faire. (*Journal des Sçavans*, 23 février 1665)
> [... but the brevity of this Journal does not allow us to do so.]

Inter. References to works other than the item in the *Journal des Sçavans* itself. Since the *Journal des Sçavans* is largely made up of book reviews this will frequently be the book under review.

> **Ce liure** est composé en dialogue. (*Journal des Sçavans*, 23 février 1665)
> [This book is written as a dialogue.]

Exist. These occur in existential clauses where the theme simply indicates the existential nature of the clause.

> **Il** y en a trois citez dans la letre. (*Journal des Sçavans*, 20 juin 1695)
> [There are three of them quoted in the letter.]

Field. References to a specific field of study. This is a relatively rare category: there is only one example in the whole of the *Journal des Sçavans* corpus.

> **L'Architecture navale** est quelque chose de si ingenieux, & ce que les Grecs avec les Romains ont fait voir dans leurs exercices sur mer, dans leurs batailles, dans leurs disciplines, dans leurs loix & leur coûtumes est quelque chose de si extraordinaire, qu'une histoire de toutes ces choses peut estre que tres-agreable. (*Journal des Sçavans*, 1 juillet 1675)
> [Naval architecture is so ingenious, and what the Greeks and Romans have shown with their exercises at sea, their battles, their disciplines, and their laws and customs is so extraordinary, that an account of all these things can only be very pleasant.]

Ment. Mental processes, or the argumentation structure of the text itself.

> **Sa conjecture** est fondée sur ce que la mer est fort basse entre Calais & Douvres. (*Journal des Sçavans*, 21 février 1695)
> [His conjecture is based on the fact that the level of the sea is very low between Calais and Dover.]

Time. Expressions of time.

> **En 1676**, ayant esté elu Professeur de Theologie en l'Université de Salamanque, il l'augmenta de beaucoup, & ne put neanmoins le publier

à cause de divers obstacles qui lui survinrent. (*Journal des Sçavans*, 3 janvier 1695)
[In 1675, having been elected Professor of Theology at the University of Salamanca, he augmented it considerably, but was nevertheless unable to publish it because of various obstacles which have survived him.]

Rad. Expressions of radical modality.

Il faut observer qu'encore auiourd'huy à Rome, il y a differentes manieres de compter l'année. (*Journal des Sçavans*, 9 mars 1665)
[It has to be noted that even today in Rome there are different ways of calculating the year.]

Math. Mathematical expressions. There are no examples of this in the *Journal des Sçavans* corpus.

Sit. Spatial location.

Ce fut là qu'il composa ses livres de la Peinture des Anciens qui furent imprimez à Amsterdam, & qu'il mit beaucoup de temps à l'étude des langues du Nort. (*Journal des Sçavans*, 21 février 1695)
[It was there that he wrote his books on the painting of the ancients which were printed in Amsterdam, and that he devoted a great deal of time to the study of northern languages.]

Table 19 gives the distribution of the categories in the *Journal des Sçavans* sample.

Table 19. Semantic categories of themes in the *Journal des Sçavans*.

	1665	*1675*	*1685*	*1695*	*Total*	*%*
Obj.	82	98	83	161	424	22%
Exp.	–	4	16	1	21	1%
Equip.	2	–	–	–	2	*
Obs.	1	–	3	–	4	*
Auth.	40	26	45	12	123	6%
Oth.	142	188	159	230	719	37%
Meta.	12	1	6	–	19	1%
Inter.	107	70	59	73	309	16%
Exist.	22	9	9	14	54	3%
Field	–	1	–	–	1	*
Ment.	36	48	31	61	176	9%
Time	6	9	11	44	70	4%
Rad.	5	2	–	7	14	1%
Math.	–	–	–	–	–	–
Sit.	–	3	4	7	14	1%

Table 20. Percentages of semantic categories in the *Journal des Sçavans.*

	1665	*1675*	*1685*	*1695*
Obj.	18%	21%	19%	26%
Exp.	–	1%	4%	*
Equip.	*	–	–	–
Obs.	*	–	1%	–
Auth.	9%	6%	11%	2%
Oth.	31%	41%	37%	38%
Meta.	3%	*	1%	–
Inter.	24%	15%	14%	12%
Exist.	5%	2%	2%	2%
Field	–	*	–	–
Ment.	8%	10%	7%	10%
Time	1%	2%	3%	7%
Rad.	1%	*	–	1%
Math.	–	–	–	–
Sit.	–	1%	1%	1%

For comparisons from year to year, Table 20 gives the percentage distribution for each year.

The most frequent category is that of humans other than the author of the text (Oth.), which accounts for 37% of the themes overall. It is also the most common theme in each of the individual years, ranging from 31% in 1665 to 41% in 1675. In previous studies based on smaller samples (Banks 2010b, 2011, 2012b, c), I hypothesized that this category was made up predominately of references to the authors of books under review. Consequently, it is useful to look at this category in greater detail and to see to what extent that hypothesis is justified.

Humans other than the author

Looking at this category in greater detail, it seems possible to distinguish six distinct groups: the author or writer of a book under review (writer); a person or persons referred to in a book under review, or in the item itself where this is not a review (text sub.); the editor or publisher of a book under review (editor); the translator of a book under review (translator); references to larger groups, usually of a more general nature (general); and a person

Table 21. Other human groups in the *Journal des Sçavans.*

	1665	*1675*	*1685*	*1695*	*Total*	*%*
Writer	55	106	64	69	294	41%
Text sub.	49	31	52	129	261	36%
Editor	13	8	16	15	52	7%
Translator	1	9	3	–	13	2%
General	19	21	10	7	57	8%
Person/s	5	13	14	10	42	6%

or persons introduced by the writer of a review (person/s). The category of humans other than the author of the review has been analysed in terms of these six groups, and the results are given in Table 21.

For comparison between different years, Table 22 gives the percentage distribution for each year. The first point to be made is that the hypothesis previously made, that the 'other human' category is due to the presence of themes relating to the writer of a book under review, is to a large extent confirmed, insofar as this is the largest group in the other human category, accounting for 41% of the examples. It is also the largest group in three of the four years concerned, never falling below 39%. The second largest group is that of persons referred to in the book under review or in the item in those cases where this is not a book review. This group accounts for 36% overall, and although its rate is relatively low in 1675 (16%), it is the largest group in 1695, where it accounts for 56% of the sample. This might indicate a difference in style between the then editor, Cousin, and his predecessors. Whereas previous editors tended to thematize writers rather than persons constituting the subject matter, Cousin does the reverse, thematizing persons occurring in the subject matter more than the writers of the material.

Table 22. Percentage distribution of other human groups.

	1665	*1675*	*1685*	*1695*
Writer	39%	56%	40%	30%
Text sub.	35%	16%	33%	56%
Editor	9%	4%	10%	7%
Translator	1%	5%	2%	–
General	13%	11%	6%	8%
Person/s	4%	7%	9%	6%

In referring to the writer of a book under review, the author of the review frequently uses the word *auteur* [author] itself, and this may be followed by a series of pronouns referring back to this term, all of them functioning as theme:

> **L'Auteur de ce livre** rejette le premier de ces sentimens, **il** doute de la solidité du second, & **il** approuve fort le troisiéme : mais **il** en ajoûte un quatrième fondé sur l'authorité des Conciles & des Peres, qui donnent le nom de Canon à une certaine regle, descipline, ou genre de vie qui est conforme aux Canons & aux Maximes que les SS. Peres nous ont laissées dans leurs Ouvrages. (*Journal des Sçavans*, 11 mars 1675)
> [The author of this book rejects the first of these proposals; he doubts the soundness of the second, but he approves the third. He adds a fourth based on the authority of the Councils and the Fathers, who give the name of Canon to a certain rule, discipline or lifestyle which conforms to the Canons and maxims which the Church Fathers have left us in their writings.]

In the same way, though less frequently, the author of a book under review may be referred to by name, and this again may be followed by a series of pronouns referring back to him, all of them functioning as theme:

> **M. Catherinot** dit qu'Vfano Capitaine de l'artillerie au chasteau d'Anvers observe qu'en Portugal on garde encore par curiosité quatre anciens Canons dont l'un est nommé Indien parce qu'il fut fondu dans les Indes. **Il** ajoute à cela le nom des autres pieces de cette nature les plus extraordinaires que l'on a faites, comme celle qu'on appelloit la Diablesse de Boldue & le Triquetraque de Rome conservé dans le Chasteaux S Ange, lequel tire 5. coups de suite. **Il** vient après aux differents pîeces d'Artillerie & aux peuples à qui elles doivent leur nom & leur invention ; ainsi **il** remarque que les moscovites inventerent le mousquet, les Arabes la carabine que l'on nommoit Arabine, & les Italiens de Pistoye les pistolets qu'on qu'on appella d'abord pistolles. (*Journal des Sçavans*, 30 juillet 1685)
> [M. Catherinot says that Ufano, artillery captain at Antwerp Castle, observes that four old canons, one of which is called 'Indian' because it was made in India, are still kept in Portugal through curiosity. He adds the names of the most extraordinary pieces of the same type that have been made, like the one called the 'Diablesse de Boldue' and the 'Triquetraque de Rome', preserved in Castel Sant'Angelo, which can fire five times in succession. Next he comes to other pieces of artillery and to the peoples who invented them, and to whom they owe their names; thus he notes that the Muscovites invented the musket, the Arabs the carbine, which was first called the 'arabine', and the Italians of Pistoia pistols, which were first called 'pistolles'.]

The thematization of persons mentioned in a book under review occurs most frequently where the author of the review summarizes the contents of the book. This often happens in the case of books of a historical nature:

> **Henri IV**. qui commença à regner en 1399. fut qualifié d'*Excellente Grace.* **Edouard IV**. en 1461. se fit apeler *Haut & puissant Prince.* **Henri VIII**. eut d'abord la qualité d'*Altesse*, puis celle de *Majesté.* (*Journal des Sçavans*, 21 février 1695)
> [Henry IV, who began his reign in 1399, was called *Excellent Grace.* In 1461, Edward IV had himself called *Great and Powerful Prince.* Henry VIII had first the title of *Highness*, and then that of *Majesty*.]

In items other than book reviews, these persons are those mentioned and thematized in the text, as in this example, which is adapted in the *Journal des Sçavans* from an item in the *Philosophical Transactions*:

> **M. Coxes** vient d'en faire de nouvelles en Angleterre sur ce sujet, & **il** écrit qu'ayant tiré beaucoup de sel de Fougere, & qu'en ayant fait dissoudre une partie à l'air humide apres l'avoir fait secher, le reste de la lessive estant filtré devint rouge comme du sang pur. (*Journal des Sçavans*, 11 mars 1675)
> [Mr. Coxes has just carried out some new ones on this question, and he writes that having drawn a large quantity of Fougère salt, and having dissolved part of it in humid air after drying it, the rest of the wash was filtered and it became red like pure blood.]

None of the other groups accounts for as much as 10% of the total. That relating to larger and more general groups accounts for 8% overall, and from 6% to 13% in individual years. These often occur in the introductory sections of reviews:

> **Quelques-uns** l'ont attribué à Gerson Chancelier de Paris ; mais **ils** n'avoient pas pris garde que l'Auteur du livre de l'Imitation se donne plus d'une fois la qualité de Moine, & que Gerson ne le fut jamais. **Peu de personnes** ont suivi le sentiment de ceux qui l'ont attribué à un Chartreux, ou à un Thomas Prieur de Vendeshem, parce qu'il n'y a pas eu des raisons assez fortes pour l'appuyer. (*Journal des Sçavans*, 1 juillet 1675)
> [Some have attributed it to Gerson, Chancellor of Paris, but they didn't take into account the fact that the author of the *Imitation* more than once says he is a monk, which Gerson never was. Few have followed the opinion of those who have attributed it to a Carthusian, or to a certain Thomas, Prior of Vendeshem, because there was insufficient evidence to support it.]

The impersonal pronoun, *on*, is sometimes used with this general function:

> **On** nous donne tous les jours de nouveaux systemes sur les fiévres. (*Journal des Sçavans*, 15 janvier 1685)
> [Every day we are given new accounts of fevers. Literally: People give us ...]

Quite a number of the books reviewed are collections of writings by authors, usually from earlier periods, including ancient Greece and Rome. Hence, these books have an author, the original writer, and also an editor, the person who put the collection together, often adding notes and other information. Also included in this group are publishers, that is, those who bring the work into the public domain in multiple copies. At that time the distinction between editor and publisher was not particularly clear. Henry Oldenburg, the editor of the *Philosophical Transactions*, refers to himself as 'the publisher'. In the following example the themes indicate an editor in the contemporary sense of the term:

> Quoy qu'il en soit **celuy qui a pris soin de nous donner icy les œuvres de Lactance, ce Ciceron Chrestien comme on l'appelle**, nous assure qu'il les a reveües sur les anciennes éditions & sur cinq differens Mss. **Il** ajoût à la fin le livre de Lactance *de Mortibus Persecutorum* que nous devons depuis ces dernieres années aux soins de M. Baluze, & **il** y insere les notes de cet infatigable auteur. (*Journal des Sçavans*, 4 juin 1685)
> [Even so, the person who has taken the trouble to give us here the works of Lactance, the so-called Christian Cicero, assures us that he has compared them with the former editions and with five different MSS. He adds at the end Lactance's book *De Mortibus Persecutorum*, for which we have been indebted for the last few years to the efforts of Mr. Baluze, and he inserts the notes of that tireless author.]

The *on* in the following example seems to be more like a publisher, or several publishers:

> **On** a fait en mesme temps trois editions de ce liure. (*Journal des Sçavans*, 12 janvier 1665)
> [Three editions of this book have been made at the same time. [Literally: They have made ...]

The writer of a review may introduce other persons into his discussion of the book under review, other than those who are mentioned in the book itself, or simply refer to other persons in items which are not book reviews. These also can be thematized; the following is a piece of information supplied by the reviewer.

> **Pachimere** y a travaillé autrefois ; (*Journal des Sçavans*, 6 mai 1675)
> [Pachimeres worked on it at one time;]

A number of the books reviewed are translations, particularly from the classics, and the translators are sometimes thematized. In the following example Anne Le Fèvre is the translator of the Greek author Callimachus:

> **Mademoiselle Le Fevre** a reparé heureusement ces deux défauts : **elle** y a ajouté quelques fragmens qui avoient esté ômis dans toutes les autres editions ; (*Journal des Sçavans*, 11 mars 1675)
> [Fortunately, Mademoiselle Le Fevre has corrected these two faults: she has added some fragments that were omitted from all the previous editions.]

Hence we see that themes referring to the writer of a book under review and references to persons mentioned in such books together make up 77% of the themes referring to humans other than the author. The writer of the book is the most frequent, accounting for 41%, with persons mentioned in the books accounting for 36% of the themes. The other groups are relatively rare, never accounting for more than 8%.

Objects of study

In previous studies carried out on a small sample (Banks 2010b, 2011, 2012b, 2012c), the second most frequent type of theme was references to other texts (Inter.). This larger corpus indicates that the second largest category is that of objects of study (Obj.), which seem to have been underestimated by the small sample. Here they account for 22% of the themes. However, as pointed out above, object of study, in the *Journal des Sçavans*, must be interpreted fairly widely; it refers frequently to the subject matter, rather than objects in a physical sense, and can ultimately be totally abstract:

> **LA question** estoit de sçavoir, si le Pape accordant vne dispense de mariage au second degré de consanguinité, peut legitimer les enfans venus auparavant le mariage.
> **Le fait** estoit, que Charles Barbier auoit eu deux enfans de Barbe Barbier sa niepce, auparauant de l'avoir espousée. (*Journal des Sçavans*, 12 janvier 1665)
> [The question is to ascertain whether the Pope, after granting a dispensation for a marriage at the second degree of consanguinity, can legitimize the children born before the marriage.
> The fact is that Charles Barbier had two children by Barbe Barbier, his niece, before he married her.]

Those objects of study that are purely physical tend to be more numerous in those items which are not book reviews. The following occurs in an item adapted for the *Journal des Sçavans* from the *Philosophical Transactions*:

> Ainsi **le sel** estoit comme tartareux & essential ; **estant seché par grand feu** il diminua beaucoup en poids, & devint plus blanc, parce qu'il y avoit auparavant de l'huyle & de l'acide. (*Journal des Sçavans*, 11 mars 1675)
> [Thus the salt was somewhat tartarous and essential; after being dried by a large fire, it diminished considerably in weight and became whiter, because earlier there had been oil and acid in it.]

These references to the subject matter, as already noted, are the most common type of theme in the 1695 sample, after having been the second most common in the three other years considered. This seems to indicate that Cousin's interest, in terms of thematic choice, centred on the subject matter of the books reviewed, whereas his predecessors' interest centred on the writers of those books.

Other texts

References to other texts, that is, texts other than the *Journal de Sçavans* text itself, form the third most frequent type of theme, accounting for 16% overall. However, its frequency declines over time, falling from 24% in 1665 to 12% in 1695. In previous studies on a small sample (Banks 2010b, 2011, 2012b, 2012c), where this type of theme was the second most frequent, it was suggested that these would be essentially references to the book under review. This group has been analysed into those referring to the book under review, those referring to books other than that under review, and those referring to texts other than books. The results are given in Table 23. The percentage distributions for individual years are given in Table 24.

Table 23. References to other texts in the *Journal des Sçavans*.

	1665	*1675*	*1685*	*1695*	*Total*	*%*
Book under review	90	53	44	51	238	77%
Other books	12	14	8	7	41	13%
Other texts	5	3	7	15	30	10%

Table 24. Percentage distribution of references to other texts.

	1665	*1675*	*1685*	*1695*
Book under review	84%	76%	75%	70%
Other books	11%	20%	14%	10%
Other texts	5%	4%	12%	21%

It is evident that the hypothesis that the importance of the 'other text' category as theme derives from references to books under review is amply vindicated. More than three-quarters (77%) of the 'other text' category are of this type, and though it is possible to note a steady fall in the rate from 84% in 1665 to 70% in 1695, this last figure is still relatively high. One frequent format is a reference to the book as a whole, followed by references to different parts, each of the references functioning as theme:

> **Ce liure** est diuisé en trois parties.
> **La premiere** contient les Regles des Peres de l'Orient, comme de saint Antoine, de saint Macaire, de saint Pacome &c.
> **La seconde** contient celles des peres de l'Occident, de saint Benoist, de saint Colomban &c.
> Enfin **la troisesme** comprend les Regles des autres Peres de l'Eglise pour les Religieuses, comme de saint Augustin, de saint Cæsarius &c. (*Journal des Sçavans*, 9 mars 1665)
> [This book is divided into three parts.
> The first contains the rules of the Eastern Fathers, such as Saint Anthony, Saint Macaire, Saint Pachomius, etc.
> The second contains those of the Western Fathers, such as Saint Benedict, Saint Columban, etc.
> Finally, the third includes the rules of other Church Fathers for nuns, like Saint Augustine, Saint Caesarius, etc.]

The relatively rare themes that refer to books other than that under review can refer to individual works or groups of books introduced in comparison with the one reviewed:

> **DE quatre cent ouvrages differens que la Republique des letters doit aux Femmes Sçavantes**, & qu'un curieux a pris plaisir de ramasser soigneusement, il n'y en a pas de plus hardy que celuy-cy. (*Journal des Sçavans*, 11 mars 1675)
> [Of the four hundred different books which the Republic of Letters owes to learned women, and which an inquiring mind has with pleasure carefully collected, there is none more daring than this one.]

This category also includes some cases where the work referred to is not a book which has actually appeared, but one which might do so in the future or which the reviewer hopes might be written:

> **En attendant que cet Auteur traite dans un plus gros livre de toutes les autres parties de la Navigation**, il en explique icy les principes … (*Journal des Sçavans*, 16 avril 1685)
> [While waiting for this author to deal, in a longer book, with all the other aspects of navigation, he here explains the principles …]

Themes which relate to texts other than books include references to such things as letters, edicts and manuscripts:

> ... **le manuscript** est à la Biblioteque de Cluny ... (*Journal des Sçavans*, 6 mai 1675)
> [... the manuscript is in the Cluny library ...]

The reviewer

All of the other categories are relatively rare, none of them exceeding 10%; in fact, the most frequent of these is the category of mental processes and argumentation, which accounts for 9% of the themes. The lack of frequency of these themes means that in general they do not require any comment. However, the category of themes referring to the author of a review merits some comment simply because it is so relatively rare. Indeed, it accounts for only 6% of the themes.

This category includes not only the author of a review, but also the authors of items other than reviews, or of groups to which these authors belong. Of the 123 occurrences in the category, 17 are in items other than reviews, such as extracts from letters. The remaining 106 cases therefore can be considered as referring to the author of a review or a group to which he belongs. Of these, 87 (82%) are occurrences of the impersonal pronoun, *on*. In some cases the pronoun *on* does refer uniquely to the writer of the review, but much more frequently it refers to a more general group with which the reviewer associates himself, or even from which he cannot be excluded. There are in addition a small number of occurrences of *je* [I], *nous* [we], *tout le monde* [everyone], *personne* [no one], and (once) *ce Journal* [this Journal], interpreted as referring to the editor rather than the publication. Table 25 gives the distribution of these. *On* referring to the reviewer is given as '*on* (rev.)'; *on* with general reference is given as '*on* (gen.)'.

Table 25. The reviewer as theme in the *Journal des Sçavans*.

	1665	*1675*	*1685*	*1695*	*Total*	*%*
on (gen.)	23	20	26	7	76	72%
on (rev.)	9	–	2	–	11	10%
je	–	–	–	2	2	2%
nous	–	2	9	1	12	11%
tout le monde	1	1	–	–	2	2%
personne	–	2	–	–	2	2%
ce Journal	1	–	–	–	1	1%

Hence, 72% of the themes referring to the author of a review or a group to which he belongs are occurrences of the impersonal pronoun *on* with general reference:

> **On** n'y trouve pas autant d'éloquence que dans les autres ouvrages de ce Père, parce que les sujets n'en sont pas capables : **On** en découvre pourtant assez en plusieurs endroits pour convaincre d'erreur ceux qui les ont attribuez à Eustathe Evesque de Sebaste qui est mort dans l'arianisme, dont le caractere n'estoit nullement d'estre éloquent. (*Journal des Sçavans*, 6 mai 1675)
> [One does not find as much eloquence in it as in the other books by this Father, because the subject does not lend itself to it. One discovers enough of it, however, in several places, to confound those who have attributed them to Eustathius, the bishop of Sebaste, who died professing Arianism, whose character is in no way to be eloquent.]

Only 10% of these cases can be considered references to the reviewer as an individual:

> ... & **on** ne doute point que le monde ne fust bien aise d'apprendre dans trois feüilles de papier, ce qui demanderoit, sans ce secours, de années entieres. Mais **on** differera l'execution de ce dessein, iusqu'à ce que ce Iournal soit entierement estably, & qu'on ait trouué des personnes capables de bien traiter dans toutes les sciences, ces sortes de sujets. (*Journal des Sçavans*, 23 février 1665)
> [... and we have no doubt that the world will be delighted to learn in three sheets of paper that which would require entire years without this aid. But we will postpone carrying out this plan until the Journal is firmly established, and we have found persons capable of dealing with these questions well in all the disciplines.]

However, it will be noted that of the 11 occurrences of this type that turn up, nine are in the 1665 sample under the editorship of de Sallo. It is possible therefore that this trait, even though it is not particularly common, is a feature of his personal style.

There are in addition 12 occurrences (11%) of *nous* [we]. Exactly half of these have a fairly general sense, and are hence similar to the general *on*:

> **Nous** avons encore un autre nouveau system sur les fiévres par M Minot Docteur en Med. Il se vend à Paris chez R. Pepie. (*Journal des Sçavans*, 15 janvier 1685)
> [We have yet another new account of fevers by M. Minot, M.D. It is on sale at R. Pepie's in Paris.]

The other half refer specifically to the reviewer himself:

> **Nous** avons parlé ailleurs de la premiere partie de cet ouvrage qui ne passe pas pour la meilleure piece de cet auteur. (*Journal des Sçavans*, 4 juin 1685) [We have spoken elsewhere about the first part of this work, which cannot be thought to be the best piece by this author.]

Examples of *nous* are concentrated in the 1685 sample, where nine of the 12 examples occur. De la Roque was then editor, so, again, despite the small number, this may be related to his personal style, just as the use of *on* to refer to the reviewer may be linked to de Sallo.

There are only two occurrences of *je* [I], and these appear in adjacent sentences in the final issue of our sample:

> **J'**AI parcouru dans l'onziémé Journal de cete année tous les ouvrages de feu M. Aubery. **Je** m'arrêterai maintenant un peu davantage à ce dernier, auquel il semble avoir raporté tous les autres. (*Journal des Sçavans*, 8 août 1695) [I gave an overview of the complete works of the late M. Aubery in the 11th issue of this year's Journal. I shall now give a little more time to this latest, in which he seems to recapitulate all the others.]

This means that, of the 106 examples where the theme includes reference to the reviewer himself, 86 (81%) are of general import (general uses of *on*, six examples of *nous*, plus the examples of *tout le monde* and *personne*), and only 20 (19%) refer specifically to the reviewer as an individual (examples of *on* referring to the reviewer, the other six examples of *nous*, the examples of *je*, and the example of *ce Journal*). So the presence of the reviewer as theme is even less than that which the 6% for the author category would lead us to believe, since only 13% of the cases included in this figure refer specifically to the reviewer; in the other cases he is potentially present but simply as a member of a much larger and more general group. Hence the impact of the reviewer as theme is very small indeed.

The overall picture of theme in the *Journal des Sçavans* is, then, that the major type of theme is that of reference to other texts, mainly books under review, followed by themes relating to the subject matter of the items in the journal, followed by references to humans other than the author of the *Journal des Sçavans* item, mainly the authors of books under review. In addition, we can note that references to the reviewers of books are almost infinitesimal.

The *Philosophical Transactions*

As in the *Journal des Sçavans*, all four major grammatical functions can function as theme, though in vastly differing degrees. The subject is the unmarked theme, accounting for almost two-thirds of the sample, and adjuncts are the major marked type of theme, accounting for almost a third. The following are examples with subject functioning as theme:

> **I** Cannot enough wonder at the strange agreement of the thoughts of the acute French Gentleman Monsieur *Auzout*, in the *Hypothesis* of the Comets motion, with mine; and particularly, at that of the *Tables*. (*Philosophical Transactions*, 3 April 1665)

> **The Ships in the Harbour** at *Port-Royal* felt it; and **one who was Eastward of the Island coming thither then from *Europe***, met with, as he said, at the same time, and Hurricane. **One riding on horseback** was not sensible of it. (*Philosophical Transactions*, March/April 1694)

> **Whether this be to be ascribed to the Snow, which comes from the North and North East, and is stored with Nitre, (the reputed cause of fertility;)** is considered by our Author. (*Philosophical Transactions*, 22 November 1675)

Of those adjuncts which function as theme, many are simple adverbs or adverbial groups:

> ... & **in some of our Seas** there float sometimes such bulky masses of Ice, that are far greater than the Objects, which we are assured, we can see in the *Moon*. (*Philosophical Transactions*, December 4 1665)

However, there are also a significant number of examples where the adjunct theme has the form of a clause, sometimes finite, as in the following:

> ... but, **after it begins to ebb**, the Current runs on still Eastward 12 hours together, that is all day long, from about 9½ in the morning, til about 9½ at night. (*Philosophical Transactions*, 5 June 1665)

While others are non-finite (or gerundive):

> **The other Horn of the Womb being not then opened**, I layd it in a Box on a moist paper for 16 hours ... (*Philosophical Transactions*, 22 August 1685)

There are relatively few examples of complements functioning as theme. The following is one example:

> ... and **as many of them as I could** I took into the Boat, and still row'd on till I came where I thought my House had stood, but could not hear of neither Wife nor Family; so returned again to that little part remaining above Water. (*Philosophical Transactions*, March/April 1694)

Included in this group are those where the thematized item forms part of a more complex unit. For example, in the following, the discontinuous non-finite clause, *this ... to be the most frequent cause of ordinary Damps*, functions as the complement of the clause, but only the deictic pronoun is thematized:

> And **this** they take to be the most frequent cause of ordinary Damps. (*Philosophical Transactions*, 22 November 1685)

In some cases the whole of a clause functioning as the complement is thematized:

> **Whether this great diversity proceeds from the Various breaths of the *Pyrites*, and the *lapis Calcarius*, whilst under their different states, and changes, or from other sorts of effluviums**, (the store of nature being vast, and very copious) I dare not determine ... (*Philosophical Transactions*, 23 March 1685)

Predicators functioning as theme are even less frequent; when these occur they are typically in the form of imperatives:

> ... then **place** it upon an Oven, continually but moderately, kept warm, or in a hot Sand-furnace ... (*Philosophical Transactions*, 22 February 1675)

However, other types do occasionally occur:

> ... yet **amounts** it to no more, than an alteration; which whether the Heavens will admit of, we may justly question. (*Philosophical Transactions*, 26 July 1675)

There are a small number of extraposed matrices functioning as theme, for example:

> ... so that **it will not be improper** to insert here the History in short of that Remarkable Distemper. (*Philosophical Transactions*, March/April 1694)

However, cleft items functioning as theme are virtually absent, a single example having been identified in the whole of the *Philosophical Transactions* subcorpus:

> **It was in the Age of *Augustus Cæsar***, that *Gratius*, their best Cynegetical Poet, compared the *British* Dogs for courage and stout performance with the *Molossian*, and for craft or skill with the *Athamanian*, *Thessalian* and *Epirote* Dogs, which, in those differing faculties, were the best in the World, that were then known at *Rome*, where from remote parts they were often tried in the Theatre. (*Philosophical Transactions*, 22 November 1675)

The details of the distribution of themes in terms of grammatical function are given in Table 26. From this, it can be seen that the subject functions as theme in almost two-thirds (62%) of the examples, and as the adjunct in almost a further third (31%). Intuition would suggest that the incidence

Table 26. Grammatical functions of themes in the *Philosophical Transactions.*

Function	*1665*	*1675*	*1685*	*1694*	*Total*	*%*
Subject	259	400	307	331	1297	62%
Predicator	8	17	1	1	27	1%
Complement	12	24	20	20	76	4%
Adjunct	161	213	153	126	653	31%
Cleft	–	1	–	–	1	*
Extraposition	8	14	4	18	44	2%
Total	448	669	485	496	2098	

of adjuncts functioning as theme is here rather more than it would be in present-day English. However, it is difficult to find figures which are comparable. Biber *et al.* (1999) claim that in academic prose adverbs occur in initial position in 15% of cases, and prepositional phrases in 15%. While this is a statement about structure, and not thematization, it does suggest that thematization of adjuncts is of the order of 25% in contemporary academic writing. If so, this indicates a drop of about 6% since the late seventeenth century. The same authors also say that the 'fronting of core elements is relatively rare', where 'core elements' seems to correspond roughly to our predicators and complements, and that there are only about '200–300 occurrences per million words in academic prose and fiction' (Biber *et al.* 1999: 909). This works out at about 0.02% to 0.03%, infinitesimal compared to the 5% found here. Table 27 shows the percentage distribution for individual years.

These figures seem to indicate that there is a small but steady rise in the percentage of subjects functioning as theme. This rises from 58% in 1665 to 68% thirty years later. This is matched by a corresponding fall in the percentage of adjuncts functioning as theme, which falls gradually from 36% in 1665 to 25% in 1694. The complement functioning as theme is rare, but

Table 27. Percentages of grammatical function as themes (*Philosophical Transactions*).

Function	*1665*	*1675*	*1685*	*1694*
Subject	58%	60%	63%	68%
Predicator	2%	3%	*	*
Complement	3%	4%	4%	4%
Adjunct	36%	32%	32%	25%
Cleft	–	*	–	–
Extraposition	2%	2%	1%	4%

Table 28. Numbers of clausal adjuncts as theme (*Philosophical Transactions*).

Clause type	*1665*	*1675*	*1685*	*1694*	*Total*	*% of adjuncts*
Finite	41	43	54	29	167	26%
Non-finite	40	55	19	18	132	20%
All clause types	81	98	73	47	299	46%

Table 29. Clausal adjuncts as percentage of adjunct themes (*Philosophical Transactions*).

Clause type	*1665*	*1675*	*1685*	*1694*
Finite	25%	20%	35%	23%
Non-finite	25%	26%	12%	14%
All clause types	50%	46%	48%	37%

remains steady at about 4%. Predicators functioning as theme are even rarer, and virtually disappear after 1675. Equally rare are extraposition matrices functioning as theme, though there are slightly more in the 1694 sample, while cleft examples are virtually absent.

A significant number of adjuncts have clausal form, some of which are finite and others non-finite. The distribution of these is given in Table 28. Almost half (46%) of adjuncts functioning as theme are of the clausal type, a quarter (26%) of them being finite clauses, and a fifth (20%) non-finite. Table 29 gives the percentage distribution for each year.

This seems to indicate a fall in the percentage of clausal types in the 1694 sample. This is largely due to the fall in the frequency of non-finite clauses functioning as adjunct themes from 1685 onwards, compensated for in 1685 by an unusually high percentage of finite clauses. On the basis of this, it is possible to establish a hypothesis that towards the end of the seventeenth century, not only was there a fall in the use of adjuncts as theme, but where they do occur they are less likely to have clausal form.

Textual and interpersonal themes

The incidence of textual and interpersonal themes is given in Table 30. Textual themes are most frequently simple conjunctions:

> **And** *Milford haven* was once famous for plenty of rich Wine from the mountains of *Wales*, and may be so again hereafter, if we go on, as we begin to do; **and** 'tis as cheap to try the Vines of *Smyrna*, and *Greece*, of the *Canaries*, of *Montefiasco*, the *Falernian* and *Chian*, as any vulgar vine; ***but*** *for Vines in our Northern climates we should choose the Southern declivity,*

Table 30. Textual and interpersonal themes in the *Philosophical Transactions.*

	1665	*1675*	*1685*	*1694*	*Total*	*%*
Textual	110	264	182	207	769	37%
Interpersonal	25	67	22	27	135	7%

> *and make a trench to carry off the rain above, before the stream falls into the trenches of Vines.* (*Philosophical Transactions*, 26 July 1675)

There are some examples of two adjacent textual themes, but these are not particularly common:

> ... **and then** drawing out this new Air that was made, he made the gage-water subside again by degrees, in like manner as when the common Air is drawn out ... (*Philosophical Transactions*, 22 November 1675)

Textual themes occur in over a third (37%) of the ranking clauses.

Interpersonal themes are relatively rare, occurring in only 6% of the ranking clauses. These are often modal in nature, like the following example:

> **Perhaps** he will say, he has transfer'd the *Libratory Circle* from the *Orbis magnus* to the transverse diameter of the Ellipsis. (*Philosophical Transactions*, 26 July 1675)

Interpersonal themes of a modal type also commonly occur in the form of an extraposition matrix which functions as a grammatical metaphor of modality:

> **'Tis also probable**, that the *Aqua fortis* and the Spirit of Wine would boyl always when they are mingled ... (*Philosophical Transactions*, 22 November 1675)

A small number of vocatives, usually *Sir*, function as interpersonal themes. These normally occur at the beginning, but occasionally in the middle, of letters:

> Now **Sir** if these worthy *Gent.* thought it worth their while, laboriously to make such *Observations* without the helps that you have afforded us, how supine had we been, if we had forborn to prosecute it ... (*Philosophical Transactions*, 23 March 1685)

Also included in the interpersonal count are a small number of cases where the finite appears in thematic position because of the presence of a negative item, as in:

> ... nor **do** they fall out according to the four seasons of the year. (*Philosophical Transactions*, 22 February 1675)

Table 31. Percentages of textual and interpersonal themes in the *Philosophical Transactions.*

	1665	*1675*	*1685*	*1694*
Textual	25%	39%	38%	42%
Interpersonal	6%	10%	5%	5%

There is a small inflation of interpersonal themes due to the fact that a small number of items, notably one item in 1665 and one in 1675, have a cluster of queries introduced by the word *whether*, functioning as an interrogative marker; in thematic position this functions as an interpersonal theme. An item in the 1675 sample, entitled *Divers Rural and Oeconomical Inquiries, recommended to Observation and Tryal*, has a whole series of this type of clause:

> 4. **Whether** any Trees will live, of which a part is unbarked round about? Some affirming, that the *Alder* will thrive, notwithstanding its being thus unbarked.
> 5. **Whether** the often transplanting of Wild trees does really turn them into Garden-trees?
> 6. **Whether** it agrees with Experience what *Laurembergius* affirms, that Gilly-flowers transplanted twice a year, Spring and Harvest, become the fuller and more beauteous?
> (*Philosophical Transactions*, 22 February 1675)

In all, there are 28 of these queries in this item. The overall effect of these clusters is of the order of 1%.

The percentage distribution of textual and interpersonal themes for different years is given in Table 31. From an initial incidence of 25%, the frequency of textual themes rises in 1675, but remains relatively stable thereafter at roughly 40%. Interpersonal themes are relatively rare, but fairly stable at just over 5%, with perhaps a peak in 1675.

Thematic progression

Thematic links of the linear type are more common than constant links, and this is true for each individual year. This is shown in Table 32.

Table 32. Thematic progression in the *Philosophical Transactions.*

	1665	*1675*	*1685*	*1694*	*Total*	*%*
Constant	126	220	116	139	601	29%
Linear	227	247	242	192	908	43%

Table 33. Percentage distribution of thematic progression in the *Philosophical Transactions.*

	1665	*1675*	*1685*	*1694*
Constant	28%	33%	24%	28%
Linear	51%	37%	50%	39%

Overall, 43% of the ranking clauses were identified as presenting a thematic link of the linear type, that is, having a theme derived from a preceding, though not necessarily immediately preceding, rheme. Links of a constant type, derived from a preceding theme, were identified in 29% of the ranking clauses.

The percentage distribution for individual years is given in Table 33. In each of the individual year samples, linear progression is more frequent than constant progression, but to differing degrees depending on the year. For 1685 there is a large difference of 16 percentage points between the incidence of linear and constant progression; however, for 1675 the difference is only 4 percentage points. Nevertheless, to the extent that linear progression can be linked to a more argumentative type of discourse, and constant progression to a discourse of a more descriptive or narrative type, it seems reasonable to say that in the *Philosophical Transactions* the discourse tends to present a more structured argumentation.

Semantic categorization of themes

The distribution of the 15 semantic categories of themes is given in Table 34. By far the most common type of theme is that referring to an object of study. These account for a massive 45% of the themes, showing that the object of study is the dominant thematic interest of these writers. These objects of study are the physical objects or phenomena on which the interest of the writers is centred; objects of study of a more abstract nature are rare.

> **Our Air** is very healthy all the year long. **The Diseases, which the inhabitants are most subject to**, are the Colick and Leprosy. (*Philosophical Transactions*, 22 February 1675)

> **The following bodys** were poured gently into the vessel, and **those in the 12 first Experiments** were weighed in scales turning with 2 ounces, but **the last** 7 were weighed in scales turning with one ounce. (*Philosophical Transactions*, 23 March 1685)

> **As to the Number of the Pillars**, we could not guess that they are fewer than One Hundred Thousand; but **the shape of the Causeway** is so irregular, that we could not number the Columns of one side or end, in order to

Table 34. Semantic categories of themes in the *Philosophical Transactions.*

	1665	*1675*	*1685*	*1694*	*Total*	*%*
Obj.	143	327	192	281	943	45%
Exp.	18	39	33	6	96	5%
Equip.	7	4	4	1	16	1%
Obs.	10	3	3	1	17	1%
Auth.	58	86	86	54	284	14%
Oth.	96	80	41	63	280	13%
Meta.	7	9	25	6	47	2%
Inter.	26	28	22	20	96	5%
Exist.	8	11	26	10	55	3%
Field	–	1	1	–	2	*
Ment.	51	46	27	29	153	7%
Time	11	17	23	22	73	3%
Rad.	1	–	–	–	1	*
Math.	1	6	–	1	8	*
Sit.	11	12	2	2	27	1%

> make a probable Computation of them all; **some** are very long, and higher than the rest; others short and broke; some for a pretty large space of an equal height ... (*Philosophical Transactions*, July/August 1694)

Only two other categories concern more than 10% of the themes; these both deal with persons: references to the author account for 14% of the themes and those referring to persons other than the author, 13%. The author here is Oldenburg in those items which he has drafted himself, including book reviews, or the original writer in those items he has printed verbatim. This is particularly the case in letters and letter extracts, and articles which came to him in the post. The following example occurs in a book review:

> **I** shall only add, that about three hundred years after *Gratius, Nemesian* gives the precedent to *British* Greyhounds for velocity ... (*Philosophical Transactions*, 22 November 1675)

The following is from a long extract from a letter by van Leeuwenhoek:

> **I** examined the *Ovarium*, and found in it 2 or 3 water bladders which lay deep and were half hid, and one that was reddish, the rest that stuck out more, being the greater number, were of an ash-colour and consisted of Glandulous parts. **I** lookt also how the Eggs might have a passage to come down, but could find none. (*Philosophical Transactions*, 22 August 1685)

Although Oldenburg does not specifically say so, this was presumably translated from Dutch, since van Leeuwenhoek, unlike most other intellectuals of his time, knew no other language. It will be noticed that authors have no compunction about using the first person pronoun to refer to themselves.

Humans other than the author are a more diverse group, but they include references to other intellectuals, like this reference to Robert Plot:

> **The learned Dr. *Plott***, in his late book, *De Origine Fontium*, mentions some fountains in *England* ... (*Philosophical Transactions*, 23 March 1685)

Or this one to Robert Boyle:

> **Honorable Mr. *Boyle***, according to his usual accurateness, hath given us an account of the antecedent, concomitant, and following changes of Air and Weather, and very black Winds, when the Earthquake was about *Oxford*, *Januar*. 19. 1685; recited in *Numb*. 11. *p*. 176. *of your Tracts*. (*Philosophical Transactions*, 26 July 1675)

They can also simply be persons in the environment, such as inhabitants of a region being described, or workmen in a technical situation:

> **The Labourers** work for a *Julio* a day, which is not above 6 or 7 pence, and indure not long; for, although none stay underground above 6 hours; all of them in time (some later, some sooner) become *paralitick*, and dye *hectic*. (*Philosophical Transactions*, 3 April 1665)

In items of a medical nature, the patient may be thematized:

> ... **he** began to be indisposed the Saturday before with running pains, yet so well as to be abroad next day at Church ... (*Philosophical Transactions*, 23 March 1685)

And in book reviews, as in the *Journal des Sçavans*, the author of the book under review may be thematized:

> **This Author** (for whom his former *Treatises* had prepared a welcome in the world) divides the Practice of *Physick* into ordinary and extraordinary ... (*Philosophical Transactions*, 22 August 1685)

Of the other types, only three account for as much as 5% of the corpus. Thematization of references to mental processes and argumentation occurs in 7% of the ranking clauses, such as:

> But now, **to know the moment, or very near the moment of the said Equinox**, the author of this Secret imparts also the way of finding that out with certainty. (*Philosophical Transactions*, 26 July 1675)

> **This supposed**, we must for our purpose measure or make an Estimate of some River, as it runs from its very source to a place where some Rivolet

> enters into it, and see, whether the Rainwater that falls about the course thereof, if it were put into a Conservatory, would be sufficient to make it run a whole year. (*Philosophical Transactions*, 22 November 1675)

References to an experiment or the experimental process account for 5% of the themes.

> **A needle being driven into the Brain of a Dog, between the first *Vertebræ*, and the *Os Occipitis*,** the Dog seem'd as of struck with an Epilepsy, and died in a little time. (*Philosophical Transactions*, 23 March 1685)

In some cases the word 'observation' is used when it is clearly in the context of an experimental process. The following example occurs in an item dealing with the dissection of animals and involves the use of equipment such as a microscope. Such cases have been included in the experimental type, rather than that of observation.

> **The preceding Observations** were made in a moderately dry season, but 2 days after when it was rainy weather, I lookt for the same Salts, but they were melted, and run among the brown Globules. (*Philosophical Transactions*, 22 August 1685)

Also accounting for 5% are those examples referring to texts other than the *Philosophical Transactions* itself. The majority of these occur in book reviews, where the text referred to is the book under review or part of it:

> **The Second Part** treats of the Quadratures of those Spaces, whose *Quadratix's* are *Mechanical* or Transcendent Curves, as he (after Mr. *Leibnitz*) chooses rather to call them; where he gives a general Method for finding their Tangents. (*Philosophical Transactions*, March/April 1694)

However, other examples do occur:

> SIR,
> It may seem, **by the curious Remarks sent to you from Scotland**, that we are yet to seek out the Causes and original Source, as well as the Principles and Nature of *Frosts*. (*Philosophical Transactions*, 26 July 1675)

Of the types of theme that occur less frequently, it is perhaps worth noticing that of mathematical expressions, which, although infrequent at this period, would become significant in the physical sciences from the late nineteenth century onwards (Banks 2008a).

> … and **supposing the same diameter of the Libratory circle**, the same Æquations will be found to a second … (*Philosophical Transactions*, 26 July 1675)

The least frequent thematic type is that of radical modality, of which only a single example was identified in the whole of the *Philosophical Transactions* subcorpus:

> ... nay, **if it be necessary** (without much trouble, especially in the grinding of longer Glasses) the whole *Concave Surface* of the *Tool* may be made to touch a Glass. (*Philosophical Transactions*, 5 June 1665)

Table 35 shows the percentage distribution of semantic categories for individual years. The object of study is by far the most common semantic category in any individual year, rising from 32% in 1665 to 57% in 1694. The rise is particularly noticeable in the final year; this might indicate an increasing focus on the object of study, as scientific activity became established, or a difference in the attitude of the then editor, Richard Waller. However, since there is a considerable amount of verbatim material used, this second possibility may seem less plausible. References to the author as theme are relatively stable, between 11% and 13%, with a slight peak to 18% in 1685. The same could be said of references to persons other than the author, which, after an initial fall from 21% to 12%, remains within the range 8% to 13%. Similarly, mental processes fall from 11% to 7%, but then remain in the 6% to 7% area. The experimental category shows a fall in 1694, but the other categories, although the figures are small, never vary by more than 3% at most.

Table 35. Percentages of semantic categories in the *Philosophical Transactions.*

	1665	*1675*	*1685*	*1694*
Obj.	32%	49%	40%	57%
Exp.	4%	6%	7%	1%
Equip.	2%	1%	1%	*
Obs.	2%	*	1%	*
Auth.	13%	13%	18%	11%
Oth.	21%	12%	8%	13%
Meta.	2%	1%	5%	1%
Inter.	6%	4%	5%	4%
Exist.	2%	2%	5%	2%
Field	–	*	*	–
Ment.	11%	7%	6%	6%
Time	2%	3%	5%	4%
Rad.	*	–	–	–
Math.	*	1%	–	*
Sit.	2%	2%	*	*

Some elements of comparison

Table 36 shows the overall percentage distribution of the grammatical functions of themes in the two journals. This shows that the *Philosophical Transactions* thematizes subjects less frequently and adjuncts more frequently than the *Journal des Sçavans*. The difference in each case is of the order of 10 percentage points. However, the difference between the two journals reduces as time goes on: 16 percentage points in 1665, 12 in 1675, 9 in 1685, and 5 for the two final samples (1695 for the *Journal des Sçavans* and 1694 for the *Philosophical Transactions*). To the extent that thematizing the adjunct provides a circumstantial frame (e.g. Thompson 2004), thus creating first the circumstantial surroundings (time, place, reason, etc.) within which the event occurs, then one can say that this practice is rather more prevalent in the English journal than in the French.

A considerable proportion of the adjuncts have the form of a finite or non-finite clause. The percentages of adjuncts which have clausal form in the two journals are given in Table 37. Where an adjunct is thematized, the *Journal des Sçavans* has recourse to a clausal form slightly more frequently than the *Philosophical Transactions*, but in both cases finite clauses are more frequent than non-finite clauses to roughly the same degree.

Table 36. Percentage distribution of grammatical functions.

	Journal des Sçavans	*Philosophical Transactions*
Subject	73%	62%
Predicator	1%	1%
Complement	*	4%
Adjunct	22%	31%
Cleft	2%	2%
Extraposition	2%	*

Table 37. Percentages of adjuncts with clausal form.

	Journal des Sçavans	*Philosophical Transactions*
Finite clause	31%	26%
Non-finite clause	22%	20%
Total	52%	48%

Table 38. Percentages of textual and interpersonal themes.

	Journal des Sçavans	*Philosophical Transactions*
Textual	29%	36%
Interpersonal	3%	7%

Table 38 gives the incidence of textual and interpersonal themes in the two journals. When textual themes as a percentage of ranking clauses are compared, it is found that the percentage for the *Philosophical Transactions* is higher than that for the *Journal des Sçavans*. Some may find this result surprising, insofar that present-day English accepts implicit links more readily than present-day French. Nevertheless, it is clear here that for these two journals at least, links in the form of textual themes are more common in the English journal. It might also be noted that while the percentage of textual themes in the *Journal des Sçavans* reduces (from 41% to 17% of clauses) over time, that in the *Philosophical Transactions* increases (from 25% to 42% of clauses) over time. Interpersonal themes are not common in either of the journals; however, to the extent that they occur, they are over twice as common in the *Philosophical Transactions* as in the *Journal des Sçavans*. This may be due to the fact that, since the editors of the *Philosophical Transactions* used more verbatim material, the authors of these letters and articles might be more likely to implicate themselves by thematizing their own attitudes. Another contributing factor may be that after the initial difficulties of Denis de Sallo, and calls for the *Journal des Sçavans* to simply report new publications, without any critical evaluation, editors may have had a tendency to reduce personal implication, and thus its thematization, to a minimum.

The degree of constant and linear progression is virtually the same in each of the journals. This is shown in Table 39.

Thus both journals display a preference for linear progression, and this is true of each individual year for both of the journals, with differences ranging from 8 to 15 percentage points in individual years in the *Journal des Sçavans*, and rather more, from 4 to 26 percentage points, in the *Philosophical Transactions*. This means that both journals prefer constructed argument over simple description and narrative with a ratio of roughly 4:3.

When the semantic categories of themes are considered, some stark differences are apparent between the two journals. Table 40 gives the percentage distributions of semantic categories for the two journals.

Table 39. Percentages of constant and linear progress.

	Journal des Sçavans	*Philosophical Transactions*
Constant	30%	29%
Linear	41%	43%

Table 40. Percentages of semantic categories of themes.

	Journal des Sçavans	*Philosophical Transactions*
Obj.	22%	45%
Exp.	1%	5%
Equip.	*	1%
Obs.	*	1%
Auth.	6%	14%
Oth.	37%	13%
Meta.	1%	2%
Inter.	16%	5%
Exist.	3%	3%
Field	*	*
Ment.	9%	7%
Time	4%	3%
Rad.	1%	*
Math.	–	*
Sit.	1%	1%

The most frequent category in the *Journal des Sçavans* is that of other humans (Oth.), within which the author of a book under review figures largely. This category accounts for 37% of the themes. In the *Philosophical Transactions,* although it is the third largest category, it accounts for only 13% of the themes, and this, in particular, includes references to other intellectuals. So, the references to other humans functioning as theme are much less common in the *Philosophical Transactions,* and even when they do occur, the reference is not to the same type of person. References to the author himself functioning as theme (Auth.) are just as common in the *Philosophical Transactions* as references to other humans, accounting for 14% of the themes. However, in the *Journal des Sçavans* this type accounts for only 6% of the themes, and since the majority of items are reviews, this is most commonly the reviewer, who is usually the editor of the journal himself.

By far the commonest type of theme in the *Philosophical Transactions* is that of the object of study (Obj.), this type of theme accounting for 45% of the sample. Although this is the second largest group in the *Journal des Sçavans*, it is much less common than in the *Philosophical Transactions*, accounting for only 22% of the themes. The only other type of theme occurring in significant proportions is that of references to other texts (Inter.), which is the third largest group in the *Journal des Sçavans*, accounting for 16% of the themes. The majority of these are references to a book under review. By comparison, the *Philosophical Transactions* has few themes of this type, and they account for only 5% of the themes.

Thus the thematic focus of the *Journal des Sçavans* is primarily on people, and secondarily on things and subjects of study, with texts providing a third centre of interest. In the *Philosophical Transactions* the focus is much more strongly on things, with people providing only a fairly weak secondary interest. The interest in people and texts in the *Journal des Sçavans* derives directly from the editorial decision to base the journal on book reviews covering the whole range of new thought, and this decision itself is part and parcel of the general historical situation, in which the journal had been set up as part of a strategy of state control of new thought. Hence, there is a causal string which stretches from the general historical situation through the decisions of the actors in this scenario, and ultimately down to the linguistic features of the texts they produced. Similarly, the prevalence of themes relating to things, objects of study, in the *Philosophical Transactions* derives from the decision to restrict the content of the journal to science and technology. This results from Oldenburg's need to find new sources of revenue and using his network of correspondence to provide a newsletter for the members of the Royal Society and like-minded people. Once again, the historical situation, motivating the decisions of Oldenburg, leads ultimately to the features we find in the pages of the *Philosophical Transactions*.

6 Transitivity: actions, events, states

The Systemic Functional concept of transitivity goes far beyond the traditional notion of transitive and intransitive verbs. It is concerned with the whole relationship within the clause between processes, the participants in those processes, and the circumstances in which they occur (Halliday 2014). Here I shall concentrate mainly on the types of process used, and for this purpose I shall use a system of five processes (Banks 2005): material processes, which are actions and events of a physical nature; mental processes, which are events of a cerebral nature; relational processes, which are states and relationships between items or between an item and a characteristic; verbal processes, which are processes of communication; and existential processes, which simply state the existence of an entity. Mental processes can be subdivided into those which are cognitive (ways of thinking), perception (ways of perceiving) and affective (ways of liking). Some analysts distinguish a desiderative type (ways of wishing), but this I consider to be included in the cognitive type. Relational processes can be subdivided into attributive, which is basically descriptive, identifying, which is defining, and possessive, which in addition to possession includes inclusive relationships. I shall not use the category of behavioural process, used by many within the Systemic Functional framework, because I feel that this category involves inherent contradictions (Banks 2016), and that the phenomena it is intended to cover can be dealt with perfectly well within the five transitivity types I have outlined.

O'Donnell *et al.* (2008) have shown that within the systemic community there is a range of criteria used for analysing process types. Although there is wide variation, different practitioners tend either towards criteria which are conceptual or towards those which are syntactic. My analysis falls very much towards the conceptual end of that cline; thus it is semantic without having to conform to strict grammatical criteria. For example, I treat all processes of communication as being verbal process, whether or not they can, grammatically, be accompanied by direct or indirect speech, or 'project' in systemic terminology.

The *Journal des Sçavans*

The distribution of process types for each of the years in the sample is shown in Table 41. The analysis relates to all finite verbs, but does not take into account non-finite forms or nominalizations. The latter will be considered later as a form of grammatical metaphor.

Table 42 gives the percentage distribution for individual years. There is a total of 5790 finite verbs in the *Journal des Sçavans* corpus, varying from 1313 to 1657 for individual years. Since the *Journal des Sçavans* subcorpus contains an estimated 66,447 words, the average number of words per finite clause is almost eleven and a half (11.48). The commonest process type is that of relational process, which accounts for 31% of the total. Moreover, it will be noted that this rate is stable over the period, remaining within the range 30% to 33% in each of the four years concerned. Relational processes are basically static; they do not involve any type of action or event, with the exception of that which is the coming about of a state. Hence the major process type of the *Journal des Sçavans* tends to present the world as it is; it is descriptive and non-dynamic. As stated above, relational processes can be divided into attributive, identifying and possessive. Attributive relational processes are basically descriptive, giving characteristics, in the form of adjectival phrases, indefinite nominal groups, spatial location, and so on.

Table 41. Process types of finite verbs in the *Journal des Sçavans*.

	1665	*1675*	*1685*	*1695*	*Total*	*%*
Material	218	365	423	479	1485	27%
Mental	196	217	224	252	889	15%
Relational	431	454	407	512	1804	31%
Verbal	389	381	265	361	1396	24%
Existential	79	29	55	53	216	4%
Total	1313	1446	1374	1657	5790	

Table 42. Percentage distribution of process types in the *Journal des Sçavans*.

	1665	*1675*	*1685*	*1695*
Material	17%	25%	31%	29%
Mental	15%	15%	16%	15%
Relational	33%	31%	30%	31%
Verbal	30%	26%	19%	22%
Existential	6%	2%	4%	3%

Ces choses **sont** rare & curieuses; & on ne doute point que le monde ne **fust** bien aise d'apprendre dans trois feüilles de papier ce qui demanderoit, sans ce secours, des années entieres. (*Journal des Sçavans*, 23 février 1665)
[These things are rare and curious; and it cannot be doubted that everyone was well pleased to learn in three sheets of paper what would, without this aid, take years.]

Les deux letters qui suivent ont esté tirées d'un Ms. de trois cens ans d'ancienneté, qui **est** dans la Bibliotheque d'Oxford. (*Journal des Sçavans*, 30 juillet 1685)
[The two letters which follow have been taken from a three-hundred-year-old MS, which is in the Oxford Library.]

Identifying relational processes define an item:

De treize ou quatorze Empereurs dont Herodien décrit le regne dans son histoire, Severe **est** le seul qui soit mort dans son lit. (*Journal des Sçavans*, 1 juillet 1675)
[Of the thirteen or fourteen Emperors whose reign is described by Herodian in his history, Severus is the only one who died in his bed.]

L'une est qu'il est difficile de ne pas croire que le souper rapporté par les Evangelistes **est** la Pâque dont ils ont décrit la préparation. (*Journal des Sçavans*, 3 janvier 1695)
[One of them is that it is difficult not to believe that the supper recounted by the Evangelists is the Pascal meal whose preparation they had described.]

Possessive relational processes, in addition to possession properly so-called, include types of abstract possession, such as inclusion, and some spatial relationships.

On **a** de luy vne method pour la quadrature des paraboles de tous les degrez. (*Journal des Sçavans*, 9 février 1665)
[We have, by him, a method for the quadrature of parabolas of every degree.]

Elle **a eu** un grand Roy pour fondateur, des Papes tres-pieux & tres sçavans pour Panegyristes ; & ce qui est encore plus considerable pour sa gloire, elle **a** toujours **esté remplie** de personnes illustres & celebres par leur doctrine. (*Journal des Sçavans*, 9 septembre 1675)
[It had a great king for founder, pious intellectual popes as panegyrists; and what is even more important for its glory, it has always been full of people famed and celebrated for their doctrine.]

Table 43. Types of relational process in the *Journal des Sçavans.*

	1665	*1675*	*1685*	*1695*	*Total*	*%*
Attributive	255	295	264	270	1084	60%
Identifying	63	55	43	89	250	14%
Possessive	113	104	100	153	470	26%
Total	431	454	407	512	1804	

Table 43 gives the distribution of the three types of relational process. It can be seen that 60% of relational processes are of the attributive type, hence the major function of relational process is for descriptive purposes. The possessive type accounts for a further quarter (26%); many of these relate to the contents of books under review. The identifying type, with basically a defining role, is the least frequent of these types, occurring in 14% of the examples. So the relational process type is the most common in this corpus of the *Journal des Sçavans,* and its most usual function is of a describing nature.

The second most common process type is that of material process, accounting for 27% of the processes in the *Journal des Sçavans.* Material processes express actions, events and happenings of a physical nature.

> Il en trouve de mesme dans ce qu'il dit de toutes sortes de miroirs : mais il ne sçauroit se persuader ce que l'Histoire nous apprend d'Archimede, qui par le moyen d'un miroir concave **mit** le feu à la flotte des Romains qui **assiegeoient** la ville de Syracuse où il estoit. (*Journal des Sçavans,* 14 janvier 1675)
> [The same thing can be found in what he says about all sorts of mirrors: but he is unable to convince himself of what History tells us about Archimedes, who by means of a concave mirror set fire to the Roman fleet that was laying siege to the town of Syracuse where he was.]

> Dés que la saison **commence** à s'échaufer, la mouche **pond** sur le fromage; & le vermisseau qui **sort** de son œuf **serpente** & **se promene** dessus en prenant sa nourriture sur le lieu de sa naissance. (*Journal des Sçavans,* 8 août 1695)
> [As soon as the season begins to warm up, the fly lays its eggs on the cheese and the young worm which comes out of its egg wanders about on it taking its nourishment from its place of birth.]

Unlike relational process, the frequency of material process is not stable over time. From a fairly low 17% in 1665, it almost doubles in the following twenty years to 31% in 1685. The rate then remains relatively stable with 29% in 1695. This could be due to an increase in the general interest in matters of a physical nature, or it could be that the personal interests of the editors were directed more clearly towards physical questions in the second half of our period, or perhaps a combination of both. De Sallo himself only edited the journal for 13 issues, and Gallois who took over may have had some penchant for scientific matters. According to Camusat, in an early history of the journal:

> Il paroit que M. Gallois a principalement excellé en ce qui regarde les Mathematiques, la Physique, l'Histoire naturelle, & la Medecine ; car une ardeur incroïable de tout sçavoir l'avoit porté à etudier les choses les plus eloignées de sa profession. (Camusat 2011 [1734]: 237)
> [It would seem that M. Gallois mainly excelled in things relating to mathematics, physics, natural history and medicine, for an incredible desire to know everything pushed him to study things the farthest removed from his profession.]

Birn (1965) says that Gallois was particularly attentive to the quality of information he received about scientific progress in France. De la Roque was a tireless journalist rather than a genuine intellectual. However, he may have had a leaning towards medicine, but, on the other hand, his status as a priest led him, according to Paris (1903), to avoid certain types of medical question. Cousin was much more of an intellectual than his predecessor, and, although he was a lawyer by training, Birn describes him as '... savant respecté, traducteur des historiens grecs et latins, mathematician et naturaliste' (Birn 1965: 25) [... respected intellectual, translator of the Greek and Latin historians, mathematician and naturalist].

Hence, some of the editors may be thought of as having a leaning towards scientific questions, but there is insufficient evidence to show that, for example, de la Roque was significantly more so inclined than Gallois. However, it is quite possible that there was a general increase in scientific interests, and it is an intriguing historical fact that the Académie Royale, which throughout this period published its findings only in limited luxurious editions that were not widely distributed, decided in 1699 to begin publishing and distributing its findings on a much wider basis. The first volume of these *Mémoires* actually appeared in 1702 (McClellan 2001). The publication and distribution of the work of the Académie Royale from the beginning of the eighteenth century onwards can therefore be seen as a concretization of the increasing interest in scientific matters evidenced by the increasing use of material processes in the pages of the *Journal des Sçavans*, particularly between 1665 and 1685, but then maintained at that level. Although this can be no more than a hypothesis, it is nevertheless an interesting and intriguing one and, to the extent that it is valid, it shows to what extent the linguistic details of the language used in the writings of the time derive from the historical context which produced them.

Verbal processes are only a little less frequent than material processes, accounting for 24% of the processes.

> Car il **pretend** qu'il **ne** l'**auoit pas escrit** pour estre publié. (*Journal des Sçavans*, 23 février 1665)
> [For he claims that he did not write it in order to be published.]

> Les Empereurs Valentinien & Marcien **congratulent** le Pape par cette lettre de la victoire remportée sur les Euticheens dans le Conc de Calcedoine. Ils **l'informent** ensuite de la prééminence que le Patriarche de Constantinople y avoit obtenuë sur ceux d'Alexãdrie & d'Antioche au prejudice des quels le premier rang apres celuy de Rome luy avoit esté octroyé. (*Journal des Sçavans*, 30 juillet 1685)
> [In this letter, the Emperors Valentinian and Marcian congratulate the Pope on the victory over the Eutichians at the Council of Chalcedon. They then inform him of the pre-eminence which the Patriarch of Constantinople had obtained there over those of Alexandria and Antioch, to whose detriment the first rank after that of Rome had been granted him.]

The distribution of verbal process over time is virtually the mirror image of that of material process. From 30% in 1665, it drops to 26% in 1675, and then to 19% in 1685. It then remains fairly stable, with only a slight rise to 22% in 1695. Thus we can say that the rise over time of material processes is matched by a corresponding fall in verbal processes. This is confirmed by the fact that the total of material plus verbal processes is almost stable: 47% – 51% – 50% – 51%. Thus, while communication seems to have been of high significance for de Sallo, it became increasingly less so for his successors, though still remaining at about one in five of processes at the end of the period.

Mental processes seem to be of less significance than relational, material and verbal processes. Overall, they account for 15% of the processes.

> On **a douté** long temps si la chose pouvoit se faire. (*Journal des Sçavans*, 11 mars 1675)
> [For a long time we had doubted whether it could be done.]

> En quittant ce pays il **resolut** de convertir tout son Royaume, & il amena pour cet effet avec luy un Evesque, deux Prêtres & quelques Diacres. (*Journal des Sçavans*, 16 avril 1685)
> [In leaving this country he decided to convert the whole of his kingdom, and for this purpose, brought with him a bishop, two priests, and some deacons.]

Table 44. Types of mental process in the *Journal de Sçavans.*

	1665	*1675*	*1685*	*1695*	*Total*	*%*
Cognitive	179	199	183	231	792	89%
Perception	13	16	37	15	81	9%
Affective	4	2	4	6	16	2%
Total	196	217	224	252	889	

The incidence of mental processes is stable over time, remaining at a steady 15% to 16% over the whole of the period. If the examples of mental process are considered in terms of their subtypes – cognitive, perception and affective – the examples found in the *Journal des Sçavans* are overwhelmingly cognitive. Table 44 shows the distribution of the different types of mental process.

So, although mental process is far from being the most common, where it does occur, in nine cases out of ten (89%) it is of the cognitive type. This means that mental processes are usually a question of cognitive thought processes. This is the case of the two examples above and of the following:

> Comme plusieurs personnes **font** leur diuertissement du Iournal, sans en vouloir faire leur occupation, ils **s'interessent** si peu au succez qu'il peut auoir, que tout ce que l'on écrira pour le combatre, demeurera sans replique. (*Journal des Sçavans*, 9 mars 1665)
> [Since some people make the Journal their entertainment, without wanting to make it their profession, they are so little interested in the success it might have, that everything that one writes to fight it remains without reply.]

> Il y a déjà long temps que l'on **remarque** que tous Messieurs les Protestants qui **travaillent** sur les Peres de l'Eglise, **ne s'avisent** gueres d'aller au delà du III. siecle, sans doute de peur d'y trouver leur condamnation. (*Journal des Sçavans*, 4 juin 1685)
> [For quite some time it has been noticed that Protestant gentlemen who work on the Church Fathers scarcely dare to go beyond the 3rd century, without doubt through fear of finding their own condemnation.]

One particular type of thought process which forms a small but significant subtype within this group is that of wishing and wanting, sometimes classified separately as a desiderative type, but here considered to be a form of cognitive mental process.

> Ainsi ils ne sont pas seulement les Maistres en l'Art de bien parler ; ils **veulent** encore apprendre aux autres, par ce qu'ils font, la manière de bien, écrire. (*Journal des Sçavans*, 14 janvier 1675)
> [Thus they are not only masters of the art of speaking well, they want, moreover, to teach others, through what they do, how to write well.]

> Or il est clair à M. de Tillement par l'Evangile, que quand les Apôtres demanderent à N.S. où il **vouloit** qu'ils lui préparassent la Pâque, ils estoient au premier jour des Azimes, auquel il faloit immoler la Pâque, & par consequent au 14. du mois. (*Journal des Sçavans*, 3 janvier 1695)
> [But it is clear to M. de Tillement from the Gospels, that when the Apostles asked Our Lord where he wanted them to prepare the pascal meal for him, it was the first day of unleavened bread, when the pascal lamb had to be sacrificed, and so it was the 14th day of the month.]

Examples of perception mental processes are not particularly common and account for less than one in ten (9%) of mental processes.

> De là viennent les tremblemens de terre, qui ont abîmé quelquefois des Villes toutes entires, & qui ont fait paroistre des forests & des lacs, où l'on **voyoit** auparavant des montagnes inaccessibles. (*Journal des Sçavans*, 11 mars 1675)
> [From there come the earthquakes which have sometimes destroyed whole towns, and made forests and lakes appear there, where previously we could only see inaccessible mountains.]

> Le fait dont il s'agit, & qui est arivé à une femme de Lion nommée Caterine Crepieu, doit estre mis au nombre des plus curieux & des plus rare que l'on **ait** encore **observé** parmi les femmes grosses, quand elles ont passé les termes ordinaires de la grossesse & de l'accouchement. (*Journal des Sçavans*, 10 juin 1695)
> [The event in question which happened to a woman of Lyon called Caterine Crepieu must be counted as one of the most curious and rarest that have yet been observed among pregnant women when they have passed the normal period of pregnancy and delivery.]

Examples of affective mental processes, that is, processes of liking and disliking, are extremely rare, and account for no more than 2% of mental processes.

> ... & les choses y sont décrites d'une maniere à donner beaucoup de plaisir à ceux qui **aiment** à lire l'histoire de leur païs en une Langue étrangere. (*Journal des Sçavans*, 6 mai 1675)
> [... and the things are described in a way which will give a great deal of pleasure to those who like reading the history of their country in a foreign language.]

Thus mental processes are far from constituting the most common process type, but form nevertheless a significant minority group, accounting for roughly a quarter of processes. Where these occur they are massively of the cognitive type; processes of perception are relatively rare, and affective mental processes are totally insignificant. The ratio of affective to perception to cognitive is roughly 1:5:45. Thus thinking is relatively important in the *Journal des Sçavans*, perception is fairly rare, and liking is not a question of any importance. Since the major part of the periodical is made up of book reviews, this might seem initially surprising. However, on reflection, it probably indicates that, for the editors, the fact that they liked a work or not was not in itself important; what was important were the arguments that could be brought to defend its value. Nevertheless it should be remembered that direct criticism was not appreciated, and this may account for the fact that description, and hence relational processes, are more frequent than mental processes.

The last category with which we must deal is that of existential processes. This is a small group, which accounts for only 4% of processes. This again is a stable figure, since existential process never accounts for more than 6%, or less than 2% in individual years.

> On sçait qu'il y **avoit** plusieurs especes de Sacrificateurs. (*Journal des Sçavans*, 15 janvier 1685)
> [We know that there were several kinds of sacrificers.]

> Elle avoit cependant la mesme dureté que celles des autres enfans, aussi bien que la mesme grosseur ; & il n'y **paroissoit** qu'un tache rouge à l'un des costez sur le derriere. (*Journal des Sçavans*, 30 juillet 1685)
> [It nevertheless had the same strength as those of the other children, as well as the same thickness, and there was a red patch on one of the sides at the back.]

It is possible then to say that the vision of the world as conveyed through the process types of finite verbs in the *Journal des Sçavans* is one that is primarily static, non-dynamic, and mainly related to describing the world as it is. This is constant throughout the period studied. Events and happenings in the physical world provide a secondary interest, and this interest tends to increase over the period, probably under the influence of a generally increased interest in matters of a scientific nature. The increased interest in physical events is matched by a decreasing interest in communication, which provides a third centre of interest, albeit one which decreases over time. Mental events are only of minor interest, but where they occur they are overwhelmingly of a cognitive type. Simple existence, as expected, is a fairly marginal category. Thus this world view could be sketched as being primarily descriptive, secondarily about physical events, and thirdly about communication.

A note on passive clauses

The passive form is not particularly frequent in French. It is much less common than in English, where it is particularly prevalent in scientific writing. This has been noted in numerous works from Barber's seminal article (1962) onwards (e.g. Turner 1972; Tarone *et al.* 1981, 1998; Banks 1994a). Since this book aims to compare the French of the *Journal des Sçavans* with the English of the *Philosophical Transactions*, it is useful to consider the use of what is for French a minor verb form, in order to compare this with the use of the passive in the *Philosophical Transactions*. The incidence of passives in the *Journal des Sçavans* is given in Table 45.

Table 45. Passives in the *Journal des Sçavans*.

	1665	*1675*	*1685*	*1695*	*Total*	*%*
Passives	94	56	85	171	406	7%

Table 46. Processes of passives in the *Journal des Sçavans*.

	1665	*1675*	*1685*	*1695*	*Total*	*%*
Material	34	33	51	97	215	53%
Mental	14	5	8	22	49	12%
Relational	6	7	6	10	29	7%
Verbal	40	11	20	42	113	29%
Total	94	56	85	171	406	

As can be seen, a relatively small 7% of finite clauses are passive in form. When these are distributed in terms of their process types, some interesting points emerge. This is shown in Table 46. A typical passive form would probably be thought of in terms of material process, so it is unsurprising that material process forms that largest category. On the other hand, at just over half (53%), the incidence might be thought to be relatively modest.

> Quand la fougere **fut brûlée** elle estoit entre seche et vert. (*Journal des Sçavans*, 11 mars 1675)
> [When the fern was burnt, it was between dry and green.]

> Les deux catalogues qui font la seconde partie du volume, **n'avoient jamais esté imprimez**. (*Journal des Sçavans*, 21 fevrier 1695)
> [The two catalogues which constitute the second part of the volume have never been printed before.]

What is perhaps more surprising is that verbal process accounts for 29% of the passive clauses. Perhaps this indicates a desire to talk about communicated messages without having to attribute them to a source, though of course that source would usually be available elsewhere in the text.

> Car tous les raisonnemens y **sont proposez** en la forme qui **est vsitée** dans l'Escole, & **énoncez** avec la seicheresse qui est familiaire aux lulistes. (*Journal des Sçavans*, 23 février 1665)
> [For all the argumentation is put forward in the form which is used by the Schoolmen, and announced with the dryness common among the Lullists.]

> Ceux qui voudront voir l'histoire, la description & l'usage de cette inustion des Chinois, n'ont qu'à consulter le IX. Journ. de l'Année derniere où il en **a esté** amplement **parlé**. (*Journal des Sçavans*, 4 juin 1685)
> [Those who wish to read about the history, description and use of this cauterization by the Chinese need only consult the ninth issue of last year's Journal where it was extensively discussed.]

Mental processes in passive clauses are rare, accounting for only 12% of the passive clauses.

> Il **a esté regardé** comme un des maistres de nostre Langue. (*Journal des Sçavans*, 9 septembre 1675)
> [He has been considered one of the masters of our language.]

> Il explique aussi l'opinion des Millenaires qui **a esté suivie** non seulement par des Heretiques & par des juifs, mais aussi par des Saints & par des Martyrs. (*Journal des Sçavans*, 3 janvier 1695)
> [He also explains the opinion of the millenarians, which has been followed not only by heretics and Jews, but also by saints and martyrs.]

It is not surprising that relational processes in passive clauses are even rarer. This is a type of process which does not lend itself easily to passivization, though some examples do occur and they account for 7% of the passive clauses.

> Cette assemblée **est composée** de deux Chambres, la haute, & la basse. (*Journal des Sçavans*, 21 février 1695)
> [This assembly is made up of two chambers, the higher and the lower.]

There are no examples of existential processes in passive clauses.

A further point emerges when the percentage distribution for individual years is considered. This is shown in Table 47. While the figures for 1675 onwards are of the same order for each year, with material process accounting for 57% to 60% of the passives, and verbal process for 20% to 25%, the percentages for 1665 are significantly different. For 1665 the commonest

Table 47. Percentage distribution of passive clauses.

	1665	*1675*	*1685*	*1695*
Material	36%	59%	60%	57%
Mental	15%	9%	9%	13%
Relational	6%	13%	7%	6%
Verbal	43%	20%	24%	25%

Table 48. Material process passives in the *Journal des Sçavans*.

	1665	*1675*	*1685*	*1695*
Affected-Material	30	30	37	63
% of Material	88%	91%	73%	65%
% of all passives	32%	54%	44%	37%

type of passive is verbal process, which accounts for no less than 43%, with material process accounting for 36%. If the hypothesis, that use of verbal process passives is a way to avoid stating the source of communication, is correct, then this tendency is much stronger in the issues edited by de Sallo than in those by the editors who followed him. It is not impossible that this is related to the heated controversies of de Sallo's short-lived editorship.

While material process might be thought of as the prototypical type of passive, the typical material process passive might be thought of as that which has an affected functioning as subject. Indeed, roughly three-quarters of the material process passives are of this form. This can be seen in Table 48.

The vast majority, roughly nine out of ten, of material process passives have an affected subject in the 1665 and 1675 samples. Thereafter the percentage falls, though this formulation remains the most common.

> Ils augmenterent le lendemain depuis midy jusqu'au soir ; & environ les 9 heures, apres un tremblement des plus violens, trois grandes pierres enflamées en forme de globes, **furent poussées** prés d'une demy lieuë en l'aire, & y crevérent comme des grenades avec un bruit terrible. (*Journal des Sçavans*, 4 juin 1685)
> [The following day they increased from midday until the evening, and at about 9 o'clock, after one of the most violent quakes, three large flaming globe-shaped stones were thrown about half a league into the air, and there burst like grenades with a terrible noise.]

As a percentage of all passives, the incidence of material process passives with an affected subject increases sharply between 1665 and 1675, but thereafter it again decreases, but never falling as low as the 1665 figure. Hence, on this point too, de Sallo distinguishes himself from later editors.

It is also worth pointing out that although passive forms occur throughout the corpus, where there are concentrations of passive forms, this is usually in items other than book reviews, including a number of items adapted from the *Philosophical Transactions*; it is to this periodical that we will now turn.

The *Philosophical Transactions*

The distribution of the processes of finite verbs in the *Philosophical Transactions* sample is given in Table 49. Table 50 gives the percentage distribution for individual years.

A total of 6257 finite clauses were identified in the *Philosophical Transactions* subcorpus, for an estimated total of 77,295 words. This means that the average number of words per finite clause is over 12 (12.35). The commonest process type in the *Philosophical Transactions* is material, accounting for over a third of the total (35%). This indicates the interest of the writers of the journal in physical events and actions.

Table 49. Processes in the *Philosophical Transactions.*

	1665	*1675*	*1685*	*1694*	*Total*	*% of total*
Material	448	763	454	511	2176	35%
Mental	387	302	222	277	1188	19%
Relational	478	517	407	501	1903	30%
Verbal	267	258	136	135	796	13%
Existential	65	33	57	39	194	3%
Total	1645	1873	1276	1463	6257	

Table 50. Percentages of processes in the *Philosophical Transactions.*

	1665	*1675*	*1685*	*1694*
Material	27%	41%	36%	35%
Mental	24%	16%	17%	19%
Relational	29%	28%	32%	34%
Verbal	16%	14%	11%	9%
Existential	4%	2%	4%	3%

> The generality of our people **use** no salt; those that **do make** use of what **is imported**. Our Sea-water in clear nights being struck with Oares, **shineth** like fire bursting out of a furnace. The *tydes* **observe** the motion of the Moon. The Sea **swells** about the Moons rising and setting; and it **falls** when she is Southerly and Northerly. (*Philosophical Transactions*, 22 February 1675)

> I **bought** a female Rabbet and **let** it take Buck 3 times in my presence, (which **was** quickly **done**) and then **killed** it, but **did not open** the womb, till a quarter of an hour after; about an Inch from the beginning of one of the Horns, I **found** a little fluid matter containing some few living animals of the Male seed ... (*Philosophical Transactions*, 22 August 1685)

It will be noted that this interest was much less in the 1665 sample, where the percentage of material processes is 27%, a little less than the percentage of relational processes, which constitute the commonest processes for that year. However, by 1675, this has risen to 41%, and thereafter settles in the mid-thirties, 36% in 1685 and 35% in 1694. Since Oldenburg, who founded the journal, was still editor in 1675, it can be said that he presided over the initial explosion in the use of material processes.

The second most common process type is that of relational process. Describing the world as it is was particularly important for the members of the Royal Society, and fitted well into their Baconian conception of scientific activity. According to Jones:

> Perhaps the most important service which Bacon contributed to the cause of science lies in this very fact, that he forcefully called men's attention back to the physical world, made them distrust the sheer operations of the mind divorced from material reality, and taught them the value and necessity of sensuous observations of nature as a sine qua non of scientific knowledge. More than once he calls attention to the fact that he himself dwelt constantly among the data of nature, withdrawing his intellect from them no farther than was necessary to perceive them properly, and his continual conversancy with the external world, he claims, possessed more value than his wit, for truth was to be sought not in the mind but in the world. (Jones 1982: 50–1)

The incidence of relational process is stable between 1665 and 1675, where the percentages are 29% and 28% respectively, and it is stable between 1685 and 1694, 32% and 34% respectively, but there is a significant rise from 28% to 34% between 1675 and 1685. Hence, description seems to have gained importance in the second half of our period in relation to the first half. Within the category of relational process, attributive relational processes describe in terms of qualities and properties, identifying relational processes

Table 51. Types of relational process in the *Philosophical Transactions.*

	1665	*1675*	*1685*	*1694*	*Total*	*%*
Attributive	346	370	309	396	1421	75%
Identifying	34	44	27	10	115	6%
Possessive	98	103	71	95	367	19%
Total	478	517	407	501	1903	

give alternative expressions for the same entity, while possessive relational processes, as well as possession properly so-called, englobe relations such as containing and spatial location. The distribution of these three types of relational process is given in Table 51.

As can be seen, attributive processes constitute by far the largest category, accounting for 75% of all relational processes. These are basically descriptive.

> I have been perplext in observing my self, an hundred times, the difference of Heat and Cold between two villages, within a mile of each other, where we could discern no disparity of Hills and Rivers; only the Springs in the one **were** all shallower, in the other some **were** deeper. In a large Tract of Land the surface **was** of so hot a ferment, that at every step I trod up to the ankles. (*Philosophical Transactions*, 26 July 1675)

> That part which is now standing, **is** part of the end of that neck of Land which **runs** into the Sea, and **makes** this Harbour (at the Extremity of which **stands** the Fort, not shook down, but much shatter'd by the Earthquake, and **is** now a perfect island ... (*Philosophical Transactions*, March/April 1694)

Use of attributive relational processes rises slightly over time from 72% of all relational processes in 1665 to 79% in 1694.

Possessive relational processes cover the areas of possession, both physical and abstract, containment, spatial relations and so on. These account for 19% of the relational processes.

> What then, *saith he*, would becom of a Glass of 10000 feet, which, according to the said Table **would have** more than four feet, or four feet and nine inches, or five feet, seven inches *Aperture*, and of which the *Ring*, though it were two feet nine inches, **would have** but one minut of *Inclination*, and the Glass of 5 feet *Aperture* **would have** but 4 minuts, and the curvity of it would be less than the hundred part of a Line. (*Philosophical Transactions*, 5 June 1665)

> Among the several *figured Stones* already described by Authors, I find none that **has** more agreement with those that **compose** our *Giants Causway*,

> than the *Entrochos*, the *Astroites*, or *Lapis Stellaris*, and the *Lapis Basanus*, or *Basaltes*: And yet for all the great Resemblance they **have** in some particulars, they differ very much in others ... (*Philosophical Transactions*, July/August 1694)

Use of possessive relational processes decreases slightly over time, possibly mirroring the increase in attributive processes. From 21% in 1665 the rate falls to 19% in 1694, though it had fallen to 17% in 1685.

Identifying relational processes are relatively rare, accounting for only 6% of all relational processes, showing that identification, which includes defining, was not a priority for the writers of these texts.

> The general opinion of our workmen **is**, That there are some Damps which kill by reason of the noisome steam, and others merely by want of air ... (*Philosophical Transactions*, 22 November 1675)

> That the imperfection of Voice, as well as the difficultie of swallowing **were** the effects of the *paralysis*, may probably be allowed, & be a satisfactory reason why the Person *Dr. Lister* mention's, could not *use the Quill* which was given him to suck with. (*Philosophical Transactions*, 23 March 1685)

Identifying relational processes range from 7% to 9% in the years 1665 to 1685, but the rate drops to only 2% in 1694.

Thus we can say that the functions covered by the use of relational process, notably that of description, are important to the writers of these texts. Moreover, the distribution of the three types of relational process is relatively stable over time, attributive processes remaining within the range 72% to 79%, though the tendency is to rise, possessive processes remaining within the range 17% to 21%, and identifying processes within the range 7% to 9% for the years 1665 to 1685, with a fall to 2% in 1694. This is shown in Table 52.

Mental processes account overall for 19% of process types. Thus, while being relatively significant, they are much less so than either material or relational processes. Like relational processes, mental processes can be divided into three subtypes: cognitive, basically processes of cognitive activity like thinking; perception, such as seeing, hearing and so on; and affective, which are processes of liking. The distribution of these three subtypes is shown in Table 53.

Table 52. Percentage distribution of relational processes.

	1665	*1675*	*1685*	*1694*
Attributive	72%	72%	76%	79%
Identifying	7%	9%	7%	2%
Possessive	21%	20%	17%	19%

Table 53. Types of mental process in the *Philosophical Transactions.*

	1665	*1675*	*1685*	*1694*	*Total*	*%*
Cognitive	294	212	144	181	831	70%
Perception	89	87	78	93	347	29%
Affective	4	3	–	3	10	1%
Total	387	302	222	277	1188	

Thus it can be seen that where mental processes occur it is those of the cognitive type which are by far the most common, accounting for 70% of all mental processes.

> He told me he bled freely at the wounds the *Fox* had made, and that they healed without any farther trouble, than now and then a little girding pain on that hand & arm; and further said, (to please his friends,) he had taken a *white Powder* of an Apothecarie, and **believed** himself in no danger of what **was feared** (for I had **discovered** the danger I **apprehended** in his condition:) tho' the *Aquæ Pavor* did not yet appear, his heat was much increased ... (*Philosophical Transactions*, 23 March 1685)

> But till we have a better stock of more accurate Histories of them, and **be** further **acquainted** with their nature and progress, I **do not think** it so proper to the Design of those that candidly **prosecute** Philosophical Enquiries to determine any thing as yet in this Point. (*Philosophical Transactions*, March/April 1694)

Even though occurring much less frequently than cognitive processes, perception processes account for a fairly significant 29% of the mental processes. This shows the relative importance of observation for these early scientists. The world and its wonders were there to be recorded for posterity, but to be recorded they had to be seen. Related to this is the importance of witness. It was important for these men to record what had been seen but also what they had heard.

> The full Discovery of which particular also he makes to be a part of *Cassini's* and *Campani's* work, seeing that they so distinctly **see** the inequalities in the *Belts*, and **see** also sometimes other *Spots* besides the *shadows* of the *Satellites* ... (*Philosophical Transactions*, 5 June 1665)

> No. 6 Is part of a Letter, dated the *6th*. of *March*, 1693. From another Observing Gentleman there present in the same Earthquake of the *7th.* of *June*, 1692. Giving an Account of what he **saw** himself, and **heard** of others about it. (*Philosophical Transactions*, March/April 1694)

Affective mental processes, on the other hand, are virtually absent, accounting for only 1% of mental processes. The fact that there are only ten examples in the whole of the *Philosophical Transactions* subcorpus means that on average an example occurs only once per 7730 words of text. Even the few examples that occur may be considered marginal by some.

> I Am very much obliged for the last pacquet which came safe, and I **was** not a little **transported** with joy in the perusal of Honorable Mr. *Boyles Essay Instrument*, as he hath expressed the five principal uses of it ... (*Philosophical Transactions*, 26 July 1675)

> Next Morning I went from one Ship to another, till at length it **pleased** God that I met with my Wife and two of my Negroes. (*Philosophical Transactions*, March/April 1694)

Thus, expressing likes and dislikes can be said to be virtually excluded from the discourse of the writers of these texts. For them it is the objective facts which are important, not their own subjective reactions to them.

When the percentage distribution of types of mental process for individual years is considered, it can be seen that there is a distinct rise in the use of perception process at the expense of cognitive process between the years 1665 and 1685, after which it remains stable, thus supporting the idea that observation was of increasing importance to these early scientists. This is shown in Table 54.

Verbal processes are less common, accounting for 13% of the total. These tend to occur more frequently in book reviews than in other items.

> He **concludeth** with two Celestial Observations; whereof the one **imports**, what multitudes of Stars are discoverable by the Telescope, and the variety of their magnitudes ... (*Philosophical Transactions*, 3 April 1665)

A small number are simple interpolations attributing a statement to others.

> In the beginning of Frebuary I received from a Butcher, the *Uterus* of a Sheep, which had taken the Ram 17 days before (as they **said**) I found in one of the *Cornua* thereof, a small body wrapt up in Membranes of a red fleshy colour. (*Philosophical Transactions*, 22 August 1685)

Table 54. Percentage distribution of types of mental process.

	1665	*1675*	*1685*	*1694*
Cognitive	76%	70%	65%	65%
Perception	23%	29%	35%	34%
Affective	1%	1%	–	1%

The use of verbal processes decreases over time from 16% in 1665 to 9% in 1694.

Existential processes, as might be expected, are few in number, accounting for 3% of all processes. However, the few that occur usually do so in a context of description, and to that extent might be considered to conflate with relational process, making the difference with material process somewhat less.

> But, *saith he*, there **are** so many Rocks, and such bleak winds in *Scotland*, that they can hardly draw in the same yoke with *England* for Gardens and Orchards. (*Philosophical Transactions*, 26 July 1675)

> ... that there **is** not the least sign of Morter, or any equivalent Cement, to joyn the Commissures or Sides of the Columns together; that there **are** no foot-steps of the strokes of Tools or Chissels, in the Surface of any part of the Stone; that there **are** other parcels of the like Stone, which lye still in their Native Beds, as they were first produced in the adjoining Mountain. (*Philosophical Transactions*, July/August 1694)

The use of existential processes is stable over time, remaining within the narrow range of 2% to 4%.

Hence we can say that the interest of the writers of the texts in the *Philosophical Transactions*, as evidenced by the processes of their finite clauses, is centred on actions and events, encoded in material processes. Their interest, then, is in what is happening and what is done. This is almost equalled by an interest in description, shown by their use of relational process. Thus, the world as it is is also a major interest. What is thought is a minor interest, shown by the low incidence of mental processes, and the very low incidence of verbal process shows that what men say is not of great importance for them.

A note on passives

In the *Philosophical Transactions* subcorpus 14% of the finite verbs are passive in form. Though well below the 30% or more to be found in many twentieth-century scientific articles (Banks 2008a), this is nevertheless a significant rate, and as it was from this base that use was to rise to the twentieth-century figure it merits attention. The figures are shown in Table 55.

Table 55. Incidence of passive finite verbs in the *Philosophical Transactions*.

1665	*1675*	*1685*	*1694*	*Total*	*%*
223	278	178	176	855	14%

Table 56. Process types of passive clauses in the *Philosophical Transactions*.

	1665	*1675*	*1685*	*1694*	*Total*	*%*
Material	116	168	118	102	504	59%
Mental	55	64	35	46	200	23%
Relational	6	14	7	5	32	4%
Verbal	46	32	18	23	119	14%
Total	223	278	178	176	855	

The rate is relatively stable over the period: 14% in 1665 and 1685, 15% in 1675, with a slight fall to 12% in 1694. The distribution of passive clauses in terms of their process types is given in Table 56.

As might be expected, there are no existential processes which are coded in a passive form. Otherwise, the most common process type with a passive form is material process. Again this would be expected.

> ... and since our Old Philosophers do allow the Sun to give a potent assistance in the generation of all things that **are generated**. But may not Mines **be discovered** by examining the juices of Vegetables growing on the place, and by the Waters which issue thence, as elsewhere I have proposed? (*Philosophical Transactions*, 26 July 1675)

> ... so that I believe what Oak **was undermined** by the water, **was covered** with mud, and so **petrified** into Stone, and of this sort might that be which the Fishermen found; for if some part of that ground which **is** now **covered** by water, was formerly wood, as is on good grounds believed by those that live thereabouts ... (*Philosophical Transactions*, 22 August 1685)

Mental processes account for 23% of the passive clauses. This is perhaps rather more than might have been expected.

> But if any will make use of two *Object-glasses*, whereof the *Focus's* **are known**, the distance of them **will be known**. If it **be supposed**, that the Focus of the *first* be B. and *that* of the *second* C. and the distance given, B+2D, and that D minus C be equal to F ... (*Philosophical Transactions*, 4 December 1665)

> But the evaporous *effluvia* of Water, having a greater degree of refraction than the *Common Air*, may suffice to bring those Beams down to the Eye, which when the Water is retired, and the Vapours subsided with it, pass above, and consequently the Objects seen at the one time, **may be conceived** to disappear at the other. (*Philosophical Transactions*, July/ August 1694)

Verbal processes occur much less frequently, accounting for only 14% of the sample.

> THE Noble Authors design in this Discourse being to shew, that the *Philosophical* Difficulties, urged against the *Possibility* of the RESURRECTION, are nothing so insuperable, as they **are** by some **pretended**, and by others **granted**, to be ... (*Philosophical Transactions*, 22 February 1675)

> So that here we have two different sorts of steams causing these boylings, yet neither of the fountains are Medicinal, or so much was arm;[7] the like **is related** by *Varenius*, [*primo lapide à culma* (says he,) ... (*Philosophical Transactions*, 23 March 1685)

Relational processes in a passive form are, as would be expected, rare, though a few do occur, accounting for 4% of the sample.

> The Country of *Feroe* **is provided with** many well-tasted and wholsom Fountains, springing on high hills. (*Philosophical Transactions*, 22 November 1675)

> *Whether the Earth, or Sand about this* Lough ***be indued with*** *this Qualitie?* (*Philosophical Transactions*, 22 August 1685)

When the percentage distribution for individual years is considered, it can be seen that it is not totally stable over the period considered. This is shown in Table 57. There is a tendency for the percentage of material process passive clauses to rise. From 52% in 1665, it rises to 62% by 1685, though it falls back slightly to 58% in 1694. This is mirrored by a corresponding fall in the percentage of verbal process passive clauses, which fall from 21% to 10% over the period 1665 to 1685 and rise slightly to 13% in 1694. Mental process and relational process passive clauses are both relatively stable over this period. Mental process passive clauses have a range of 20% to 26%, and the fairly rare relational processes one of 3% to 5%.

Table 57. Percentage distribution of passive clauses.

	1665	*1675*	*1685*	*1694*
Material	52%	60%	62%	58%
Mental	25%	23%	20%	26%
Relational	3%	5%	4%	3%
Verbal	21%	12%	10%	13%

---

7 Presumably, *was arm* is a printer's error for *as warm*.

Table 58. Material process passives with an affected subject.

	1665	*1675*	*1685*	*1694*
Affected-Material	68	131	93	76
% of material	59%	78%	79%	75%
% of passive	39%	47%	52%	43%

Table 58 gives the figures for material process passives with an affected subject, which I have suggested is the prototypical form of a passive clause. As can be seen, material process passive clauses with an affected subject, as a percentage of all material process passives, account for 59% in 1665, but this figure rises sharply thereafter to 78% in 1675, remaining at that level until the end of the period, within the range 75% to 78%. As a percentage of all passives, that variation is rather greater, but shows the same general tendency. From 39% in 1665, that rate rises to 47% in 1675, and then remains within the range 43% to 52%. Hence material processes with an affected subject are the preferred form of passives, accounting for roughly three-quarters of material process passives from 1675 onwards, and almost half of all passives.

Some elements of comparison

The overall results for the two journals are given in Table 59. Both journals display an equal interest in description, with an incidence of relational process of almost a third (31% for the *Journal des Sçavans* and 30% for the *Philosophical Transactions*). So both periodicals have an extensive interest in describing the world as it is. However, in the case of the *Philosophical Transactions*, this interest is superseded by an interest in physical actions and events, indicated by the incidence of material process of 35%. So for these writers, even more important than the static description of what is, is what happens in that world, and what men do in that world; this encompasses

Table 59. Process types in both journals.

	Journal des Sçavans	*Philosophical Transactions*
Material	27%	35%
Mental	15%	19%
Relational	31%	30%
Verbal	24%	13%
Existential	4%	3%

physical phenomena (e.g. volcanic eruptions), industrial processes (e.g. mining), as well as scientific experiments as such. In the *Journal des Sçavans,* the rate of material process is less than that of relational process, at 27%; so interest in physical phenomena and human actions is less than the interest in description, and considerably less that the same interest in the *Philosophical Transactions.* Interest in communication, indicated by the rate of verbal process, is relatively high in the *Journal des Sçavans,* with a rate of 24%, only a little less than the rate for material process. It is presumably the fact that the *Journal des Sçavans* is basically a periodical of book reviews that leads to this interest in what is said, and who says what. With a rate of only 13% for verbal process, the *Philosophical Transactions* displays only a minor interest in communication as such. This also reflects the fact that in the *Journal des Sçavans* most of the pieces are written by the same person, the editor, commenting on the writings of others, whereas in the *Philosophical Transactions* there is a wide variety of authors, usually speaking in their own voice. Both periodicals have a minor interest in thought, indicated by the incidence of mental process, 15% in the *Journal des Sçavans* and 19% in the *Philosophical Transactions.* However, in the *Journal des Sçavans* this is considerably less than the rate for verbal process, whereas in the *Philosophical Transactions* it is a little more. So the *Journal des Sçavans* tells us what men say much more frequently than what men think, but in the *Philosophical Transactions* what men think seems to be rather more important than what they say. Both journals have a small percentage of existential processes, 4% in the *Journal des Sçavans* and 3% in the *Philosophical Transactions.*

The use of material processes has a tendency to rise in both the *Journal des Sçavans* and the *Philosophical Transactions,* but whereas the main rise in the former is from 17% in 1665 to 31% in 1685, it is from 27% in 1665 to 41% in 1675 in the *Philosophical Transactions,* thereafter falling back to the mid-thirties. In both journals the rate is stable between 1685 and 1694/5. Nevertheless, it can be said that there is a general tendency to use more material processes as the end of the century approaches. The difference between the rates for 1665 and 1694/5 is 12 percentage points in both cases. Hence one can say that interest in material actions and events is increasing on both sides of the Channel.

The use of mental process is stable in the *Journal des Sçavans,* with a range of 15% to 16%. In the *Philosophical Transactions* it is a little higher in 1665 (24%), but thereafter falls back to virtually the same level (16% to 19%).

The use of relational process is also stable in the *Journal des Sçavans,* with a range of 31% to 33%, whereas in the *Philosophical Transactions* there is a small rise from 28% in 1675 to 32% in 1685, being stable before and after those dates. Thus, interest in the world as it is seems to be unchanging in the *Journal des Sçavans,* and the *Philosophical Transactions* differs only by the small rise in the middle of our period.

The use of verbal process falls over the period in both of the journals. This fall is systematic in the *Philosophical Transactions,* where it falls steadily from 16% in 1665 to 9% in 1694. The fall is greater in the *Journal des Sçavans,* where it falls from 30% in 1665 to 19% in 1675, with a small rise to 22% in 1695. Thus, there is a waning interest in what men say in both journals, and this despite the accent on book reviews in the *Journal des Sçavans.*

The use of existential processes is never high in either journal, remaining in the range 2% to 6% in the *Journal des Sçavans,* and 2% to 4% in the *Philosophical Transactions.*

The percentage distribution of different types of relational process is given in Table 60. Attributive relational processes are the most common type of relational process in both journals, but this is more marked in the *Philosophical Transactions,* where it accounts for 75% as opposed to 60% in the *Journal des Sçavans.* Thus description seems even more important for the authors of the *Philosophical Transactions* than for the editors of the *Journal des Sçavans.* Identifying relational processes are never common, but occur more frequently in the *Journal ds Sçavans* than the *Philosophical Transactions,* 14% and 6% respectively. Thus, while identification and definition are never a major consideration, they play a greater part in the French journal. Possessive relational processes are also more frequent in the *Journal des Sçavans,* 26% as opposed to 19% in the *Philosophical Transactions.* This is probably due to the nature of the book review, which frequently expresses the content of the book under review.

Table 60. Types of relational process.

	Journal des Sçavans	*Philosophical Transactions*
Attributive	60%	75%
Identifying	14%	6%
Possessive	26%	19%

Table 61. Types of mental process.

	Journal des Sçavans	*Philosophical Transactions*
Cognitive	89%	70%
Perception	9%	29%
Affective	2%	1%

The distribution of different types of mental process is given in Table 61. Cognitive mental processes are by far the most common type in both journals; however, this is more marked in the *Journal des Sçavans* with 89% as opposed to 70% in the *Philosophical Transactions*. This is balanced by the rates for perception mental processes, which are much more common in the *Philosophical Transactions*, where they account for 29% compared with only 9% in the *Journal des Sçavans*. This shows the importance that the writers of the *Philosophical Transactions* attached to observation and witness. What they had seen, or in some cases heard, was of major importance. This seems to constitute a major difference between the approaches of the two journals, since perception mental processes take a much more minor role in the *Journal des Sçavans*. This is probably another reflection of the difference between those in the Baconian tradition and those in the Cartesian tradition. For those in the Baconian tradition the important thing was to build up factual knowledge of the world, hence the necessity of observation. For those in the Cartesian tradition, the prime necessity was the establishment of hypotheses, which then could be tested, but the hypotheses come first, hence the dominance of cognitive processes.

One would expect passive clauses to be more common in the English journal than in the French; they are in fact twice as frequent, accounting for 14% of finite clauses in the English periodical, but only 7% in the French. However, 14% is still a far cry from the 30% and more to be found in late-twentieth-century academic articles (Banks 1994a, 2008a) and this is presumably still the sort of rate to be found today. Table 62 gives the percentage distribution of passive clause by process type.

As can be seen, where passive clauses occur, they tend to be material rather more frequently in the *Philosophical Transactions* (59%) than in the *Journal des Sçavans* (53%). The difference in the case of mental process is even more striking, since 23% of passive clauses in the *Philosophical Transactions* are mental, but this is the case of only 12% in the *Journal des Sçavans*. Relational process clauses are relatively rarely passivized, as one would expect – 7% in the *Journal des Sçavans* and 4% in the *Philosophical*

Table 62. Process types of passive clauses.

	Journal des Sçavans	*Philosophical Transactions*
Material	53%	59%
Mental	12%	23%
Relational	7%	4%
Verbal	29%	14%

Transactions. However, passivized verbal process clauses are relatively common in the *Journal des Sçavans*, accounting for 29% of passive clauses, whereas the equivalent figure is only 14% in the *Philosophical Transactions*. Thus, where passive clauses are used, these are likely to be material in both journals, but the second most common type of passive clause is verbal in the *Journal des Sçavans* and mental in the *Philosophical Transactions*.

7 Modality: possibility, ability, obligation

Modality covers a number of linguistic strategies whereby a speaker comments on the content of his discourse. The ways in which this area has been categorized are various, and sometimes highly detailed. I shall take a relatively simple approach, and for the purposes of this study, which considers only texts in French and English, I shall identify three types of modality. Epistemic modality is that which pertains to thought processes and knowledge, and is basically a way of evaluating the likelihood of the content of a clause corresponding to external reality. Modality which is not epistemic can be called root modality, and this can be subdivided into two types. Deontic modality is that which concerns the moral world, hence questions of permission and obligation. Dynamic modality concerns questions about the physical world, notably physical possibility and ability (Palmer 1974, 1986, 2003; Larreya 1984; Coates 1983; Perkins 1983). Halliday refers to epistemic modality as modalization, and root modality as modulation (Halliday 2014).

While there is a vast literature on the question of modality in English, the same is not true of French. Indeed, in French grammars the question of modality is frequently conflated with that of mood, since the French word *modalité* covers both (Riegel *et al.* 2009). Caffarel (2006) treats modality in French on Hallidayan lines, along a cline of high-median-low, distinguishing probability and usuality (modalization), and obligation and readiness (modulation).

The *Journal des Sçavans*

Grammatical structure

In French, there are a number of ways in which modality can be encoded. The most obvious way is that of using auxiliary verbs: Vb (Aux.). Those found in the corpus are *pouvoir* and *devoir*. In the grammar of French it is these 'auxiliaries' which are finite, that is, conjugated, and they are followed by an infinitive.

> Car il nous apprend beaucoup de circonstances du Regne de Henry III. & de Henry IV. qu'on **ne peut** apprendre ailleurs. (*Journal des Sçavans*, 12 janvier 1665)
> [For he tells us a great deal about the circumstances of the reigns of Henry III and Henry IV which we would not be able to learn elsewhere.]

> Il remarque pourtant qu'encore qu'en **doive** recevoir toutes les expressions mises en usage par ce Père de l'eloquéce Romaine, il n'est pas necessaire de s'abstenir de tous les mots qu'il a condamnés ; puisqu'il s'en est servi quelquefois luy même ... (*Journal des Sçavans*, 4 juin 1685)
> [However, he remarks that while we should accept all the expressions used by this Father of Roman eloquence, it is not necessary to refrain from using all the words he condemned, for he sometimes used them himself ...]

Rowlett (2007), writing in a generative framework, calls these 'pseudo-modals'. In addition there is an impersonal verb [Vb (Imp.)], *falloir*, which only ever appears in the third person.

> Quelques-vns mesprisent ces sortes d'ouurages : cependant il n'y en a point de plus difficiles : & comme la science est toute dans ces principes ; **il faut** aussi en auoir vne connaissance parfaite pour les bien expliquer. (*Journal des Sçavans*, 26 janvier 1665)
> [Some despise this type of book; however, there are none more difficult, and since science is totally determined by its principles, it is necessary to have perfect knowledge of them in order to explain them well.]

To this group I have assimilated a single example of the impersonal modal expression *il se peut.*

> Mais **il ne se peut** rien souhaiter de plus acheué, que la plaidoyé de Monsieur l'Aduocat General Bignon, où sans rien perdre des graces que demandoit la matière, ny de cette noblesse de style, qui conuient à la dignité de sa Charge ... (*Journal des Sçavans*, 9 mars 1665)
> [But it is not possible to wish for anything more complete than the plea of Advocate General Bignon, who, without losing anything of the eloquence that the subject demanded, or the nobility of style, which is appropriate to the dignity of his position ...]

There are, furthermore, a number of finite verbs which have modal sense, such as *sembler, paraître* and *obliger* [Vb (Oth.)].

> ... il les rapporte à ce que nous avons de plus sensible, qui sont les quatre élemens qui composent ce bas monde : & c'est ce qui l'**a obligé** de donner

à son ouvrage le nom de monde Mathematique. (*Journal des Sçavans*, 14 janvier 1675)
[... he links them to the most perceptible things we have, which are the four elements which make up this world here below, and it is this which obliged him to call his book 'Mathematical World'.]

Ces accidens **semblerent** ne s'arrester pour quelque temps le Mercredy d'apres, qu'afin de recommencer ensuite comme ils firent, avec encore plus de violence qu'auparavant. (*Journal des Sçavans*, 4 juin 1685)
[The following Wednesday, these incidents seemed to stop for a short time, only to start again, as they did, with even more violence than before.]

Modality can also be expressed with adverbs (Adv.).

Ces sçavans Religieux auront **sans doute** de la peine à luy accorder ce point, & ils ne seront **peut-estre** pas les seuls de ce sentiment. (*Journal des Sçavans*, 15 janvier 1685)
[These religious intellectuals will no doubt have difficulty in acceding to this point, and they will perhaps not be the only ones to feel this way.]

Adjectives (Adj.) can function in a similar way.

... mais parce qu'il s'imagine que cette façon de parler est **capable** de choquer les Suisses, & que ce *sub me* peut passer pour vne enterprise contre leur liberté. (*Journal des Sçavans*, 9 mars 1665)
[... but he imagines that this way of talking can shock the Swiss, and that this *sub me* can be taken as an attack on their liberty.]

However, most adjectival forms with a modal reading occur in the form of extraposed structures (Extra.), or 'thematized comment' as Thompson (2004) calls them. These function as grammatical metaphors of modality, and since they have this special status it is useful to count them separately, distinct from adjectives properly so-called.

Sans m'arrester icy à recherché s'**il est possible que** l'œil puisse se comprimer par le moyen des muscles qui l'environnent ... (*Journal des Sçavans*, 30 juillet 1685)
[Without stopping here to see whether it is possible for the eye to contract by using the muscles around it ...]

This includes examples of the now obsolete phrase *il est constant que*.

... il est certain que le Pape, qui represente l'Eglise, en peut dispenser : & suppose qu'il le fasse, **il est aussi constant que** cét obstacle estant leué, la dispense a vn effet retroactif ... (*Journal des Sçavans*, 12 janvier 1665)
[... it is certain that the Pope, who represents the Church, can give a dispensation, and if he does so, it is also clear that since this obstacle has been removed, the dispensation has a retroactive effect ...]

Table 63. Forms of modality in the *Journal des Sçavans.*

Form	*1665*	*1675*	*1685*	*1695*	*Total*	*%*
Vb (Aux.)	87	72	69	58	286	61%
Vb (Imp.)	15	12	3	11	41	9%
Vb (Oth.)	20	5	6	23	54	11%
Adv.	5	4	10	5	24	5%
Adj.	1	4	7	3	15	3%
Extra.	11	14	19	6	50	11%
Total	139	111	114	106	470	

Table 64. Percentage distribution of modal forms.

Form	*1665*	*1675*	*1685*	*1695*
Vb (Aux.)	63%	65%	61%	55%
Vb (Imp.)	11%	11%	3%	10%
Vb (Oth.)	14%	5%	5%	22%
Adv.	4%	4%	9%	5%
Adj.	1%	4%	6%	3%
Extra.	8%	13%	17%	6%

In a previous pilot study (Banks 2013a) of a small 1665 sample, it was found that Vb (Aux.) accounted for 53% of the sample, Vb (Imp.) for a further 16% and Vb (Oth.) for 15%. The distribution for the corpus used here is given in Table 63. A total of 470 modal expressions were identified, which means that a modal expression occurs on average once per 12.3 finite clauses. The percentage distribution for individual years is given in Table 64.

It can be seen that the preferred method of expressing modality is that of modal auxiliaries, accounting overall for 61% of the modal expressions. This is the case in each individual year, though the rate falls slightly from a peak of 65% in 1675 to 55% in 1695. The rate for modal auxiliaries is rather higher than in the pilot study, whereas the rates for impersonal and finite modal verbs are rather lower, though all are of the same order. Of the two auxiliaries concerned, *pouvoir* accounts for four out of five (79%) of the occurrences. This is shown in Table 65.

Table 65. Modal auxiliaries in the *Journal des Sçavans.*

	1665	*1675*	*1685*	*1695*	*Total*	*%*
pouvoir	72	58	51	44	225	79%
devoir	15	14	18	14	61	21%

Examples of *pouvoir* tend to be dynamic in nature.

On **ne peut pas** en avoir au delà de ce qu'il en a toûjours fait paroître, & peu de personnes **peuvent** joindre une plus grande politesse, à une vivacité noble, solide, & éclairée par une connoissance parfaite des belles Lettres. (*Journal des Sçavans*, 9 septembre 1675)
[It is impossible to have more than what he has always displayed, and few people can add great politeness to a noble robust liveliness, enlightened by perfect knowledge of literature.]

Un anglois **ne peut** estre obligé à loger des gens de guerre, pas mesme en payant, ni à porter les armes hors de sa Province, à moins que ce soit pour chaser les ennemis qui seroient entrez dans le royaume. (*Journal des Sçavans*, 21 février 1695)
[An Englishman cannot be forced to billet soldiers, even against payment, nor to carry arms outside his province, except to chase enemies who have entered the kingdom.]

However, there are a small number of examples which are epistemic;

... il apprend de quelle maniere il **pouvoit** avoir esté bâti, & il avouë qu'un vaisseau de cette nature **pourroit** estre fort utile à une Ville assiegée, pour y apporter des nouvelles & pour y faire entrer du secours sans que les ennemis peussent s'en apercevoir. (*Journal des Sçavans*, 14 janvier 1675)
[... he tells us how it might have been built, and he claims that a vessel of this type could be very useful to a besieged town, to bring news and help without the enemy noticing.]

On the other hand, *pouvoir* with a deontic sense is very rare.

Que les Ministres des Chateaux & Maisons des Seigneurs, ***ne pourront*** *exercer leur Ministére plus de 3. ans dans un mesme lieu.* (*Journal des Sçavans*, 30 juillet, 1685)
[That Ministers of the palaces and houses of the nobility cannot exercise their ministry for more than 3 years in the same place.]

Most examples of *devoir* are also dynamic.

... & si l'on fait la mesme chose pour l'objet éloigné de six pieds, il **doit** paroitre aussi simple suivant cette Hypothese. (*Journal des Sçavans*, 30 juillet 1685)

> [... and if the same thing is done for the object at a distance of six feet, it should also appear single, according to this hypothesis.]

However, a significant number are also deontic.

> ... il fait voir quant au premier, que l'Eglise qui est visible, perpetuelle & infaillible **doit** aussi decider des controverses ... (*Journal des Sçavans*, 4 juin 1685)
> [... as for the first, he shows that the Church, which is visible, eternal and infallible must also decide in controversies ...]

Impersonal verbs account for 9% of the sample. The rate is stable at 10% to 11% except in 1685, when it falls to 3%. These are, with a single exception, examples of the verb *falloir*. Examples of *falloir* are typically deontic.

> **Il faloit** examiner si la multiplication de ces sieges episcopaux au lieu d'etre utile à la religion, n'y seroit point prejudiciable, & si les peuples estoient disposez à recevoir avec respect ces nouveaux Prelats. (*Journal des Sçavans*, 25 avril 1695)
> [It was necessary to study whether the multiplication of these episcopal sees, rather than being useful to religion, was not detrimental and whether the people were ready to receive these new prelates with respect.]

However, there are also a small number which are dynamic.

> ... & cependant ce ne sont que des prolegomenes, qu'**il faut** sçauoir pour estre capable de l'estude des Medailles ... (*Journal des Sçavans*, 23 février 1665)
> [... however, these are only prolegomena which it is necessary to know in order to be capable of studying medals ...]

Finite verbs functioning with a modal sense are the second largest group, accounting for 11% of the total. The rate for 1665 is 14%, falling to only 5% in 1675 and 1685, but rising fairly sharply to 22% in 1695. So one can say that the uses of finite verbs with modal sense is fairly variable but at most accounts for about one in five of modal expressions. The verbs that occur in the corpus are *obliger, paraître, sembler* and *permettre*. Their distribution is shown in Table 66.

Table 66. Finite modal verbs in the *Journal des Sçavans*.

Verb	*1665*	*1675*	*1685*	*1695*	*Total*
obliger	8	1	1	4	14
paraître	5	2	1	7	15
permettre	2	1	1	10	14
sembler	5	1	3	2	11
Total	20	5	6	23	54

Thus it can be seen that there are roughly the same number (from 11 to 15) of occurrences of each of these verbs, and that they all tend to occur rather more at the beginning and the end of the period. The verb *obliger* is used with a deontic sense.

> CE Liure est si plein d'esprit, & remply de tant de nouuelles descouuertes, qu'on a creu **estre obligé** de remarquer vne partie des beautez qui s'y rencontrent. (*Journal des Sçavans*, 12 janvier 1665)
> [This book is so full of wit, and filled with so many new discoveries, that we felt we had to point out some of the beautiful things to be found there.]

The use of *paraître* is epistemic.

> Le raisonnement sur lequel M. Conringius apuye ce paradoxe, ne lui **paroit** convainquant. (*Journal des Sçavans*, 8 août 1695)
> [The reasoning on which M. Conringius bases this paradox does not seem to him to be convincing.]

The verb *permettre* is usually deontic, though dynamic examples occasionally occur.

> En prenant le mot probable au premier sens, le P. Genzalez demeure d'accord qu'il **est permis** de suivre l'opinion la moins probable qui favorise la liberté contre la loi ... (*Journal des Sçavans*, 3 janvier 1695)
> [In taking the word 'probable' in its first sense, Fr. Genzalez still agrees that it is permissible to follow the less probable opinion which favours liberty against the law ...]

> ... & s'il en est enfin sorti, c'est que la matrice estant parvenuë au terme qui ne lui **permet** plus de se dilater & de retenir son fruit, elle a travaillé elle-mesme à se dégager d'un corps devenu étranger par un trop long sejour. (*Journal des Sçavans*, 20 juin 1695)
> [... and if he finally came out, it is because the womb, having reached a point which no longer allowed it to dilate and retain its fruit, itself worked to expel a body which had become foreign due to a overlong stay.]

The verb *sembler* is used with an epistemic sense.

> En effet il **semble** qu'on ne peut pas nier qu'il n'y ait dans le Ciel quantité d'estoiles, dont la petitesse iointe à nostre éloignement, nous derobe la veuë. (*Journal des Sçavans*, 26 janvier 1665)
> [Indeed, it seems that we cannot deny that there are numerous stars in the sky whose small size together with the distance prevents us from seeing them.]

Adverbial forms with modal sense are not particularly common, accounting for only 5% of the sample overall. The rate is 4% or 5% in individual years with a peak of 9% in 1685. The forms that occur are *assurement*,

Table 67. Adverbial modals in the *Journal des Sçavans.*

Adverb	*1665*	*1675*	*1685*	*1695*	*Total*
assurement	–	–	1	–	1
certainement	2	–	–	–	2
necessairement	1	–	–	1	2
peut estre	2	4	5	4	15
possible	–	–	1	–	1
sans doute	–	–	3	–	3
Total	5	4	10	5	24

certainement, necessairement, peut estre, possible and *sans doute.* The distribution for individual years is given in Table 67. By far the most frequent of these is *peut estre,* which accounts for 15 of the 24 occurrences. It is also the only one which occurs in all four yearly samples.

> Ce dernier fait n'estoit **peut estre** pas moins inconnu que l'autre. (*Journal des Sçavans,* 4 juin 1685)
> [This last fact was perhaps no less unknown than the other one.]

Adjectival forms with a modal sense, other than those that occur in extraposed constructions, are relatively rare, accounting for only 3% of the total, and between 1% and 6% in individual years. Those that occur in the corpus are *capable, constant, necessaire, possible, probable,* and *semblable.* Their distribution for individual years is shown in Table 68.

The very small numbers show the rarity of this form. No single one occurs in all four individual yearly samples. The most frequent is *capable,* but even here there are only five occurrences in the whole of the *Journal des Sçavans* subcorpus.

Table 68. Adjectival modals in the *Journal des Sçavans.*

Adjective	*1665*	*1675*	*1685*	*1695*	*Total*
capable	1	3	1	–	5
constant	–	–	1	1	2
necessaire	–	1	3	–	4
possible	–	–	1	–	1
probable	–	–	–	2	2
semblable	–	–	1	–	1
Total	1	4	7	3	15

> Il parle des *Talismans*, qui sont ces figures, ou medailles qui portent l'image de la planete sous laquelle elles ont esté faites, & qu'on croit **capable** de plusieures effets, comme de chasser quelques bestes venimeuses, d'adoucir les ardeurs d'une fiévre ... (*Journal des Sçavans*, 11 mars 1675)
> [He discusses talismans, which are these figures or medals which carry the image of the planet under which they have been made, and which are believed to be able to produce certain effects, like warding off certain poisonous creatures, calming the heat of a fever ...]

Extraposed structures, functioning as grammatical metaphors of modality, are rather more frequent than adverbial and simple adjectival forms, accounting for 11% of the total. They are thus as frequent as finite verbs. They range from 6% to 17% in individual years: after a peak of 17% in 1685, they fall to 6% in 1695. Their sense is usually epistemic.

> **Il est aussi evident** que la distance entre les deux objects apparens sera d'autant plus grande que les trous de la carte seront ecartez l'un de l'autre, ou que l'œil sera plus applati. (*Journal des Sçavans*, 30 juillet 1685)
> [It is equally obvious that the distance between the two visible objects will be all the greater if the holes in the card are at a great distance from each other, or if the eye is flatter.]

Modal meaning

If we now consider the modal meanings of these expressions, distinguishing between epistemic (those relating to the speaker's judgement of likelihood), dynamic (relating to physical possibility or capability) and deontic (relating to permission and moral obligation), we find the distribution shown in Table 69.

Table 69. Modal meaning in the *Journal des Sçavans*.

	1665	*1675*	*1685*	*1695*	*Total*	*%*
Epistemic	32	24	31	20	107	23%
Dynamic	82	73	66	56	277	58%
Deontic	25	14	17	30	86	18%

Table 70. Percentage distribution of modal meanings.

	1665	*1675*	*1685*	*1695*
Epistemic	23%	22%	27%	19%
Dynamic	59%	66%	58%	53%
Deontic	18%	13%	15%	28%

The percentage distribution for individual years is given in Table 70. By far the most common of the modal meanings is that of dynamic modality, accounting for well over half (58%) of the modal meanings, and ranging from 53% to 66% in individual years. Thus, of the possible modal meanings, it is that related to the physical world, describing physical possibility and ability, that most commonly occurs.

> Pour voir si les astres **peuvent** causer dans les hommes quelques inclinations, il recherche la cause des differentes humeurs. (*Journal des Sçavans*, 11 mars 1675)
> [To see whether the heavenly bodies can produce certain inclinations in men, he looks for the cause of different humours.]

> Le seconde partie distinguée en vint chapitres est une relation des dernieres revolutions d'Angleterre, qui **doit** estre d'autant plus fidele, que les emplois de l'Auteur dans les pays étrangers lui ont donnée lieu de voir par lui-mesme ce qu'il en a écrit, & que d'ailleurs il l'apuye par des actes authentiques inserez dans cete seconde partie. (*Journal des Sçavans*, 21 février 1695)
> [The second part divided into twenty chapters is an account of the most recent revolutions in England, and must be all the more truthful in that the employment of the author in foreign countries has given him the opportunity to see for himself the things that he writes about, and moreover he supports this with authentic acts inserted into the second part.]

The other two types of modality are far behind in terms of frequency of use. Epistemic modality accounts for just under a quarter (23%) of the modal expressions, with a range of 19% to 27% in individual years. The highest yearly rate is 27% in 1685 and this drops to 19% in 1695. Thus, expressing a judgement of the validity of the content of a clause accounts for roughly a quarter of modal uses.

> Et **certainement** sans la mort inopinée de ce sçauant homme, elle auroit esté imprimée beaucoup plustost. (*Journal des Sçavans*, 9 mars 1665)
> [And certainly, without the unexpected death of this knowledgeable man, it would have been printed much earlier.]

> ... & s'**il est possible que** quelque occasion subite puisse determiner l'œil à changer de forme pour le rendre plus fort ou plus faible, comme nous examinerons dans la suite. (*Journal des Sçavans*, 30 juillet 1685)
> [... and whether it is possible for some sudden situation to make the eye change its shape to become stronger or weaker, as we will discuss in what follows.]

The least frequent of the types of modality is deontic, which nevertheless still accounts for 18% of the total, ranging from 13% to 28% in individual years. There is a marked increase of this type of modality in the 1695 sample, where the rate is 28%, whereas the highest rate in previous years is only 18%. Thus there seems to be an increased interest in questions of a moral nature in this final year of the sample.

> Or il est clair à M. de Tillemont par l'Evangile, que quand les Apôtres demanderent à N.S. où il vouloit qu'ils lui préparassent la Pâque, ils estoient au premier jour des Azimes, auquel **il faloit** immoler la Pâque, & par consequent au 14. du mois. (*Journal des Sçavans*, 3 janvier 1695)
> [But it is clear to M. de Tillement from the Gospels, that when the Apostles asked Our Lord where he wanted them to prepare the pascal meal for him, it was the first day of unleavened bread, when the pascal lamb had to be sacrificed, and so it was the 14th day of the month.]

> ... & le Concile de Nicée a declaré que ceux qui se seroient ordonner par un autre **ne devoient point** estre mis au nombre des Evêques. (*Journal des Sçavans*, 25 avril 1695)
> [... and the Council of Nicea declared that those ordained by another should not be counted among the number of the bishops.]

The *Philosophical Transactions*

We shall now turn to the *Philosophical Transactions*, where, naturally, the forms in which modality is expressed are somewhat different to those used in French.

Grammatical form

In English the main method for expressing modality is by using auxiliary verbs. There are in English nine modal auxiliaries properly so-called (Aux.), that is which occur as an auxiliary with a following main verb in the form of the base or naked infinitive, without the intervention of the particle *to*. These are *may, might, can, could, will, would, shall, should* and *must*. All of these occur to differing degrees in the corpus.

> ... and lastly that the Uterus **may** not be fit for the Reception of Animals at one time, tho' before 2 or 3 days are past, it **may** become perfectly capable. (*Philosophical Transactions*, 22 August 1685)

> But seeing all People endeavouring to get to the Island, I went among them, in hopes I **might** hear of my Wife, or some part of my Family, but could not. (*Philosophical Transactions*, March/April 1694)

> ... and he knows not whether we **can** find such a dexterity of keeping so much of it, and for so long a time, as needs, upon the Brim of a ring that is half an Inch broad. (*Philosophical Transactions*, 5 June 1665)

> They **could** perceive no smell before the fire, but afterwards a very strong smell of brimstone. (*Philosophical Transactions*, 22 November 1675)

> So that, if he **will** by any Contrivance he hath, give me a *Plane-convex* Glass of 30, or 40 foot *Diameter*, without *Veins*, and truly wrought of that *Figure*, I **will** presently make a Telescope with it, that with a single Ey-glass shall draw a thousand foot ... (*Philosophical Transactions*, 5 June 1665)

> ... and from thence I am ascertained that it hath no other passage then at X, for if it had, the Quick-silver **would** have run out of it. (*Philosophical Transactions*, 22 August 1685)

> And, if our Silversmiths hold on their degrading mixtures, I **shall** question, whether our *Silver-plate* may not shortly come down to approach our Forefathers *Pewter* ... (*Philosophical Transactions*, 26 July 1675)

> But why the Earth **should** shake for a quarter of a Minute, and then stand still for six, or seven, or ten Days, then shake again, and so continue to shake now and then by fits ... (*Philosophical Transactions*, March/April 1694)

> ... and I **must** confess (tho' this *Bitch* was as likely as any could be wisht) I could not find any round particle in it, that was bigger than a Globule of the blood, which makes it red. (*Philosophical Transactions*, 22 August, 1685)

Other verbal means of expressing modality (Vb) have been grouped together. These are mainly finite verbs which may be used with a modal function. Those that occur in the corpus are *appear, need, oblige, require* and *seem*. To these have been added a few examples of *be* followed by the infinitive, and *ought*, also followed by the infinitive. Many include this with the auxiliaries, but it differs in that it is the full infinitive that follows with the particle *to*.

> There was a double Diaphragm meeting in the middle between the two back-bones, and making a membrane, which to me **seem'd** to be a *Mediastinum*; for it reached up to the *Thymus*. (*Philosophical Transactions*, 22 August 1685)

> And then he leaveth it to be judged, whether a Glass of such a length being found, we **ought** to hope, that a *Turn* can be firm enough to keep such a piece of Glass in the same Inclination, so that the *Mandril* do not recede some Minutes from it ... (*Philosophical Transactions*, 5 June 1665)

There are no examples of *have* followed by the infinitive with modal force in the corpus.

There are a small number of modal adverbs (Adv.). Those that occur are *certainly, doubtless, necessarily, perhaps, possibly, probably, seemingly,* and *undoubtedly*. However, several of these occur only once in the whole corpus, and only *perhaps* and *certainly* occur more than four times.

> **Perhaps** he will say, he has transfer'd the *Libratory Circle* from the *Orbis magnus* to the transverse diameter of the Ellipsis. (*Philosophical Transactions*, 26 July 1675)

> If, as I shall make out in my answer to the last Quæry, this vertue of *petrifying* do's **certainly**, if not solely reside in the soil contiguous to this *Lough*, most **certainly** trees that imbibe some of this petrifying Vertue, or these Lapideous particles with their nourishment, as being already dispos'd for it, will be more easily altered into stone. (*Philosophical Transactions*, 22 August 1685)

There are also a small number of adjectives used with a modal function (Adj.). Those that occur are *able, capable, certain, impossible, improbable, likely, necessary, possible, probable, sure, unable,* and *uncertain*. Of these only *able, necessary* and *possible* occur more than four times.

> ... so that in every *little particle* of its matter, we may now behold almost as great a variety of creatures, as we were **able** before to reckon up in the whole *Universe* itself. (*Philosophical Transactions*, 3 April 1665)

> ... so as that a Ring of an inch broad may be made to touch the *Spherical Surface* of the Glass; nay, if it be **necessary** (without much trouble, especially in the grinding of longer Glasses) the whole *Concave Surface* of the Tool may be made to touch a Glass. (*Philosophical Transactions*, 5 June 1665)

The other forms that occur are rare. They are nouns (Noun), combinations (Comb.), grammatical metaphors (Meta.), and cases of extraposition (Extra.). The nouns which occur with a modal use are *certainty, impossibility, inability, likelihood, necessity, need, possibility,* and *probability*. However, of these, *likelihood* occurs three times, and the others less than that.

> Now, since in all **likelihood** the fixt Stars are suns, (perhaps of a different Magnitude) we may as a reasonable *Medium* presume they are generally about the bigness of our Sun. (*Philosophical Transactions*, March/April 1694)

Combinations occur where two lexical items function together with modal force, such as *may perhaps*, or *seem probable*. These are examples of what I have elsewhere called 'fertilized hedges' (Banks 1994b). The only one of these which occurs more than twice is the now obsolete *must needs*.

> ... but the air stagnating in very deep groves or pits, the grosser parts **must needs** at length separate themselves by their own weight, and subsiding to the bottom, there corrupt ... (*Philosophical Transactions*, 22 November 1675)

However, where adjacent modal terms are functioning separately, they have been counted separately; this is most obvious where one of the terms functions as an epistemic modal and the other as a dynamic modal.

> ... yet we may observe some of her Productions, that at least bear such an *Analogy*, or Resemblance to the Composition and Figure Remarkable in these Stones, that we shall easily conclude These as well as They **must certainly** be the Architecture of the Regular Hand of Nature. (*Philosophical Transactions*, July/August 1694)

I have used the term 'grammatical metaphor' for cases such as *I believe* or *I think*, where these function simply as items of epistemic modality. This includes two instances of the now obsolete *me thinks*.

> **Me thinks**, I say, that *these* changes are considerable enough in the force of the reflexions of Light to be observed, since we see so many differences of Lights in the *Moon*. (*Philosophical Transactions*, 4 December 1665)

Finally, those cases of extraposition which have been counted separately are those where the extraposition matrix functions as a grammatical metaphor of modality.

> ... **nor is it certain**, that the *Romans* or *Britains* were then much addicted to Coursing, or could soon know the worth of those Greyhounds ... (*Philosophical Transactions*, 22 November 1675)

A total of 1120 modal expressions were identified. The distribution of the grammatical forms is given in Table 71.

Table 71. Forms of modality in the *Philosophical Transactions*.

	1665	*1675*	*1685*	*1694*	*Total*	*%*
Aux.	325	269	127	136	857	77%
Vb	41	23	11	23	98	9%
Adv.	15	10	15	9	49	4%
Adj.	24	8	5	12	49	4%
Noun	2	2	4	4	12	1%
Comb.	5	5	4	3	17	1%
Meta.	8	5	1	8	22	2%
Extra.	3	5	4	4	16	1%
Total	423	327	171	199	1120	

Table 72. Percentages of forms of modal expression.

	1665	*1675*	*1685*	*1694*
Aux.	77%	82%	74%	68%
Vb	10%	7%	6%	12%
Adv.	4%	3%	9%	5%
Adj.	6%	2%	3%	6%
Noun	*	1%	2%	2%
Comb.	1%	2%	2%	2%
Meta.	2%	2%	1%	4%
Extra.	1%	2%	2%	2%

The vast majority of modal expressions are those with an auxiliary; these account for over three-quarters (77%) of the total. Other verbal forms account for 9%, adverbs and adjectives for 4% each. The other forms never account for more than 2%. The number of modal expressions identified gives an average rate of one modal expression per 5.6 finite clauses. However, this rate decreases from one per 3.9 clauses in 1665 to one per 7.4 clauses in 1694. The percentage rate for each year is given in Table 72.

The rate for auxiliaries ranges from 68% to 82%. Other verbal forms range from 6% to 12%. None of the other forms ever accounts for more than 10% in any individual year.

Since auxiliaries are the commonest grammatical form for the expression of modality, it is interesting to look at this form in greater detail. Table 73 gives the incidence of individual auxiliaries. As can be seen, *may* is the

Table 73. Modal auxiliaries in the *Philosophical Transactions.*

	1665	*1675*	*1685*	*1694*	*Total*	*%*
may	57	70	26	36	189	22%
might	11	9	13	6	39	5%
can	47	26	15	20	108	13%
could	20	21	27	24	92	11%
will	58	69	8	12	147	17%
would	51	29	11	17	108	13%
shall	25	20	10	7	62	7%
should	30	10	12	5	62	7%
must	26	15	5	9	55	6%
Total	325	269	127	136	857	

Table 74. Percentage rates of modal auxiliaries.

	1665	*1675*	*1685*	*1694*
may	18%	26%	20%	26%
might	3%	3%	10%	4%
can	14%	10%	12%	15%
could	6%	8%	21%	18%
will	18%	26%	6%	9%
would	16%	11%	9%	13%
shall	8%	7%	8%	5%
should	9%	4%	9%	4%
must	8%	6%	4%	7%

commonest modal auxiliary, accounting for 22% of the total, followed by *will*, with 17%. The auxiliaries *can* and *would* account for 13% each, and *could* for 11%. The other auxiliaries account for less than 10% each. Huddleston's (1971) study of mid-twentieth-century scientific texts does not distinguish between *may* and *might*, *can* and *could*, etc., but for *may* + *might* gives 27%, which corresponds to the figure here. However, for *can* + *could* he gives 36%, compared to 24% here, and 22% for *will* + *would*, compared to 30% here. Hence, as one would expect, there seems to have been considerable development over the three-century gap. The rates for individual years are given in Table 74.

The auxiliary *may* is the most common in each individual year, ranging from 18% to 26%, with *will* providing as many in the 1665 and 1675 samples. The evolution of the use of *will* is peculiar, in that it is much more common in the first half of the period than the second: 18% and 26% in 1665 and 1675, but only 6% and 9% in 1685 and 1694. The pattern for *could* is the opposite, with a much larger percentage in the second half of the period: 6% and 8% in 1665 and 1675, but rising to 21% and 18% in 1685 and 1694. The other auxiliaries are fairly stable, including *can*, ranging from 10% to 15%, and *would*, ranging from 9% to 16%.

Other verbal forms, although the second most frequent of our categories, account for only 9% of all modal expressions. The most common of these is the verb *seem*, with 46 occurrences in the corpus.

> This doth **seem** to shew the manner of petrification. (*Philosophical Transactions*, 26 July 1675)

> If this place be nothing but Sand (as some would have it, that are it's no Well-wishers) it **seems** strange that the Force of the Earthquake did

> not dissipate and dissolve the very foundation of it ... (*Philosophical Transactions*, March/April 1694)

The only other form with more than ten examples is *ought*, which occurs 11 times.

> Besides, that the strength of Man is so limited, that he is unable to work Glasses beyond a certain bigness, so as to finish and polish them all over so well, as *small* Glasses; whereas yet, the bigger they are, the more compleat they **ought** to be ... (*Philosophical Transactions*, 5 June 1665)

The verb *be* followed by the infinitive occurs 11 times, *require* and *need* have four occurrences each, and *appear* and *oblige* three.

Of the modal adverbs which occur, *perhaps* is the most common, with 27 occurrences.

> ... or **perhaps**, if the *Mercurial Baroscope* had been more generally spread in the hands of many sagacious Gentlemen, I conceive, we should have heard less noise against the Gravity and Gravitation of the Air. (*Philosophical Transactions*, 26 July 1675)

The only other adverbial modal which has more than ten occurrences is *certainly*, which has 11.

> This **certainly** proves the soil to have this petrifying Vertue, which was never yet proved of the water. (*Philosophical Transactions*, 22 August 1685)

Of the others, *probably* occurs four times, *necessarily* twice, and *seemingly, possibly, doubtless,* and *undoubtedly* once each.

The only adjectival modal that occurs more than ten times is *able*, of which there are 13 occurrences.

> ... and that this absence of Vapors is perhaps the cause, that no *Crepuscle* is there, as it seems there is none, my selfe at least not having hitherto been **able** to discerne any mark thereof ... (*Philosophical Transactions*, 4 December 1665)

Of the others, *necessary* occurs eight times, *possible* seven, *impossible* four, *capable, likely* and *certain* three times each, *unable, requisite* and *probable* twice each, and *improbable* and *uncertain* once each.

Although there are a small number of nouns with a modal function, none have any degree of frequency: *likelihood* occurs three times, *necessity* and *probability* twice, and *certainty, possibility, need, inability,* and *impossibility* all occur once each.

Of the combinations, the now obsolete *must needs* occurs eight times.

> But I suppose, all would be visible, had we a convenient light to view them by, because, be they either thicker or thinner than the Air, that density or thinness will occasion a refraction, and that **must needs** render them visible. (*Philosophical Transactions*, 22 November 1675)

Of the others *may perhaps* occurs twice as a combination, as does *may seem*, others only once.

The grammatical metaphors which occur in this function are mainly either *I think* (ten occurrences) or *I believe* (eight occurrences).

> And this our Judicious Author is, **I think**, the first that may justly be called an English author of fruitful Gardens. (*Philosophical Transactions*, 26 July 1675)

> ... it forced its passage out from the Hill in (**I believe**) twenty or thirty several places, some more forcibly than others ... (*Philosophical Transactions*, March/April 1694)

Modal meaning

When the modal meanings of the expressions found in the *Philosophical Transactions* subcorpus are analysed in terms of epistemic, dynamic, and deontic modality, it is found that just over three-quarters (76%) of the modal expressions are cases of dynamic modality, with a further 20% being epistemic modality. Deontic modality, however, is fairly rare, accounting for only 4% of the modal expressions. This is shown in Table 75. The percentage rates for individual years are given in Table 76.

Table 75. Modal meanings in the *Philosophical Transactions.*

	1665	*1675*	*1685*	*1694*	*Total*	*%*
Epistemic	70	52	45	60	227	20%
Dynamic	337	261	118	137	853	76%
Deontic	16	14	8	2	40	4%

Table 76. Percentages of modal meanings.

	1665	*1675*	*1685*	*1694*
Epistemic	17%	16%	26%	30%
Dynamic	80%	80%	69%	69%
Deontic	4%	4%	5%	1%

Dynamic modality is by far the commonest form of modality found in the *Philosophical Transactions* corpus, reflecting the prime interest of its readers in questions of a physical nature. Thus, when modality is used, it is the area which concerns physical ability, physical possibility and future events, which constitute the main area of modal expression. It will, however, be noted that there is a distinct drop in the incidence of dynamic modality from 80% in 1665 and 1675 to 69% in 1685 and 1694, a drop of roughly 10 percentage points. This seems to be mainly due to a rise in the incidence of epistemic modality. From 16% in 1675, the incidence of epistemic modality rises to 30% in 1694. This must be balanced against the fact that the incidence of modality in general is somewhat less in the second half of the period. Nevertheless, it does indicate that where modality is resorted to, there is an increasing likelihood that it will be epistemic in nature. Epistemic modality expresses a judgement of validity on the part of the speaker, and is thus a tactic of hedging (Hyland 1998; Salager-Meyer 1994, 1995; Alonso-Aleida 2012), whereby the speaker mitigates the force of his statement. One might hypothesize that while in the early years of the journal simple unadorned observations would frequently be all that was necessary, as time went on, it became more necessary to give a more closely constructed argument to the discourse, including foreseeing possible objections, and protecting oneself against possible counter-arguments. This would involve a greater degree of hedging, and hence of epistemic modality. If correct, this hypothesis would account for the increase in the percentage of epistemic expressions at the expense of dynamic modality, which nevertheless remains by far the most frequent form of modality. The use of deontic modality is never great, and from an already very low 4% to 5% in the years 1664 to 1685, it falls to a totally insignificant 1% in 1694. This indicates that questions related to the moral sphere were not of interest to the readers of the *Philosophical Transactions.*

Some elements of comparison

In the *Journal des Sçavans* a modal expression occurs once per 12.3 clauses; in the *Philosophical Transactions*, a modal expression occurs once per 5.6 clauses. Hence modal expressions can be said to be more than twice as frequent in the English journal as in the French. This is probably due to the nature of the texts involved. It must be remembered that in the case of the *Journal des Sçavans,* the items in any issue were for the most part written by a single person, the editor, whereas the *Philosophical Transactions* is made up of letters, letter extracts, articles, etc., all by different writers. In the *Journal des Sçavans*, the majority of the items are book reviews, where giving a synopsis of the content of the book is a major priority; this will not usually require a great deal of qualification or hedging, and can be fairly straightforward. This may be the reason why the use of modality seems comparatively restrained. The case of the *Philosophical Transactions* is quite different, for here writers are expressing their own observations, recounting their own experiments, putting forward their own hypotheses and explanations. Hence there may be much more need to qualify and hedge against possible attack, contradiction, or counter-examples. In the light of this it seems reasonable that there should be a much greater incidence of modality in the *Philosophical Transactions*.

It might, however, be noted that the incidence of modality falls in both of the periodicals over the period concerned. In the *Journal des Sçavans* it falls from one modal expression per 9.4 clauses in 1665 to one per 15.6 clauses in 1695; in the *Philosophical Transactions*, it falls from one modal expression per 3.9 clauses in 1665 to one per 7.3 clauses in 1694. This, however, in no way detracts from the fact that modality is much more common in the English journal.

Some might object that English uses the system of modality to express future time, whereas French has a genuine future tense. Consequently, expressions of the future will be assimilated to modality in English but not in French, thus increasing the incidence of modality in English in relation to French. If, in view of this objection and for the sake of argument, we presume that expression of future time in English is basically the use of the modal auxiliaries *will* and *shall*, and we remove *will* and *shall* from our count of modal expressions, we then find that a modal expression (excluding *will* and *shall*) occurs once per 6.6 clauses. The difference is fairly minimal, and even with this figure, modal expressions still remain almost twice as frequent in the English periodical.

A further objection might be that French possesses a conditional tense. Whether the French conditional tense constitutes a form of modality is a moot point, but it is true that it would frequently be translated in English by a modal auxiliary. There are 62 occurrences of the conditional tense in the *Journal des Sçavans* subcorpus. If, for the sake of argument, we include these in the count of French modals, we find that the rate of modal expressions is one per 10.9 clauses. This still leaves us with a frequency rate for the French journal which is much less than the rate for the English journal, even if *will* and *shall* are excluded: 10.9 for the French journal if the conditional tense is included, and 6.6 for the English journal if *will* and *shall* are excluded. Hence, even in these circumstances, the conclusion that modality is much more prevalent in the *Philosophical Transactions* than in the *Journal des Sçavans* stands.

It is evident that the grammatical forms of French are not directly comparable with those of English. Nevertheless, some comparison is possible if in each language we group all of the verbal means of expressing modality together. For French this would be Vb (Aux.) + Vb (Imp.) + Vb (Other), and for English, Aux. + Vb. If this is done, we find that verbal forms of expressing modality account for 81% of the modal expressions in the *Journal des Sçavans* and 85% of the modal expressions in the *Philosophical Transactions.*

However, probably the most interesting comparison in relation to modality concerns the type of modality involved. Table 77 compares the percentages of types of modal meaning in the two journals. From this it can be seen that where modality is used, it is most likely to be of the dynamic type in both journals. However, this is true to a much greater degree in the *Philosophical Transactions,* where the rate is 76%, than in the *Journal des Sçavans,* where it is 59%. On the other hand, epistemic modality is of the same order in both, 23% in the *Journal des Sçavans* and 20% in the *Philosophical Transactions.* The difference noted for dynamic modality seems to be mirrored by a difference in the incidence of deontic modality; even though this is the least frequent form of modality in both journals, nevertheless it accounts for 18% of the modal expressions in the *Journal des Sçavans,* but is virtually insignificant in the *Philosophical Transactions,* where it accounts for only 4%. It seems reasonable to suppose that the greater use of dynamic modality in the *Philosophical Transactions* reflects the greater interest in questions of a physical nature in the English journal, even if there is a fall in the second half of the period. The difference in the use of deontic modality probably results from the fact that the *Journal des Sçavans* includes numerous items from non-scientific disciplines, notably theology and law, where an interest in questions of a moral nature are much more likely. These are disciplines which do not appear in the pages of the *Philosophical Transactions.* This is compounded by the fact that the rate of deontic modal use in the *Journal des Sçavans* appears to be on the increase towards the end of the period, whereas the already low rate in the *Philosophical Transactions* seems to be falling.

Table 77. Types of modal meaning.

	Journal des Sçavans	*Philosophical Transactions*
Epistemic	23%	20%
Dynamic	59%	76%
Deontic	18%	4%

Thus we can say that modal use reflects a greater interest in questions of a physical nature in the *Philosophical Transactions* and an interest in moral questions in the *Journal des Sçavans* which is absent in the *Philosophical Transactions.*

8 Nominalization: reifying processes

Grammatical metaphor, which has been called the driving force of scientific writing (Banks 2008a, 2008b; Halliday 1988, 1998; Halliday and Martin 1993), is the use of a non-congruent form. For example, processes are expressed congruently as verbs; where they are encoded by other forms, such as nouns or adjectives, this constitutes a grammatical metaphor. There are numerous forms which grammatical metaphors can take, ideational, as in this example, interpersonal, etc. (Ravelli 1988; Taverniers 2003). The form of grammatical metaphor which consists in nominalizing processes has become particularly common in scientific writing (Banks 2001, 2003), and so that is the form that will be concentrated on here. That does not mean that other forms of grammatical metaphor do not occur; cursory reading shows that there are also quite a number of examples of adjectivalized processes, and a significant number of modals occurring as the matrix of an extraposed structure function as interpersonal grammatical metaphors. These cases notwithstanding, nominalized processes are of particular interest, partly because of their capacity to reify the processes involved, thus presenting them as presupposed and incontrovertible. This is so because nouns typically encode entities, and entities have a relatively permanent status compared to processes, so presenting a process in nominal form makes it seem solid and permanent, more like a truth which cannot be denied.

The *Journal des Sçavans*

Examples of grammatical metaphor in the form of nominalized processes occur in the *Journal des Sçavans* with a frequency of about 24 per 1000 words of running text, or on average one nominalized process per 43 words of text. The results for individual years are given in Table 78. The frequency is stable for individual years, with only 1675 being a little lower than the other yearly samples.

Table 78. Frequency of nominalized processes.

	1665	*1675*	*1685*	*1695*	*Whole corpus*
Frequency/1000 words	24	20	24	25	24
Words per nominalization	41	50	41	40	43

Table 79. Process types of nominalized processes.

	1665	*1675*	*1685*	*1695*	*Total*	*%*
Material	146	132	221	249	748	48%
Mental	99	84	74	115	372	24%
Relational	4	1	8	17	30	2%
Verbal	112	62	70	161	405	26%
Existential	3	–	2	2	7	*
Total	364	279	375	544	1562	

Table 80. Percentage distribution of nominalized processes.

	1665	*1675*	*1685*	*1695*
Material	40%	47%	59%	46%
Mental	27%	30%	20%	21%
Relational	1%	*	2%	3%
Verbal	30%	22%	19%	30%
Existential	1%	*	1%	*

When the examples identified are considered in terms of the process types they represent, the results given in Table 79 emerge. To all intents and purposes, the nominalization of processes concerns material, mental and verbal processes. As might be expected, given the nature of the processes involved, relational and existential processes are rare: relational processes account for only 2% of the total, and existential processes for less than 0.5%. The percentage distribution of nominalized processes for individual years is given in Table 80.

Although existential process does not lend itself to nominalization, rare cases do occur, but these never account for more than 1% of the nominalized processes in a given year.

> ... & dans l'Amérique où elles ont donné leur nom à un des plus grands fleuves du monde, on ne pourroit pas cependant en rien inferer contre l'**existence** des anciennes Amazones ... (*Journal des Sçavans*, 16 avril 1685)

[... and in America where they have given their name to one of the greatest rivers in the world, it would be impossible to infer anything from that against the existence of the ancient Amazons.]

... qu'il est impossible que les expressions communes des Peres qui marquent vne **presence** reelle ayent esté entenduës par les peuples en vn sens metaphorique. (*Journal des Sçavans*, 9 février 1665)
[... that it is impossible that the common expressions of the Fathers, which indicate a real presence, should have been understood by the people in a metaphorical sense.]

The same thing might be said of relational processes, which account for only 2% overall and never more than 3% in an individual year. Of the rare cases that occur, roughly half are attributive (53%) and half are possessive (47%). No examples of nominalized identifying processes were identified in the corpus. This is shown in Table 81.

There seem to be rather more examples in 1695, but the figures are too small to make any firm claim. The following two extracts have examples that were encoded attributive and possessive respectively.

Quand le Peintre a inventé un sujet, il en trace le dessein, & observe les proportions que la nature y a mises, sur tout s'il fait un portrait, & qu'il veuille attrapper la **ressemblance**. (*Journal des Sçavans*, 21 février 1695)
[When the painter has created a subject, he draws the outline and notes the proportions which nature has given it, especially if he is doing a portrait, and he wants to capture the likeness.]

Cependant comme ils n'ont observé aucun ordre dans leurs remarques, & qu'il est certain qu'il y en a une infinité dont la parfait intelligence dépend de leur **liaison** & de leur **rapport**, il nous manquoit une methode pour s'en servir commodement. (*Journal des Sçavans*, 16 avril 1685)
[However, since they have observed no particular order in their remarks, and it is obvious that there is an infinite number whose perfect understanding depends on their links and connections, we lacked a method for using them easily.]

Material nominalized processes are dominant in all four yearly samples, accounting for 48% overall. Moreover, their incidence rises sharply from

Table 81. Types of nominalized relational process.

	1665	*1675*	*1685*	*1695*	*Total*	*%*
Attributive	1	–	4	11	16	53%
Identifying	–	–	–	–	–	–
Possessive	3	1	4	6	14	47%

40% in 1665 to 59% in 1685, before dropping back to 46% in 1695. These processes tend to occur more frequently in items of a more scientific nature, but they also occur relatively frequently in historical items. This is the case in the following item from the field of astronomy.

> ... les Cometes ne sont qu'vn amas de plusieurs petites estoilles errantes, qui suiuant la nature des autres planetes qui ont des **mouuemens** inegaux, se doiuent necessairement ioindre ensemble de temps en temps, & se rendre visibles par cette **vnion**. (*Journal des Sçavans*, 26 janvier 1665)
> [... comets are only a mass of several small wandering stars, which like other planets that have irregular motion must necessarily join together from time to time, and make themselves visible by this union.]

And the following is from an item in the field of history.

> Elle comprend la **naissance** & le **progrez** d'une guerre civile dont le souvenir ne sçauroit estre adouci que par celui du plus grand Roy du monde, que la fortune destinoit dés-lors pour le bon-heur & pour la gloire de la France ... (*Journal des Sçavans*, 6 mai 1675)
> [It includes the beginning and progress of a civil war whose memory can only be mellowed by that of the greatest king in the world, whom fate had selected from then on for the happiness and glory of France ...]

In general, nominalized material processes in the astronomical sphere are natural phenomena, or sometimes the actions of the protagonists in the event. Those in the historical sphere are historical actions and events.

The second most common nominalized form is that of verbal process, but at 26% of the total it is only a barely significant two percentage points ahead of nominalized mental processes, which account for 24% of the total. Moreover, verbal processes are the second most common form in 1665 and 1695, whereas mental processes are the second most common in 1675 and 1685, albeit only by a single percentage point in this last case. The fact that nominalized verbal process is so common is no doubt partly due to the fact that the majority of the items are book reviews and hence discourse is at the centre of the preoccupations of the editors of the journal. However, it probably also underlines their interest in communication on a wider level than the book-review format of their publication. Items dealing with law constitute one of the fields where nominalized verbal processes are frequent.

> Ils auoient depuis obtenu **dispense**, portant **legitimation** des enfans qu'ils auoient eu auant leur mariage. Apres la mort de Charles Barbier, les enfans du premier lict interjetterent **appel** comme d'abus de la **dispense**. (*Journal des Sçavans*, 12 janvier 1665)
> [They subsequently obtained a dispensation which made the children that they had had before their marriage legitimate. After the death of Charles

Barbier, the children of the first marriage made an appeal against this as an abuse of the dispensation.]

Dans le corps de cete **requête** ils representent en termes fort patetiques la triste necessité où ils seroit réduits par la derniere **déclaration**, ou de renoncer à une profession dans laquelle ils ont vieilli, ou pour en continuer l'exercice de se remettre sur les bancs avec des cheveux gris ... (*Journal des Sçavans*, 21 février 1695)
[In the body of this request, they describe in moving terms the sad necessity to which they would be reduced by the last declaration: either to give up the profession within which they had matured or in order to continue to exercise it, to place themselves again on the bench with their grey hair ...]

In the case of mental process, the vast majority of examples are of the cognitive type, which account for 83%, with a further 11% of the perception type, and 7% affective. Thus the distribution of nominalized mental processes is similar to that of finite mental process verbs, where the corresponding percentages were 89%, 9% and 2%. The details of the distribution of nominalized mental processes are given in Table 82.

Thus, as in the case of finite verbs, nominalized mental processes are predominantly cognitive.

Mais quelque lumiere & quelque **discernement** qu'il ait fait paroistre dans cét Ouurage, il n'a pas empesché que l'on n'en ait fait des **iugemens** bien differens. (*Journal des Sçavans*, 9 mars 1665)
[But whatever the clarity and discrimination he displayed in this work, he did not prevent others making completely different judgements.]

En 1592. Michel Salonius Religieux de l'Ordre de saint Augustin, fit imprimer à Venise un traité de la Justice & du Droit, où il soutint que de deux **opinions** probables chacun peut dans la pratique choisir la moins probable, & que c'estoit là la **pensée** de plusieurs Docteurs, entre lesquels il y en avoit de l'Ecole de saint Thomas. (*Journal des Sçavans*, 3 janvier 1695)
[In 1592, Michel Salonius, a monk of the Augustinian order, published in Venice a treatise on justice and law, where he maintains that of two probable opinions, it is, in practice, possible to select the less probable, and that that was the view of several doctors, including some from the school of St Thomas.]

Table 82. Types of nominalized mental process.

	1665	*1675*	*1685*	*1695*	*Total*	*%*
Cognitive	81	77	46	103	307	83%
Perception	14	4	22	–	40	11%
Affective	4	3	6	12	25	7%

Examples of nominalized perception mental processes are relatively rare, only accounting for roughly one in ten of the nominalized mental processes.

> Les personnes intelligentes dans ces matieres, iugeront facilement par le peu de choses qu'on rapporte des **observations** de M. Auzout & de M. Buot, que ceux-là se sont trompez, qui se sont imaginez qu'il y auoit deux Cometes : & qu'on ne doit pas non plus estre surpris du grand chemin qu'elle a fait à nostre égard : & ils pourront aussi conclure des ces **observations**, que les cometes ont vn mouuement reglé comme les autres corps celestes. (*Journal des Sçavans*, 16 janvier 1665)
> [Those who are knowledgeable in these matters can easily judge from the little that has been said about the observations of M. Auzout and M. Buot that those who thought that there were two comets were mistaken, and that moreover we should not be surprised at the great distance they have covered in relation to us, and they can also conclude from these observations that comets have a motion regulated like other celestial bodies.]

Examples of nominalized affective mental process are even rarer, though some do occur.

> ... c'est à dire qu'il se contente d'exposer & de representer dans des avantures galantes, comme en autant de Tableaux, toutes les differentes especes de **l'amour**. (*Journal des Sçavans*, 15 janvier 1685)
> [... that is to say, he limits himself to describing and representing in courtly escapades, as in so many tableaux, all the different types of love.]

Hence the most common nominalized processes are material, with verbal and mental nominalized processes occurring with roughly the same frequency, and verbal processes being only fractionally more frequent than mental. Nominalized relational and existential processes are rare.

Halliday (1988, 1994) has argued that grammatical metaphor, particularly in the form of nominalized processes, plays an important role in the thematic structure and progression of a scientific text. This occurs when an unpacked (Ventola 1996) or non-metaphorical form occurs in the rheme of a clause, and a metaphorical form occurs as the theme of a following clause. One of his examples moves from 'the rate at which cracks grow' to 'the rate of crack growth'. This constitutes an important feature in the construction of the argumentation. However, this does not seem to be the case in the texts found in the *Journal des Sçavans*. There are no more than a handful of cases where a rhematic unpacked form is followed by a thematic metaphorical form, and even where this is the case it would be difficult to claim that the sequence played a significant role in the construction of the argument. There are one or two cases where an unpacked form is followed by a metaphorical form, but the metaphorical form is not thematic, so this does not correspond to the phenomenon which Halliday underlines.

> Le Pere d'Arroüis fit l'ouverture de la Conference, & soutint, que les Cometes ne sont qu'vn amas de plusieurs petites estoilles errantes, qui suivant la nature des autres plantes qui ont des mouuemens inegaux, se doiuent necessairement **ioindre ensemble** de temps en temps, & se rendre visible par cette **vnion**. (*Journal des Sçavans*, 26 janvier 1665)
> [Father d'Arroüis opened the conference, and maintained that comets are only a mass of several small wandering stars, which like other planets which have irregular motion, must necessarily join together from time to time, and make themselves visible by this union.]

In this example the infinitive phrase, *ioindre ensemble*, is subsumed in the noun *vnion* in the following clause. However, neither of these is the theme of its respective clause, so, while *vnion* can be considered to be a nominalization of the infinitive phrase, they do not constitute the phenomenon of thematic progression that Halliday discusses.

> Enfin il assure que dans un lieu nommé Glovolg il y a une petite Riviere qui **change** le hous, que les Anglois appellant *holly*, en une pierre verte dont les Chaudronniers se servent pour faire leurs moules. Il est mal-aisé de rendre raison de ce **changement** … (*Journal des Sçavans*, 1 juillet 1675)
> [Finally, he asserts that in a place called Glovolg, there is a small river which changes the *hous*, which the English call 'holly', into a green stone which boilermakers use to make their moulds. It is not easy to explain this change …]

Similarly, in this example, the finite verb *change* is taken up by the noun *changement*. However, once again, neither of these is thematic.

The following two examples seem closer to the structure we are looking for.

> Ce n'est pas que la partie D allant **presser** les boules qui sont en LG, **ne presse** en même temps celles qui sont en CF & CE : mais cette **pression** n'est pas considerable … (*Journal des Sçavans*, 1 juillet 1675)
> [It is not that the part D which pushes the balls in LG does not, at the same time, push those that are in CF and CE: but this pressure is not great …]

> La raison prise de ce que depuis long-temps les Archevêques de Reims **ne visitoient plus** le diocese de Cambrai n'est pas meilleure. Ces **visites** sont plutôt permises qu'ordonnées aux Archevêques, & le Concil de Trente s'en est sufisamment expliqué. (*Journal des Sçavans*, 25 avril 1695)
> [The reason given why for many years the Archbishops of Rheims no longer visited the diocese of Cambrai is not better. The Archbishops are permitted rather than ordered to make these visits, and the Council of Trent has explained this sufficiently.]

In the first of these examples the verbal forms *presser* and *ne presse* are the origin of the next theme, *cette pression*; and in the second the verb *ne visitoient plus* is the origin of the next theme, *ces visites*. However, these are isolated examples, and although locally they do enter into the scheme of thematic progression, they are insufficient to claim a strategy of argument construction. Hence, where nominalization of processes is used in the *Journal des Sçavans*, it seems to be a question of the reification of the process which is the instigation of the nominalized form.

The *Philosophical Transactions*

Examples of nominalized processes occur in the *Philosophical Transactions* part of the corpus with a frequency of about 20 per 1000 words of running text, or, on average, one nominalized process for 50 words of text. The details are given in Table 83. The frequency is relatively stable over the period considered, albeit rather less frequent in 1685 than in the other years.

The process types of the nominalized processes which occur are given in Table 84. It is immediately evident that, of the nominalized processes which occur, by far the most common are of the material process type; these account for two-thirds (64%) of the examples identified. Although they are the second most common, mental processes are much less common than material processes, accounting for 18% of the sample, and verbal processes even less frequent at 14%. Relational and existential processes, as expected, are rare.

Table 83. Frequency of nominalized processes in the *Philosophical Transactions*.

	1665	*1675*	*1685*	*1694*	*Whole corpus*
Frequency/1000 words	21	21	18	19	20
Words per nominalization	48	47	57	51	50

Table 84. Types of nominalized processes.

	1665	*1675*	*1685*	*1694*	*Total*	*%*
Material	261	351	166	216	99	64%
Mental	102	71	52	58	283	18%
Relational	9	10	7	13	39	3%
Verbal	52	76	47	48	223	14%
Existential	4	1	1	1	7	*
Total	428	509	273	336	1546	

Table 85. Percentage distribution for individual years.

	1665	*1675*	*1685*	*1694*
Material	61%	69%	61%	64%
Mental	24%	14%	19%	17%
Relational	2%	2%	3%	4%
Verbal	12%	15%	17%	14%
Existential	1%	*	*	*

Table 85 gives the percentage distribution for individual years. The figures are fairly stable over the whole period considered. Not only do material processes account for 64% of nominalized processes overall, but they are by far the most frequent type of nominalized process in all four of the years sampled, ranging from 61% in 1665 and 1685 to 69% in 1675. These material processes frequently refer to natural phenomena or events.

> Nor have I done, as some have fancied of me, who having been able to observe the Comet, the 27, 28, 29, 30, and 31. of *December*, and to see the **diminution** of its **motion**, have judged, that I had only determined that **diminution** for the time to come, conform to the **augmentation** thereof in time passed until the 29. of *December*. (*Philosophical Transactions*, 3 April 1665)

> But alas! The strange **Rents** and **Tearings** of the Mountains here, sufficiently evince, that Rocks and Sand are equally able to withstand the Force of a violent **Earthquake**. (*Philosophical Transactions*, March/April 1694)

Human actions, particularly of an experimental type, and the effects they produce are also commonly expressed in this nominalized form.

> The same **Experiment** was also made with common water, and it's **ebullition** with *Aqua vitæ*, purged of Air, was also found to be very great, when mixed *in vacuo*. (*Philosophical Transactions*, 22 November 1675)

> For I had made **trials**, as many as my leisure would permit, not without some good **success** ... (*Philosophical Transactions*, 5 June 1665)

The overall rate of nominalized mental processes is 18%, varying from 14% in 1675 to 24% in 1665. Hence, although being the second most frequent nominalized process type, they cannot be said to be particularly common. When the different subtypes of mental processes are considered, the results shown in Table 86 emerge.

Table 86. Types of nominalized mental process.

	1665	*1675*	*1685*	*1694*	*Total*	*%*
Cognitive	74	53	30	45	202	71%
Perception	27	14	21	12	74	26%
Affective	1	4	1	1	7	2%

Although not particularly common, where they do occur, nominalized cognitive processes account for 71% of the nominalized mental processes.

> And indeed, for any man to look upon the matters published by their Order of Licence, as if they were *Their* Sense, and had *Their* **Approbation**, as *certain* and *true*, 'tis extremely wide of their **intentions**, seeing they, in giving way to, or encouraging such publications, aim chiefly at this, that *ingenious* ***conceptions***, and *important philosophical matters of Fact* may be communicated to the learned and enquiring World, thereby to excite the minds of men to the **examination** and improvement thereof. (*Philosophical Transactions*, 5 June 1665)

> Thirdly, How to treat Composts, so as to render them fit for our service: Which he takes to be a difficulty worthy the heads as well as the hands of the profoundest Philosopher; since it requires a more than superficial **knowledge** and **penetration** into causes. (*Philosophical Transactions*, 22 November 1675)

Although less common, nominalized mental perception processes are relatively significant, accounting for 26% of the nominalized mental processes. This mainly reflects the interest of the readership of the periodical in observation as a means of amassing knowledge.

> Concerning the *Shadow above*, which *Campani* affirms to be made by the *Ring* upon the Body of *Saturn*, M. *Auzout* judges, that there could be no such *Phænomenon*, by reason of its *Northern Latitude* at the times, wherein the ***Observations*** were made, *vid*. In *April* 1663; in the midst of *August*, and the beginning of *October* next following, and in *April* 1664, except it were in *October*, and the *Shadow* strong enough to become *visible*. (*Philosophical Transactions*, 5 June 1665)

> But this is much too little to answer to the Experiments of the *French*, who found that it rained 19 Inches Water in a Year at *Paris*. Or those of *Mr. Townley*, who by a long continued Series of **Observations** has sufficiently proved that, in *Lancashire* at the foot of the Hills there falls above 40 Inches of Water in the Years time. (*Philosophical Transactions*, July/August 1694)

Affective mental processes rarely appear in nominalized form. There are only seven examples in the whole of the *Philosophical Transactions* subcorpus, accounting for only 2% of the nominalized mental processes.

> ... but here, the Gardiners reserved and best approv'd Arts are publish't for the more general **satisfaction** of those generous English who are willing to bestow the best Ornaments upon their native Countrey ... (*Philosophical Transactions*, 26 July 1675)

Nominalized verbal processes are even less common than mental, accounting for only 14% of the nominalized processes, and showing that, in terms of nominalization, communication is only of minor interest in the periodical.

> This Systeme has been well approved of by several good Astronomers, and Mr. Street has esteemed it so good, that he has printed a figure of it with the **description** of his Planetary instrument; but without acknowledgeing the proper Author ... (*Philosophical Transactions*, 26 July 1675)

> Among your many other exact and curious **observations**, I can't pass by that remarkable **relation** of the Hydrophobia (given by the learned and ingenious *Dr Lister*,) without applauding the curiosity of the observer, in his most exact historie of that diseas; and having lately had an opportunity of making some **remarks** upon a case not much differing ... (*Philosophical Transactions*, 23 March 1685)

There are no more than a handful of nominalized relational processes, which account for 4% of the sample. Of those that do occur, roughly two-thirds are attributive and one-third possessive. There are no examples of nominalized identifying relational processes. The details are given in Table 87.

In the following example, *resemblance* and *composition* were encoded as attributive and possessive respectively.

> ... where though we may find nothing altogether the same, yet we may observe some of her Productions, that at least bear such an *Analogy*, or **Resemblance** to the **Composition** and figure Remarkable in these stones ... (*Philosophical Transactions*, July/August 1694)

Table 87. Types of nominalized relational process.

	1665	*1675*	*1685*	*1694*	*Total*	*%*
Attributive	7	3	4	11	25	64%
Identifying	–	–	–	–	–	–
Possessive	2	7	3	2	14	36%

To all intents and purposes the corpus is virtually devoid of nominalized existential processes. There are, in fact, only seven cases encoded as such in the whole corpus, of which the following is one.

> Whether the Umbilical Vessels convey the blood of the Mother to the Child, or whether the *Fœtus* be for the most part form'd and acted by the circulating blood, before the **existence** of the Umbilical Vessels, or before the connection of the *Fœtus* with the *Uterus*? (*Philosophical Transactions*, 5 June 1665)

Only one example was noted where a rhematic non-metaphorical form was followed by a thematic nominalized (grammatical metaphor) form.

> But having beheld it with a Telescope, I soon said, that it **was joyned** with two small Stars, whereof one was pretty bright, which I had already seen, on February 28, and 29. And this **conjunction** gave the Comet that brightness, as it happens to most of the Stars of the fifth and sixth magnitude, where 2. or 3. or more **are conjoyned**, which perhaps would shew but faintly single, though by reason of their proximity to one another, they appear but one Star. (*Philosophical Transactions*, 3 April 1665)

Here, the non-metaphorical form, *are joyned*, is the origin of the metaphorical theme which follows, *conjunction*. However, the fact that there is only a single example suggests that nominalization is not being used as a method of argument structure through thematic progression. Moreover, it will be noted that the text moves back to the non-metaphorical form *are conjoyned*, later in the clause complex.

In a few other cases, there is passage from non-metaphorical to metaphorical forms, without this being a question of thematic progression. Thus, in the following example, we have the infinitive, followed by the finite verb, followed by the nominalized form.

> And as they have had the wit to lead us on **to change** the fashion of our *Pewter*, as oft as we **change** the fashion of our hats, our Pewter is in every **change** more and more embased ... (*Philosophical Transactions*, 26 July 1675)

In the following example the infinitive *plunder* is followed by the nominalized form.

> And as soon as the violent Earthquake was over, the Watermen and Sailers did not stick **to plunder** those Houses; and in the time of their **Plunder** one or two of them fell upon their Heads by a second Earthquake, where they were lost. (*Philosophical Transactions*, March/April 1694)

In this final example, the non-metaphorical *is ... petrified* is followed by the nominalized form, *petrification.*

> Sir, some years ago, I wrote to you from Sir *W. St.* mouth, that he could shew you, where water passeth very slowly over stone, and thence, drop by drop, falls down white like curdled milk, and **is** afterwards there **petrified**. This doth seem to shew the manner of **petrification**. (*Philosophical Transactions*, 26 July 1675)

This final example shows that there is a possible use of nominalization to create technical terms and to present such phenomena as being established fact. It is probable that this is a more general motivation for the use of nominalization, thus making the reification of the process, inherent in the nominalized form, the principal reason for its use.

Some elements of comparison

The frequency of nominalization is a little greater in the *Journal des Sçavans* than in the *Philosophical Transactions.* The details are given in Table 88.

The frequency is greater in the *Journal des Sçavans* in three of the four yearly samples; only in 1675 is the frequency greater in the *Philosophical Transactions.* This poses the interesting question of why this should be so, since some might have expected the frequency to be greater in the English journal. Part of the explanation may lie in the great importance that the Royal Society placed on clear, simple language. This derived from Bacon, their *maître à penser,* who, in his *Parasceve,* says,

> ... for all that concerns ornaments of speech, similitudes, treasury of eloquence, and such like emptinesses, let it be utterly dismissed. Also let all those things which are admitted be themselves set down briefly and concisely, so that they may be nothing less than words. For no man who is collecting and storing up materials for ship-building or the like, thinks of arranging them elegantly, as in a shop, and displaying them so as to please the eye; all his care is that they be sound and good, and that they be so arranged as to take up as little room as possible in the warehouse. And this is exactly what should be done here. (Bacon 1905: 403–4)

Table 88. Frequency of nominalized processes.

	Journal des Sçavans	*Philosophical Transactions*
Frequency/1000 words	24	20
Words per nominalization	43	50

This plea for clear, simple language was taken to heart by the early Royal Society, and Sprat enshrined it in his 1667 *History*. In a long section on 'Their manner of Discourse', he is eloquent in his criticism of 'fine speaking', as can be seen in the quotations from his work given earlier in this book. This is often seen as being in reaction against the florid rhetorical style of the period, and the use of so-called 'inkhorn terms' – neologisms, usually of Latin derivation – although the height of the inkhorn controversy had been in the previous century (Barber 1997; Knowles 1979). However, it is also possible that it is partly motivated by a rejection of other movements, such as alchemy and the Paracelsians, whose writings were deliberately obscure, so that their interpretation was possible only for the initiated.

> What he [Bacon] did notice and identify as his third kind of defective philosophy, calling it fantastic learning, was its loosely associated underworld of believers in magic, alchemy, astrology, in the importance and availability of practical, and not simply contemplative, knowledge of nature. The most important and representative of these occult nature-philosophers was Paracelsus ... (Quinton 1980: 15)

It is my suggestion, therefore, that the consciousness of the members of the Royal Society that they were creating a new style of writing for the new science and their insistence on clear and simple language are contributing factors in limiting the number of nominalized forms that they used.

Where the two journals use nominalized processes, the most common process type is material in both. However, the rate is much higher in the *Philosophical Transactions*, where 64% of the nominalized processes are material, than in the *Journal des Sçavans*, where they account for 48%. The details can be found in Table 89.

Thus the interest of the readers of the *Philosophical Transactions* in physical phenomena and events, and in human action to investigate them, is reflected in the rate of nominalized processes used. Though one might say that this interest is present in the *Journal des Sçavans* too, since material process is still the most frequent type, it is evidently much less so than

Table 89. Types of nominalized process.

	Journal des Sçavans	*Philosophical Transactions*
Material	48%	64%
Mental	24%	18%
Relational	2%	3%
Verbal	26%	14%
Existential	*	*

Table 90. Types of nominalized mental process.

	Journal des Sçavans	*Philosophical Transactions*
Cognitive	83%	71%
Perception	11%	26%
Affective	7%	2%

in the *Philosophical Transactions.* Natural phenomena on earth and in the heavens, experiments, medical treatment, are all found nominalized in the pages of both journals, but much more frequently so in the pages of the English periodical.

In the *Journal des Sçavans,* verbal process is the second most common type of nominalized process, followed by mental process, accounting for 26% and 24% respectively; in the *Philosophical Transactions* this order is reversed, with mental process accounting for 18% and verbal, 14%. Thus, the interest of the French periodical and its readers in questions of communication is reflected in the relatively high rate of nominalized verbal processes, which account for 26%, compared with 14% in the *Philosophical Transactions.* The rate of mental processes is also higher in the *Journal des Sçavans,* though the difference is rather less. In this case, it is interesting to note the distribution of different types of mental process. This is done in Table 90.

While it is evident that the vast majority of nominalized mental processes are of the cognitive type in both journals, 83% in the *Journal des Sçavans,* and 71% in the *Philosophical Transactions,* it is interesting to note that nominalizations of the perception type are much more common in the English journal, where they account for 26%, than in the French, with 11%. This shows the importance of observation in the English periodical, which in itself goes hand in hand with the importance of physical events. If one wishes to study physical phenomena, then naturally they have to be observed. Thus it is possible to see the whole empirical programme as encapsulated in the orientation of these nominalized processes.

The two remaining process types are fairly incidental since both are rare in nominalized form in both of the journals. This is due to the fact that neither of these types lends itself easily to nominalization, particularly existential process, of which there are only seven occurrences in each of the journals. Nominalized relational processes are fractionally more common, and to the extent that they do occur, roughly half of those in the *Journal des Sçavans* are attributive, while this is the case for about two-thirds in the *Philosophical Transactions.* This is shown in Table 91. Nevertheless, it must be noted that the numbers involved are quite small: 30, in the case of the *Journal des Sçavans,* and 39 in the case of the *Philosophical Transactions.*

Table 91. Types of nominalized relational process.

	Journal des Sçavans	*Philosophical Transactions*
Attributive	53%	64%
Identifying	–	–
Possessive	47%	36%

9 Winding up and winding down: by way of conclusion

We have seen that the first two academic periodicals grew out of very different social and historical situations. In France, the monolithic French monarchy, dominated by Louis XIV and his minister Colbert, wanted to control everything, and in this context, Colbert arranged for Denis de Sallo to start the *Journal des Sçavans*. In England, the Restoration had brought hope of stability after decades of chaos. In the scientific field the Royal Society reflected this hope, and one of its secretaries, Henry Oldenburg, decided to use his voluminous postbag as the basis of a newsletter, the *Philosophical Transactions*, which he could sell to increase his meagre income. The differing contexts which brought them into being engendered journals which were different in genre and scope. The desire of the French state to control new thought meant that it looked at the place where new thought appeared, and that was, of course, in books. Hence, in terms of genre, the *Journal des Sçavans* is basically a periodical of book reviews, which make up 79% of its content. By comparison, book reviews make up only 22% of the content of the *Philosophical Transactions*, where Oldenburg's position at the centre of a network of correspondence meant that letters were more important; and, indeed, letters and letter extracts make up 34% of its contents, and much of the rest of the content was also compiled from what he received in the post. In terms of scope, nothing was, in principle, excluded from the *Journal des Sçavans*, so that theology made up 17% of the items included, and history 13%; 58% of the items can be attributed to the humanities in general, and 33% to the sciences. For Oldenburg, on the other hand, his potential readership was interested in the new science, so scientific subjects account for at least 94% of the items in his journal, with astronomy and medicine accounting for 16% each. Thus these two journals are excellent examples of the way in which discourse is engendered by the social and historical situation in which it arises.

The features studied in this book have shown that in many ways the two journals are fairly similar, and many of these minor differences have been discussed and possible explanations suggested. But there are also a number of significant differences between them, which can be attributed to the different editorial decisions taken by de Sallo and Oldenburg, and ultimately to the social and historical situations in France and England.

In terms of thematic structure, we have seen that the grammatical functions of themes display only minor differences. In the *Journal des Sçavans* subject themes account for 73% of themes and adjunct themes for 22%, of which 52% are clausal, whereas in the *Philosophical Transactions* 62% of themes are subject, and 31% are adjuncts, of which 46% are clausal. Similarly, in the *Journal des Sçavans* 29% of the ranking clauses have a textual theme and 3% have an interpersonal theme, while in the *Philosophical Transactions* 37% have a textual theme and 7% an interpersonal theme. In terms of thematic progression, in the *Journal des Sçavans*, 30% of the clauses have a constant link, and 41% a linear link; the corresponding figures for the *Philosophical Transactions* are 29% and 43%.

It is in the area of the semantic categories into which the themes fall that we find a major difference between the two periodicals. In the *Journal des Sçavans*, the commonest category is that of humans other than the author, which accounts for 37% of the themes, of which 41% refer to the writer of the book being reviewed; the object of study accounts for 22%, and texts other than the *Journal des Sçavans* itself account for 16%, of which 77% refer to the book being reviewed. In the *Philosophical Transactions*, however, the object of study is by far the most common type of theme, accounting for 45%; the author and other humans come far behind, with 14% and 13% respectively. This shows that the thematic interest in the *Journal des Sçavans* is related to the fact that de Sallo took the editorial decision to give such a prominent place to book reviews. Hence the fact that books under review and their authors play such an important role in the thematic structure of the text. The dominant thematic interest in the *Philosophical Transactions* is in the object of study, and this is related to Oldenburg's decision to restrict his scope to scientific matters. Science deals with physical objects and physical phenomena, and this is reflected in the fact that by far the commonest type of theme is the object of study type.

Further differences are brought out by looking at the process types of finite verbs. Although the two journals have virtually the same percentage of relational processes (31% in the *Journal des Sçavans*, of which 60% are attributive, and 30% in the *Philosophical Transactions*, of which 75% are attributive), this is the commonest category in the *Journal des Sçavans*, but not in the *Philosophical Transactions*, where material processes account for 35%. This shows that while both journals have a strong interest in the description of the world, the *Philosophical Transactions* has an even greater interest in physical events and actions. This, like the object of study as dominant theme, is related to the scientific stance of the *Philosophical Transactions*, where the interest is in natural phenomena and man's intervention in nature. A further difference is shown by the relatively small category of mental process, which accounts for 15% of the *Journal des Sçavans*, and 19% in the *Philosophical Transactions*. The major difference is in the incidence of perception mental processes, which account for 29% of mental processes in the *Philosophical Transactions*, but only 9% in the *Journal des Sçavans*. This shows that observation, as a means of studying natural phenomena, is of much greater importance in the *Philosophical Transactions*.

Since English and French function differently, the grammatical resources used to express modality are not directly comparable. However, the types of modality can be compared, and it is found that the majority of modal expressions are of the dynamic type in both periodicals. However, this is much more so in the *Philosophical Transactions*, where 76% of modal expressions are dynamic, than in the *Journal des Sçavans*, where they account for 58%. Thus, once again, interest in the physical world is stronger in the *Philosophical Transactions* than in the *Journal des Sçavans*. Furthermore, the incidence of deontic modality, while fairly low in both journals, is nevertheless much higher in the *Journal des Sçavans*, where it accounts for 18% of modal expressions, than in the *Philosophical Transactions*, where it accounts for only 4%. This greater interest in moral matters can probably be related to the scope of the *Journal des Sçavans*, which includes theology and law, as opposed to the *Philosophical Transactions*, which is restricted to scientific subjects where moral issues are much less likely to occur.

The use of nominalized processes is slightly more prevalent in the *Journal des Sçavans* (24 per 1000 words) than in the *Philosophical Transactions* (20 per 1000 words). Of the nominalizations used, the majority in both journals are nominalizations of material processes. However, this majority is much larger in the *Philosophical Transactions*, where it accounts for 64% of the nominalizations, than in the *Journal des Sçavans*, where it accounts for only 48%. The second largest grouping in the *Journal des Sçavans* is that of verbal processes, which account for 26% of nominalizations, whereas verbal processes are only the third largest type in the *Philosophical Transactions*, accounting for a mere 14% of the nominalizations. The second largest group in the *Philosophical Transactions* is that of mental processes, which account for 18% of the nominalizations. Mental processes are only the third largest group in the *Journal des Sçavans*, but with a higher percentage rate than that in the *Philosophical Transactions*, 24%. Thus the strong interest of the

Philosophical Transactions in matters of a physical nature is borne out by this feature too; and while the *Journal des Sçavans* might be said to have an interest, albeit much lower, in physical matters, it is characterized by a relatively strong interest in communication.

So all of the features that have been looked at in this book bring out aspects of the texts that can be related to the editorial decisions of Denis de Sallo and Henry Oldenburg. Those decisions themselves were determined by the situations in which these two editors found themselves, with Denis de Sallo cooperating in a system of state control, under the absolute monarchy of Louis XIV, in a totally stable country which was the economic and cultural centre of Europe, and Henry Oldenburg, as secretary of the Royal Society, trying to make ends meet in the new-found hope of the English Restoration after decades of chaos. This does not mean that things could not have been otherwise: I am not preaching for some sort of determinism. But it does imply that texts arise out of a particular context, and that context plays an important role in the way the texts are formed and the linguistic features they display. Hence, there is a direct and important link between a text and its context, and these early issues of the *Journal des Sçavans* and the *Philosophical Transactions* are a prime example of that principle in action.

The period we have looked at starts in 1665 with the creation of the two journals. It ends with the close of the century. This is not an arbitrary cut-off point. As we have seen, the Académie Royale des Sciences published only in limited luxurious editions.

> ... the early publications of the Académie were not aimed at members of the republic of letters (who could rarely get hold of them). Instead, they were large and elegant folios, often lavishly illustrated, printed by the Imprimerie Royale 'en grand papier', aimed at celebrating Louis's glory in the eyes of other princes. (Baglioli 1996: 222)

Moreover, the work of the Académie was conceived of as collegiate, and consequently there was no recognition of individual contributions. Everything was seen as the work of the group as a whole. As a result, those who wished to preserve their priority and individual reputation went elsewhere, notably to the *Journal des Sçavans*, or to book publication.

> ... en ne les publiant pas, l'Académie a cherché à se poser durant plus de vingt ans comme le lieu clos d'où un savoir produit en commun par les philosophes les plus éminents de leur temps dérive une autorité sans limite au sens où toute circulation de l'épreuve sous forme de texts ou de démonstrations publiques n'ajouterait aucun surcoût de persuasion et de valeur à l'épreuve expérimentale. (Licoppe 1996: 84)

> [… in not publishing them, the Académie had, for more than twenty years, attempted to position itself as the private place where knowledge produced collegially by the most eminent philosophers of their time acquired limitless authority, in the sense that any dissemination of the proof in the form of texts or public demonstrations would add nothing to the persuasive power and value of the experimental proof.]

The first cracks in this edifice began to appear in 1688, when, in an attempt to deal with the problem, it was decided that anyone who wished to publish material developed within the Académie should submit his text to the Académie for examination before publication (Hahn 1971). However, the real break came in 1699, when, in the context of a total reorganization of the Académie Royale des Sciences, the old publishing policy was abandoned in favour of a periodical publication with acknowledged named authors. The first issue of the new publication, the *Histoire de l'Académie Royale des Sciences, avec les Mémoires de Mathématique et de Physique*, actually appeared in 1702. From the beginning of the eighteenth century the *Journal des Sçavans* had a serious rival, and since the new publication was specifically scientific, it can in many ways be thought of as much closer in spirit to the *Philosophical Transactions*. Thus, the end of the seventeenth century is something of a watershed. From that point on, the situation is essentially different. The period 1665 to 1700 provides a rather unusual window; during that period, although there were many other short-lived journals, the *Journal des Sçavans* and the *Philosophical Transactions* were the only two major outlets for academic articles in vernacular languages. It is this peculiar situation which is the *raison d'être* for this book. Before 1665, there was no such thing as an academic periodical; from the beginning of the eighteenth century we have a radically new situation. It would be reasonable to suppose that the new publication brought out by the Académie Royale des Sciences would be somewhat closer to the *Philosophical Transactions* than the *Journal des Sçavans* had been up till then, but only further study and analysis will show to what extent that it true.

Appendix 1: Estimated number of words

Journal des Sçavans word count

1665	12 janvier	2,438
	26 janvier	3,502
	9 février	3,233
	23 février	2,970
	9 mars	2,888
	Total for year	15,031
1675	14 janvier	2,808
	11 mars	3,284
	6 mai	1,760
	1 juillet	2,956
	9 septembre	3,277
	Total for year	14,085
1685	15 janvier	3,335
	5 mars	1,858
	16 avril	2,714
	4 juin	3,034
	30 juillet	4,608
	Total for year	15,549

1695	3 janvier	3,849
	21 février	4,416
	25 avril	4,474
	20 juin	4,481
	8 août	4,562
	Total for year	21,782

Total for *Journal des Sçavans* corpus: 66,447

Philosophical Transactions word count

1665	3 April	5,636
	5 June	10,453
	4 December	4,506
	Total for year	20,595
1675	22 February	5,711
	26 July	6,026
	22 November	12,140
	Total for year	23,877
1685	23 March	3,731
	22 August	11,842
	Total for year	15,573
1694	March/April	4,992
	July/August	12,258
	Total for year	17,250

Total for *Philosophical Transactions* corpus: 77,295

Total corpus: 143,742 words

Appendix 2: *Journal des Sçavans* corpus

1665

12 janvier 1665

Article title	*Category*	*Subject matter*
DECRETUM SACRÆ INDICIS CONgregationis, quo damnati, prohibiti, ac respectiové suspensi fuerunt infrascripti omnes libri. Romæ, 17. Nouembris 1664.	Book review	Law
SERVATI LVPI, PRESBYTERI ET ABBATIS Ferreriensis opera. Parisiis, Par Baluzium. 8.	Book review	History
CEREBRI ANATOME : CVI ACCESSIT neruorum descriptio & vsus. Studio Thomæ Willis, in Academia Oxoniensi Philosophiæ naturalis Professoris. Londini.	Book review	Medicine
ABREGÉ DES VIES DES POETES GRECS, par M. le Febure, in 12. A Saumur.	Book review	Classics
MEMOIRES DE M. DE CHIVERNY, Chancelier de France. A Paris, in 12.	Book review	History
ARREST RENDV. A LA GRANDE CHAMBRE l'vnzième iour de Decembre 1664.	Legal report	Law

26 janvier 1665

VETERUM ALIQVOT SCRIPTORVM Spicilegium. Tom. VI. Opera Domini Luce Dascheri, Monarchi Benedictini. In 4.	Book review	History
BREVIS ET ENVCLEATA EXPOSITIO in Institutionum Instiniani libros quatuor : Authore Altesera, Antecessore Tolosano. Tolosæ. In 4.	Book review	History
IOCONDE, OV L'INFIDELITÊ DES femmes. Nouvelle, par M. de la Fontaine. A Paris. In 12.	Book review	Literature
DE LA COMETE	Scientific report	Astronomy

9 février 1665

LA PERPETVITÉ DE LA FOY DE l'Eglise Catholique, touchant l'Eucharistie, &c. A Paris. In 12.	Book review	Theology
RENATI RAPINI SOCIETATIS IESV, Hortorum libri quatuor, ex Typographia Regia. Parisiis. In 4.	Book review	Literature
ÆGIDII MENAGII, IVRIS CIVILIS Amœnitates. Parisiis. In 8.	Book review	Law
ANALECTA INAVGVRALIA, SEV diceptationes Medicæ Doctoris Ioannis Rogersij, Londini. In 8.	Book review	Medicine
RELATION DE MADRID, OV Remarques sur les mœurs de ses Habitans. A Cologne. In 12.	Book review	Sociology
RESPONSE DES ESTATS GENERAUX des Provinces Vnies des Pays bas, aux plaintes du Roy de la grande Bretagne. A la Haye. In 4. En langue Flamande & Françoise.	Book review	Law
ELOGE DE MONSIEVR DE FERMAT, Conseiller au Parlement de Toulouse.	Obituary notice	Mathematics

23 février 1665

LIBRO DE LA CONCEPTION VIRGINAL, compuesto por Raimundo Lulio, y traducido en Espagnol por don Alonso Zepeda. En Brussellas. In 8. *En Latin, & en Espagnol è regione. Il se trouve chez S. Piget, ruë S. Iaques.*	Book review	Theology
INTRODUCTION A L'HISTOIRE PAR la connoissance des Medailles, par Charles Patin. A Paris chez Iean du Bray & Pierre Varriquet, ruë S. Iaques. In 12.	Book review	Numismatics
VOYAGES D'ESPAGNE. A PARIS. In 4. *Chez Sercy, au Palais ; & in* 12. *Chez L. Billaine, au Palais.*	Book review	Geography
PHARAMOND, HISTOIRE DE France, huitiesme volume. A Paris. In 8. *Chez Sommauille, au Palais.*	Book review	History
EXTRAIT DE DEVX LETTRES. L'VNE escrite de Londres, & l'autre de la Haye, touchant l'usage des Pendules, pour trouuer les longitudes sur la mer.	Letter extracts	Physics

9 mars 1665

CODEX REGVLARVM, QVAS SANCTI Patres Monachis a Virginibus Sanctimonialibus præscripsere. Collectus olim à S. Benedicto Anianiensi Abbate. Lucas Holstenius, Vaticanæ Bibliothecæ Præfectus editit. A Paris, chez L. Billaine, au Palais.	Book review	Law
IOSEPHI LAVRENTII LVCENSIS, AMALthea onomastica. Luguni: & se trouue à Paris chez Fred. Leonard, & au Palais chez L. Billaine.	Book review	Language
CONTRADICIONES APPARENTES Sacræ scripturæ. Collectæ à P. Dominica Magrio Melitensi, Conreg. Orator. In 12. A Paris, Chez Soly, ruë S. Iaques.	Book review	Theology
DIVERS PLAIDOYEZ TOVCHANT LA CAVSE du gueux de Vernon, & autres sujets. A Paris chez Louis Billaine, au Palais.	Book review	Law
REFLEXIONS, OV SENTENCES ET Maximes Morales. A Paris, Chez O. Barbin, au Palais.	Book review	Philosophy
LA VIE DE LA SAINTE VIERGE MARIE, mere de Dieu. Par le sieur de Grandual. A Paris chez Pierre Promé, ruë de la vieille Bouclerie.	Book review	Theology
LETTRE D'VN AMY DE MONSIEVR Patin, sur le Iournal des Sçauans du 23 Fevrier 1665. *A Paris chez Variquet, ruë S. Iaques.*	Book review	Numismatics

1675

14 janvier 1675

APOLOGIA PRO S. ECCLESIÆ PATRIBVS adversus Joan. Dallæum de usu Patrum, auctore Mat. Scrivenero Presbytero. Londini Et se trouve à Paris chez F. Muguet.	Book review	Theology
LA VIE DE S. THOMAS ARCHEVESQVE DE Cantorbery & martyr. A Paris chez P. le Petit.	Book review	Biography
MVNDVS MATHEMATICVS R. P. CLAVDII Milliet Deschales Cambriensis è Sociatate Iesu. Lugduni. Et se trouve à Paris chez Sebastien Mabre-Cramoisy.	Book review	Mathematics
HARANGVES PRONONCEES DANS l'Academie Françoise. A Paris chez Pierre le Petit.	Book review	Literature

11 mars 1675

ΚΑΛΛΙΜΑΚΟΥ ΚΥΡΗΝΑΙΟΥ ΥΜΝΟΙ ΕΠΙΓΡΑΜ, ΚΑΙ ΑΛΛΑ ΑΤΤΑ. *Callimahi Cyrenæi Hymni Epigrammata & Fragmenta. In* 4. A Paris chez Sebastien Mabre-Cramoisy.	Book review	Classics
DISCOVRS PHYSIQVE SVR LES Influences des Astres. In 12. A Paris chez Jean Baptiste Coignard, ruë Saint Iacques.	Book review	Astronomy
CANONICVS SECVLARIS ET REGVLARIS. In 8. A Paris chez Jean Couterot, ruë S. Jacques.	Book review	Theology
HISTOIRE SACREÉ EN TABLEAVX avec leur explication tirèe de l'Ecriture.	Book review	Theology
NOVVELLES EXPERIENCES TIRÉES DV Iournal d'Angleterre.	Article extract	Chemistry

6 mai 1675

S. MAXIMI CONFESSORIS GRÆCORVM Theologi eximiique Philosophi opera. 2 tom. In fol. A Paris chez André Cramoisy, ruë de la Bouclerie.	Book review	Theology
LA RHETORIQVE D'ARISTOTE EN François. Traduction nouvelle. In 12. A Paris chez Denis Thierry, ruë S. Jacques.	Book review	Classics
COURS DE CHYMIE, OV L'ON EXPLIQVE par les principes des Philosophes modernes les operations qui sont en usage dans la medecine. Par Nicolas Lemery. A Paris chez l'Auteur, ruë Galande à la porte dorée.	Book review	Medicine
GVILL. DONDINI SOC. IESV. HISTORIA de rebus in Gallia gestis ab Alexandro Farnesio Parmæ & Placentiæ Duce III. Supremo Belgii Præfecto. In fol. Romæ. Et se trouve à Paris chez Seb. Marbre-Cramoisy, ruë S. Jacques.	Book review	History
LES ASCETIQVES OV TRAITTEZ Spirituels de S. Basile le Grand Archevêque de Cesarée en Cappadoce. In 8. A Paris, chez Jean du Puis, ruë S. Jacques.	Book review	Theology
EXTRAIT DV IOVRNAL D'ANGLETERRE contenant un extrait d'un mémoire de Paulus Biornonus qui est en Islande, où il répond à quelques questions qu'on luy avoit faites touchant cette Isle.	Article extract	Geography

1 juillet 1675

LIBRI DE IMITATIONE CHRISTI IOANNI Gerseni Abbati Ordinis S. Benedicti iterato adserti editio secunda. In 8. A Paris chez Loüis Billaine au Palais.	Book review	Bibliography
DV BASTIMENT ET DE LA CONDVITE DES VAISSEAUX, ou l'Architecture navale, par N. Vvitsen Hollandois. In fol. A Amsterdam.	Book review	Technology
LE SISTEME DV MONDE SELON LES trois hypotheses, où l'on explique suivant les loix de la Mechanique les apparences des astres la fabrication du Monde &c. In 12. A Paris, chez Guillaume Desprez.	Book review	Astronomy
HISTOIRE ROMAINE ECRITE PAR Herodien traduite du Grec en François par M. de Boisguilbert. In 12. A Paris, chez Guillaume de Luyne, au Palais.	Book review	History
EXTRAIT DV IOVRNAL D'ANGLETERRE, contenant quelques remarques faites & communiquées par Mr. Gregoire, touchant quelques Lacs & quelques Rivieres.	Article extract	Geography

9 septembre 1675

HISTOIRE DE L'ANCIEN TESTAMENT tirée de l'Ecriture Sainte par Mr. Arnauld d'Andilly. In 4. A Paris chez Pierre le Petit, ruë saint Jacques.	Book review	Theology
ELOGE DE MONSIEVR ARNAVD d'Andilly.	Obituary notice	Biography
RECHERCHES DE L'ORIGINE ET DV mouvement du sang, du cœur, & de ses vaisseaux, du lait, des fièvres intermittentes & des humeurs. In 12. A Paris chez Jean Couterot ruë S. Jacques.	Book review	Medicine
HISTORIA ET ANTIQVITATES Vniversitatis Oxoniensis. In fol. 2 vol. Oxonii è Theatro Sheldoniano. Et se trouve à Paris chez Olivier de Varennes, au Palais.	Book review	History
ARCHIMEDIS OPERA METHODO nova illustrata & succincte demonstrata per Isa. Barrow. Londini. Et se trouvent à Paris chez Sebastien Mabre-Cramoisy, ruë S. Jacques.	Book review	Mathematics

ABREGÉ POVR LES ARBRES NAINS ET autres, contenant tout ce qui les regarde. In 12. A Paris chez Charles de Sercy, au Palais.	Book review	Agriculture
EXTRAIT DV TRAITÉ DE LA restauration des métaux & des mines composé en Anglois par Mr. Boyle.	Book summary	Technology
	Editorial note	Editorial

1685

15 janvier 1685

PAULI G. F. P. N. MERULÆ J. C. DUM VIVE*ret in Acad. Ludg. Bat. Histor. Prof. &c. Opera varia Posthuma, juxta Autographum edita. in 4. Lugd. Bat.* 1684.	Book review	General
LES LETTRES DE S. AUGUSTIN TRA*duites en François sur l'Edition nouvelle des PP. Benedictins de la Congr. De S. Maur, où elles sont rangées selon l'ordre des temps, reveuës & corrigées sur les anciens Mss. & Augmentées de quelques Lettres, avec des Notes &c. in* 8. à Paris ches J. B. Coignard. 1684	Book review	Theology
RELATION HISTORIQUE DU *Royaume de Siam. Par le Sieur de l'Isle Geographe. in* 12. A Paris chez G. de Luynes. 1684.	Book review	History
A VIEU OF UNIVERSAL HISTORY FROM *the Creation to the year of Christ 1680. Vuherein the most memorable persons and Things in the Knouun and contries in several Columns. London.* 1684.	Book review	History
NOVARUM DISSERTATIONUM, *de morbis abstrusioribus Tractatus I. de Febribus intermittentibus &c. aut. I. Iones D. M. Hagæ Com.* & se trouve à Paris chez la V. BiestKins 1684.	Book review	Medicine
LES DIFFERENS CARACTERES DE *l'Amour. In* 12. A Paris chez Cl. Blageart. 1685/	Book review	Philosophy
EXTRAIT DU JOURNAL D'ALLEMAGNE OU EPHE*merides des Curieux de la nature, contenant quelques observations singulières.*	Article extract	Medicine
NOUVEAUTEZ DE LA HUITAINE, tant pour les Artts que pour les Sciences.	List	General

5 mars 1685

LES DIX LIVRES D'ARCHITECTURE *de Vitruve corrigez & traduites nouvellement en François, avec des Notes & des figures. 2. Edition, reveuë, corrigée & augmentée. Par M. Perrault de l'Acad. R. des Sciences, D. en Med. de la Faculté de Paris. Fol.* à Paris chez J. B. Coignard 1684.	Book review	Architecture
MEDULLA CHYMIÆ VARIIS EXPERI*mentis auctæ, multisque* Fig. *illustrata. Aut I. V. Vigani Veronensi. In 8. Lond.* & se trouve à Paris, chez la V. BiestKins.	Book review	Chemistry
LA CONCORDE DES EPITRES DE S. *Paul & des autres Apostres. in* 12. A Paris chez André Pralard. 1685.	Book review	Theology
HISTORIA VENETA DI ALESSANDRO *Maria Vianoli Nob. Ven. Venetiis.* 1684.	Book review	History
EXPERIENCE DE LA VERTU SINGU*liere du Vin rouge, pour guerir la retention d'urine, avec quelques observations sur le Qinquina, &c. in* 12. *A Londres.* Et se trouve à Paris chez Jean Cusson. 1684.	Book review	Medicine
NOVORUM BIBLIORUM POLYGLOTTO*rum Synopsis. Vltrajecti.* 1684.	Book review	Theology
OBSERVATION DE L'ECLIPSE DE LUNE *faite à l'Observatoire Royal, le* 21. *Decembre* 1684.	Article	Astronomy

16 avril 1685

COMMENTARII HISTORICI DUO *bactenus inediti, alter de Regibus veustis Norvagicis, alter de profestione Danorum in terram Sanctam circa annum 1185. Susceptam &c. cura olim & opera Cl. Ioh. Kirchmanni Lubec. Ex. Ms. Bibliothecaæ Lubecensis protracti, nunc primum editi ab hujus Nap. Bernh. Casp. Kirchmanno* J. U. D. *Amstel.* Et se trouve à Paris chez la V. BiestKins 1684.	Book review	History

NOUVEAUX ELEMENS D'HYDRO*graphie, où par une methode courte & aisée l'on peut apprendre de soy-mesme tout ce qui est necessaire pour entreprendre & achever une heureuse Navigation. Par P. Cauvete Prof. d'Hydrographie. in* 12. A Dieppe, & se trouve à Paris chez l'Auteur ; 1685.	Book review	Technology
P. PETITI PHIL ET DOCT. M. DE AMA*zonibus Dissertatio, quâ an averè extiterint necne variis ultro citroque conjecturis & argumentis disputatur &c. in* 12. A Paris chez And. Cramoisy. 1685.	Book review	History
LA GENIE DE LA LANGUE FRANCOISE, *par le Sr. D...* à Paris chez L. DHoury. 1685.	Book review	Language
HERM. WITSII ÆGYPTIACA, &c. SIVE *de Ægyptiacorum sacrorum cum Hebraicis collatione libri* 3. *De decem Tribubus Israëlis liber singularis : accessit Diatribe Legione fulminatrice Christianorum. in* 4. *Amstel.* 1684.	Book review	Theology
EXTRAIT DES NOUV. DE LA REP. DES LETTRES *concernant un fait singulier, d'un homme qui a esté quarante jours sans manger.*	Article extract	Medicine
NOUVEAUTEZ DE LA HUITAINE.	List	General

4 juin 1685

FUSTENBERGIANA LIB. IV. TRES POE*matum variorum de Ferd. Furstenbergio Episc. Ac Princ. Monast & Paderb. Aut. Leonardo Frison S.* J. *Quartus epistolas ipsius Principis Autorisque ad Principem complexus. &c. in* 12. Burdigalæ. Et se trouve à Paris chez G. DeLuynes. 1684.	Book review	Classics
TRACTATUS DE PODAGRA ET HYDRO*pe per Thom. Sydenham M. D. in* 8. *Lond.* Et se trouve à Paris chez la V. Biestkins.	Book review	Medicine
RESPONSE DE M. L'EVESQUE DE TOUR*nai aux Reflexions de M. I. M. D. L. D. V. sur les Memoires de ce Prelat touchant la Religion. in* 12 à Paris chez Cl. Barbin. 1685.	Book review	Theology

NOUVEAU CALENDRIER POUR PLU*sieurs années, avec son explication.* à Paris chez P. Sevin Ingenieur ordinaire du Roy pour les Instrumens de Mathematique. 1685.	Book review	Mathematics
LUCII CÆLII LACTANTII FIRMIANI OPEra *quæ extant ad fidem Mss. Recognita & commentariis illustrata à Th Spark A. M. ex æda Christi. in* 8. *Oxonii.* Et se trouvent à Paris à la Bibliothèque du Roy. 1684.	Book review	Theology
TABLES DES SINUS TANGENTES ET SECANTES ET *des Logarithmes &c. avec un traité de Trigonometrie par de nouvelles demonstrations &c. par M. Ozanam P. de Math. in* 8. à Paris chez Estienne Michalet. 1685.	Book review	Mathematics
EXTRAIT DU JOURNAL D'ANGLETERRE. SUITE DE *la relation des Volcans ou eruptions des feux soûterrains, arrivez dans les Isles Canaries, l'an* 1677.	Article extract	Geology
NOUVEAUTEZ DE LA HUITAINE. Tant pour les Arts que pour les Sciences.	List	General

30 juillet 1685

DISSERTATION SVR LA CONFORMITÉ DE l'œil. par Mr. De la Hire, Lecteur & Prof. R. en Math. De l'Acad. Des Sciences, envoyée à l'Auteur du Iournal. 1685.	Article	Physiology
AMBROSII AD ORIGENEM EPISTOLA, DE novis Bibliorum Poliglottorum Editionibus Vltrajecti 1684.	Letter extract	Theology
APHORISMES D'HIPPOCRATE TRADUITS *en françois. Avec explications Physiques & des Annotations curieuses.* 2. *vol. in* 12. à Paris chez Est. Michalet. 1685.	Book review	Medicine
S. ATHANASII ARCHIP. ALEX. SYN*tagma doctrinæ ad Clericos & Laicos : Valentiniani & Marciani Impp.* Epist. *duæ ad Meonem M. Theod. Abducaræ Tractatus de unione & Incarnatione.* Edente *And. Arnoldo Norimberg.* in 8. à Paris chez la V. Martin & I. Boudot. 1685.	Book review	Theology
TRAITÉ DE L'ARTILLERIE PAR M. CA*therinot.* 1685	Book review	Technology

EXTRAIT DU JOURNAL D'ANGLETERRE *contenãt quelque chose de fort singulier touchãt deux enfãs qui ont la teste transparẽte, communiqué par M. Samuel Giltber fleuriste*	Article extract	Medicine
NOUVEAUTEZ DE LA HUITAINE.	List	General

1695

3 janvier 1695

MEMOIRES POUR SERVIR A *L'HISTOIRE Ecclesiastique des six premiers siecles, justifies par les citations des Auteurs Originaux ; avec une Chronologie, &c. Tome Second. Par le Sieur D.T. In 4. à* Paris chez Ch. Robustel. 1694.	Book review	History
FUNDAMENTUM THEOLOGIÆ MORALIS *id est de recto usu opinionum probilium, in quo ostenditur, ut quis licite possit sequi opinionem probabilem faventem liberati adversus legem, omnino necessarium esse & sufficere quod post diligentem veritatis inquisitionem, ex sincero desiderio non offendendi Deum susceptam, opinio illa ipsi appareat, attenta ratione & authoritate, vel unice verisimilis, vel manifeste verisimilior quam opposita, stans pro lege adversus libertatem, ac idcirce ab ipso judicetur vera judicio absoluto, firmo & non fluctuante. Authore R. P. Thyro Gonzalez, Theologiæ Professore Salmaticensi, nunc Præposito Generali Societatis Jesu. In 4. Lugduni.* Et se trouve à Paris chez Antoine Dezallier. 1694.	Book review	Theology

21 février 1695

FRANCISCI JUNII F. F. DE PICTURA VETERUM *libri tres, tot in locis emendati, & tam multis accessionibus aucti, ut plane novi possint videri. Accedit catalogus adhuc ineditus Architectorum, Mechanicorum, sed præcipue Pictorum, Statuarium, Cælatorum, Tornatorum, aliorumque Artificum, & operum quæ fecerunt, secondum seriem litterarum digestus. In Folio. Roterodami.* & se trouve à Paris chez Jean Anisson. 1694.	Book review	Art

REQUESTE IMPORTANTE POUR LES MEDECINS *de la Chambre Royale contre les Medecins de la Faculté de Paris, sur la declaration de Sa majesté du 3. Mai 1694. Surprise au prèjudice de l'Ordonnance de Blois, & des Statuts mesmes de la Faculté. In folio.* à Paris chez Laurent d'Houry, ruë saint Jaques. 1694.	Book review	Law
VOYAGES HISTORIQUES DE L'EUROPE. TOME *quatriéme, qui comprend tous ce qu'il y a de plus curieux dans les Royaumes d'Angleterre, d'Irlande & d'Ecosse. In 12.* à Paris chez Nicolas le Gras, au troisième pilier de la Grand-sale du Palais. 1694.	Book review	Geography
ORIGINES HUNGARIÆ SEU LIBER QUO VERA *nationis Hungaricæ origo & antiquitas e veteram monumentis & linguis præcipuis panduntur. Labore & studio Francisci Foris Otrokoesii. In 8. Franequeræ.* 1693.	Book review	History
EXTRAIT D'UNE LETRE ECRITE DE FLORENCE *le 19. Novembre dernier.*	Letter extract	General
MENAGIANA, OU LES BONS MOTS, LES PEN*sees critiques, historiques, morales, & d'érudition de M. Menage, recueillies par ses amis. Tome second. In 12.* à Paris chez Florentin & Pierre de Laulne. 1694.	Book review	General

25 avril 1695

REMARQUES ET EXPERIENCES PHYSIQUES SUR *la construction d'une nouvelle Clepsidre, sur les Barometres, Termometres, & Higrometres. Par M. Amontons. In 12.* à Paris chez Jean Jombert, prés des Augustins. 1695.	Book review	Technology
LA GEOGRAPHIE ANCIENNE, MODERNE ET *historique. Tome Troisiéme, qui contient l'Allemagne. In 4.* à Paris chez la Veuve de Jean Bapt. Coignard. 1694.	Book review	Geography

MEMOIRE PRESENTÉ AU ROY AU MOI DE Janvier M. DC. XCV. *par Messire Charles Maurice Le Tellier Archevèque Duc de Reims, premier Pair de France, Legat né du saint Siege Apostolique, Primat de la Gaule Belgique, Commandeur de l'Ordre du saint Esprit, & Maistre de la Chapelle de sa Majesté, &c. Contre l'érection de l'Eglise de Cambray en Archevèché. In 4.* à Paris chez Jean Anisson, ruë saint Jaques. 1695.	Book review	Law
EURIPIDIS QUÆ EXTANT OMNIA : TRA*gœdiæ nempe XX. Præter ultimam omnes completæ : item Fragmenta aliatum plusquam LX. Tragœdiarum, & Epistole V. nunc primùm & ipsæ huc adjectæ : Scholia demum doctorum virorum in septem priores Tragœdias, ex diversis antiquis exemplaribus undequaque collecta, & concinnata ab Arsenio Monembasiæ Archiepiscopo. Præmittitur Euripidis Vita ex variis Antoribus accuratius descriptà : etiam tractatus de Tragœdia Veterum Græcorum, &c. In folio. Cantabridiæ.* Et se trouve à Paris chez Jean Anisson, ruë saint Jaques. 1694.	Book review	Classics
SERMONS DE L'OCTAVE DU S. SACREMENT ET *des Misteres de l'Ascension, de la Pentecôte & de la Trinité, prononcez en l'Eglise de saint Sulpice par le R. P. Dom Dominique de la Motte Barnabite. In 8.* à Paris chez Jean Couterot, ruë saint Jaques. 1695.	Book review	Theology

20 juin 1695

BIBLIOTHECA LATINO-HEBRAICA, SIVE DE *Scriptoribus Latinis qui ex diversis nationibus contra Judeos, vel de re Hebraïca, utcunque scripsere : additis observationibus criticis & philologico-historicis, quibus quæ circa patriam, æternem, vitæ institutum, mortemque Auctorum consideranda veniunt, exponuntur. Cum quadruplici indice, nominum, cognominum, heterodoxorum, & materium. Loco Coronidis adventus Messiæ ad Judæorum blasphemiis ac Hæreticorum calumniis vindicates, sacrarum Scripturarum, sanctorum Patrum, conciliorum, Rabbinorumque suffragiis obsignatus, &c. Auctore & vindice D. Carolo Josepho Imbonato Mediolanensi, Cong. S. bern. Ord. Cist. Monacho, &c. In fol. Romæ.* & se trouve à Paris chez Jean Anisson. 1695.	Book review	Bibliography
LETTRE D'UN DOCTEUR DE SORBONNE A UN *Benedictin de la Congregation de Saint Maur, touchant le Pecule des Religieux faits Curez ou Evèques. In 12.* à Paris chez Frederic Leonard, ruë saint Jaques. 1695.	Book review	Law
EXTRAIT D'UNE LETRE DE M. PANTHOT ME*decin du Roi, Doyen de College de Medecine de Lion.*	Letter extract	Medicine

8 août 1695

RELATION DE LA VIE ET DE LA MORT DE *Frere Palemon Religieux de l'Abbaye de la Trappe, nommé dans le monde le Comte de Santena. In 12.* à Paris chez Elie Josset, ruë saint Jaques. 1695.	Book review	Biography
LE SAUT DU VERMISSEAU QUI S'ENGENDRE *sur le fromage. Par François Poupart.*	Book review	Biology
L'HISTOIRE DU CARDINAL MAZARIN. PAR M. *Aubery Avocat au Parlement & aux Conseils du Roy. In 12. 2. vol.* à Paris chez Thomas Moëtte, rue de la Vieille Bouclerie. 1695.	Book review	Biography

FASCICULUS SECUNDUS OPUSCULORUM QUÆ *ad Historiam & Philologiam sacram spectant, &c. In 8. Roterdami.* Et se trouve à Paris chez Jean Anisson, ruë saint Jaques. 1695	Book review	General
LIVRES NOUVELLEMENT IMPRIMEZ	List	General

Appendix 3 : *Philosophical Transactions* corpus

1665

3 April 1665

Article title	*Category*	*Subject matter*
Extract of a Letter, lately written from Rome, *touching the late Comet, and a New one.*	Letter extract	Astronomy
Extract of a letter, written from Paris, *containing some Reflections on part of the precedent* Roman *Letter.*	Letter extract	Astronomy
An Observation imparted to the Noble Mr. Boyle, *by Mr.* David Thomas, *touching some particulars further considerable in the* Monster *mentioned in the first papers of these* Philosophical Transactions.	Letter extract	Biology
Extract of a Letter, lately written from Venice *by the Learned Doctor* Walter Pope, *to the Reverend Dean of* Rippon, *Doctor* John Wilkins, *concerning the Mines of Mercury in* Friuli; *and a way of producing* Wind *by the fall of* Water.	Letter extract	Technology
An Extract of a letter, containing some Observations, made in the ordering of Silk-worms, *communicated by that known* Vertuoso, *Mr,* Dudley Palmer, *from the ingenuous Mr.* Edward Digges.	Letter extract	Biology
An Account of Micrographia, *or the* Physiological Descriptions *of* Minute Bodies, *made by* Magnifying Glasses.	Book review	General

5 June 1665

A Relation of some extraordinary Tydes in the West-Isles of Scotland, *as it was communicated by Sr.* Robert Moray.	Article	Physics
Monsieur Auzout's *Judgement touching the Apertures of* Object-Glasses, *and their* Proportions, *in respect of the several* Lengths *of* Telescopes.	Book extract	Technology
Considerations of Monsieur Auzout *upon Mr.* Hook's New Instrument for grinding of Optick-Glasses.	Book extract	Technology
Mr. Hook's *Answer to Monsieur* Auzout's *Considerations, in a letter to the Publisher of these* Transactions.	Letter	Technology
Of a means to illuminate an Object in what proportion one pleaseth; and of the Distances requisite to burn Bodies by the Sun.	Book extract	Physics
A further Account, touching Signor Campani's *Book and Performances about* Optick-glasses.	Book extract	Astronomy
Signor Campani's *Answer: and Monsieur* Auzout's *Animadversions thereon.*	Book extract	Astronomy
An Account of Mr. Richard Lower's *newly published* Vindication *of Doctor* Willis's Diatriba *de* Febribus.	Book review	Medicine
A Note touching a Relation, inserted in the last Transactions.	Editorial	Biology

4 December 1665

Of Monsieur de Sons *progress in working* Parabolar *Glasses.*	News item	Technology
Monsieur Auzout's *Speculations of the Changes, likely to be discovered in the* Earth *and* Moon, *by their respective Inhabitants.*	Letter extract	Astronomy
The Instance of the same Person *to Mr.* Hook, *for communicating his Contrivance of making, with a Glass of a Sphere of* 20 *or* 40 *foot* diameter, *a* Telescope *drawing several hundred foot; and his offer of recompensing that Secret with another, teaching To measure with a* Telescope *the* Distances of Objects *upon the* Earth.	Letter extract	Technology

An Experiment of a way of preparing Liquor, that shall sink into, and colour the whole body of Marble, *causing a* Picture, *drawn on a surface, to appear also in the* inmost *parts of the Stone.*	Book extract	Technology
An Intimation of a Way, found in Europe *to make* China-dishes.	News item	Technology
An Account of an odd Spring *in* Westphalia, *together with an Information touching* Salt-Springs *and the straining of salt-water.*	Letter extract	Physics
An Account of the Rise and Attempts, of a Way to conveigh Liquors immediately into the Mass of Blood.	Book review	Medicine

1675

12 February 1675

An Account of what hath been observed here in London *and* Derby, *by Mr.* Hook, *Mr.* Flamsteed, *and others, concerning the late* Eclipse *of the* Moon, *of* Jan. 1. 167$^{4}/_{5}$	Article	Astronomy
An Account of the Observations of the same Eclipse as they were made at Paris; *communicated by the Learn'd* Bulialdus *in his Letter to the Publisher, dated* Febr. 6. 1675. st. n.	Letter extract	Astronomy
An Accompt of D. Paulus Biornonius, *residing in* Iceland, *given to some Philosophical Inquiries concerning that Country, formerly recommended to him from hence: The Narrative being in Latin, 'tis thus English't by the Publisher.*	Article	Geography
Divers Rural and Oeconomical Inquiries, recommended to Observation and Tryal.	List	Agriculture
An Extract of a Letter of Dr. *J. Wallis*, to M. *Hevelius*, from *Oxford*, December 31. 1673. Gratuatory for his *Organigraphia*; and particularly concerning *Divisions by Diagonals*, lately inserted in Mr *Hooks* Animadversions on the first part of the *Machina Cælestis* of the Honourable *Job. Hevelius*; but so faultily there printed, that it was thought fit, at the Authors desire, in his Letter to the Publisher, of *Januar*.4. 167$^{4}/_{5}$. To be here done more correctly.	Letter extract [Latin]	Mathematics

An Accompt of some Books. I. *Some Physico-Theological Considerations about the* Possibility *of the* Resurrection; *by the Honourable* Robert Boyle *Esq; Fellow of the* R. Society. London, 1674/5. *in* 8°.	Book review	Physics
II. *Waare Oeffening der PLANTEN, door* Abraham Munting, *M.D. and Prof. Botanices at* Groningen. *Printed at* Amsterd. 1672, *in* 4°.	Book review	Agriculture
III. *The Prevention of Poverty, shewing the Causes of the decay of Trade, Fall of Lands, and Want of Money: With Expedients for remedying the same, and bringing the Kingdom to an eminent degree of Riches and Prosperity. By* Rich. Haynes, *London*, 1674. in 8°.	Book review	Economics

26 July 1675

An extract of a Letter, written by a Friend to the Publisher out of the Country, July 24. 1675; *relating to the Contents of the* Tract *next foregoing.*	Letter extract	General
A way of making all sorts of Plants, Trees, Fruits, Flowers, and Legums, *grow to an extraordinary bigness, communicated in the* Journal des Scavans, *as it was taken out of the small Tract, entituled,* Instruction facile pour connoitre toutes sortes d'*Orangers & Citronniers: Here inserted for Experiment.*	Book extract	Agriculture
Advertisments, occasioned by the Remarks printed in Numb. 114, *upon Frosts in some parts of* Scotland, *differing in their Anniversary Seasons and Force from our ordinary Frosts in* England: *Of Black Winds and Tempests: Of the warm or fertilizing Temperature and Steams of the surface of the Earth, Stones, Rocks, Springs, Waters, (some in, some places, more than in other places;) Of petrifying and Metallizing Waters: With some hints for the Horticulture of* Scotland: *By the Reverend and Learned* Dr/ J. Beal, *F.R.S.; who by way of Letter imparted them to the Publisher.*	Letter	Physics

Mr. Flamsteads *Letter of* July 24. 1675. *to the Publisher, relating to another, printed in* Numb. 110. *of these Tracts, concerning M.* Horroxes *Lunar Systeme.*	Letter	Astronomy
Lunæ totaliter deficientis observationes, *Londini in* Arce Londiniensi habitæ, idque in ædibus & cum instrumentis *Jonæ More* Equ. Aurati, à *Johanne Flamsteadio*, Astr. Regio, Nocte sequente d. Junii 26. 1675. St. vet.	Article [Latin]	Astronomy
An Accompt of a Book. The Planters Manual: *Being* Instructions *for the* Raising, Planting *and* Cultivating *all sorts of* Fruit-Trees; *whether* Stone-fruits, *or* Pepin-fruits, *with* their Natures *and* Seasons; *very* useful *for such as are* curious *in* Planting *and* Grafting. *By* Charles Cotton *Esquire, in* 8°, *London.* 1675.	Book review	Agriculture

22 November 1675

Some Experiments made in the Air-pump *by Monsieur* Papin, *directed by Monsieur* Hugens, (*as appeared in the Discourse printed at* Paris, 1674.)	Article	Physics
A particular account, given by an anonymous French *Author in his book of the* Origin of Fountains, *printed* 1674 *at* Paris; *to shew, that the Rain and Snow-waters are sufficient to make Fountains and Rivers run perpetually.*	Book summary	Geology
A Letter of the Ingeneous Mr. Jessop *of* Broomha *in* York-shire *containing a further account of Damps in Mines, presented in* Numb.117. *of these Tracts*	Letter	Geology
An Account of some Books. I. *A Philosophical Discourse of EARTH, relating to the Improvement of it for Vegetation and the Propagation of Plants: By* J. Evelyn *Esq; Fellow of the R. Society*. London, *printed for* J. Martyn, *Printer to the said Society.* A.1676, *in octavo.*	Book review	Agriculture

II. *A Description of the Islands and Inhabitants of* Feroë, *&c. written in* Danish *by* Lucas Jacobson Debes *M.A. and provost of the churches there: Englished by* J.S. *Doct. of Phys. in* 12°.	Book review	Geography
III. *The Gentleman's Recreation in four Parts; viz.* Hunting, Hawking, Fowling, Fishing. *Collected from Ancient and modern authors, Forreign and Domestick, and rectified by the Experience of the most skilful Artists of these times.* London, *in octavo,* 1674.	Book review	Biology

1685

23 March 1685

A remarkable account of an Hydrophobia, *in a letter from Dr* Roger Howman, *Physician in Norwich, to* William Briggs *M. D.* Fellow *of the* Coll. *of Phys.* Lond. *and Physician of St.* Tho. Hospitall.	Letter	Medicine
An extract of a Letter from Senior Ciampini, *to Dr.* Croon, *concerning a late* Comet *seen at* Rome.	Letter extract [Latin]	Astronomy
Some Observations on Boyling Fountains, *and* Subterraneous Streams: *by Dr.* Tancred Robinson, Fellow *of the* R.S.	Article	Geology
Of the weight of a cubic foot of divers grains, &c. try'd in a vessel of wel season'd Oak, whose concave was an exact cubic foot. By the direction of the Philosophicall Society *of* Oxford.	Article	Physics
A Letter from Dr. Robert Plot *of* Oxford, *to Dr.* Martin Lister F. *of the* R.S. *concerning the use which may be made of the following* History *of the* Weather, *made by him at* Oxford *through out the year* 1684.	Letter	Physics
An Abstract of a Letter from Dr Peirce *of* Bath, *to one of the* S. *of* the R.S. *giving an instance of the effects of the* Bath *in curing the* Palsy, *and* Barenness.	Letter extract	Medicine
Caroli Drelincurtii Experimenta Anatomica, *quibus adiecta sunt plurimo Curiosa super Semine Virili, Fæmineis Ovis, Uterique Tubis, atque Fætu. Lugd. Bat.* 1684, 12°.	Book review	Biology

22 August 1685

An answer to some Quæries proposed by Mr. William Molyneaux, *concerning* Lough-Neagh: *by* Mr. Edward Smyth, Fellow *of* Trinity College *in* Dublin.	Article	Geology
Historiæ Convulsionum Periodicarum *per clariss.* D[num] Gui. Cole, *Med. Doct. Descriptæ, & communicatæ.*	Article (Latin)	Medicine
Historia Convulsivi Affectus *octonariam periodum à multis annis observantis, per Clariss.* D[num]. Gui. Cole, *M. D. descripta & communicata.*	Article (Latin)	Medicine
An Abstract of a Letter of Mr. Leeuwenhoeck *Fellow of the* R. Society, *dated March 30th*. 1685. *to the* R. S. *Concerning* Generation *by an* Insect.	Letter extract	Biology
A Discourse on the Dissection *of a* Monstrous Double Catt; *read before the* Dublin Society *by* Dr. Mullen.	Paper	Biology
MICHAELIS ETTMULLERI *opera omnia Theoretica & practica, &c. Quarto* Londini 1683.	Book review	Medicine
RAYMUNDI VIEUSSENS *D. M.* Monspeliensis *Neurographia Universalis. Fol. Lugduni* 1685.	Book review	Medicine

1694

March/April 1694

I. *A LETTER from* Hans Sloane, *M.D. and S.R.S with several Accounts of the Earthquakes in* Peru October *the* 20*th*. 1687. *And at* Jamaica, February 19*th*. 168$^7/_8$ *and* June *the* 7*th*.1692.	Letter	Geology
An Extract of a Letter of Father Alvarez de Toledo *a* Franciscan *Friar, Dated* 29 Oct. 1687. *from* Lima, *giving some Particulars of an Earthquake which happened there the* 20th *of that Month.*	Letter extract	Geology
II. *Concerning the Distance of the fixed Stars. By the Honourable* Francis Roberts, *Esq; S.R.S.*	Article	Astronomy
III. *An Account of a Stone of a Prodigious size extracted by Section out of a Woman's Bladder, now living, on the Eighth day of* November, 1693. *by Mr.* Basil Wood, *Surgeon.*	Article	Medicine

IV. *Dr.* Molineaux's *Historical Account of the late General Coughs and Colds; with some observations on other Epidemick Distempers.*	Article	Medicine
V. *Of a Stone found in the Gall-Bladder of a Woman. By Mr.* J.T.	Article	Medicine
An Account of BOOKS. I. *Tractatus Mathematicus de Figurarum Curvilinearum Quadraturis & Locis Geometricis. Autore* Johanne Craig. Londini *apud* Sam. Smith & Benj. Walford, *Soc. Regiæ Typographos.*	Book review	Mathematics
II. *The History of the* Church *of* Malabar, *from the time of its being Discovered by the* Portuguezes *in the Year* 1501. *Giving an Account of the Persecutions and violent Methods of the* Roman *Prelates to reduce them to the Subjection of the Church of* Rome, *together with the* Synod *of* Diamper, *celebrated* Anno 1599. *With some remarks upon the* Faith *and* Doctrine *of the Christians of St.* Thomas *in the* Indies, *agreeing with the* Church *of* England, *in Opposition to that of* Rome: *Done out of* Portuguez *into* English *by* Michael Geddes, *Chancellor of the Cathedral Church of* Sarum. Lond. *Printed for* S. Smith *and* B. Walford. *In octavo.* 1694.	Book review	History

July/August 1694

I. *An Account of the* Giants Causway *in the North of* Ireland: *By the Reverend Dr.* Sam. Foley.	Article	Geology
Some Notes upon the foregoing Account of the Giants Causway, *serving to further Illustrate the same. By* T. Molyneaux, *M.D.S.R.S.*	Article	Geology
II. *An Account of the Evaporation of Water, as it was Experimented in* Gresham Colledge *in the Year* 1693. *With some observations thereon. By* Edm. Halley.	Article	Physics
III. *A Letter from Sir* Dudley Cullum, *to* John Evelin, *Esq; concerning the lately invented Stove for preserving Plants in the Green House in Winter, published at the end of the* Calendarium Hortense.	Letter	Technology

References

Adamczewski, Henri (1996). *Génèse et développement d'une théorie linguistique suivi de Les dix composantes de la grammaire métaopérationnelle de l'anglais.* Perros-Guirec: La TILV.

Adamczewski, Henri (2002). *The Secret Architecture of English Grammar.* Précy-sur-Oise: EMA.

Adamczewski, Henri and Claude Delmas (1982). *Grammaire linguistique de l'anglais.* Paris: Armand Colin.

Alonso-Aleida, Francisco (2012). 'An analysis of hedging in eighteenth century English astronomy texts', in Isabel Moskowich and Begoña Crespo (eds), *Astronomy 'Playne and Simple': The Writing of Science Between 1700 and 1900.* Amsterdam: John Benjamins, pp. 199–220.

Ashley, Maurice (1964). *Life in Stuart England.* London: B. T. Batsford; New York: G. P. Putnam's Sons.

Atkinson, Dwight (1999). *Scientific Discourse in Sociohistorical Context: The* Philosophical Transactions *of the Royal Society of London, 1675–1975.* Mahwah, NJ: Lawrence Erlbaum Associates.

Avramov, Iordan (1999). 'An apprenticeship in scientific communication: the early correspondence of Henry Oldenburg (1656–63)', *Notes and Records of the Royal Society of London*, 53:2, 187–201.

Bacon, Francis (1905). *The Philosophical Works of Francis Bacon*, ed. John M. Robertson. London: George Routledge and Sons.

Banks, David (1994a). *Writ in Water: Aspects of the Scientific Journal Article.* Brest: ERLA, Université de Bretagne Occidentale.

Banks, David (1994b). 'Hedges and how to trim them', in M. Brekke, Ø. Andersen, T. Dahl and J. Myking (eds), *Applications and Implications of Current LSP Research*, Vol. 2. Bergen: Fagbokforlaget, pp. 587–92.

Banks, David (2001). 'The reification of scientific process: the development of grammatical metaphor in scientific discourse', in Felix Mayer (ed.), *Language for Special Purposes: Perspectives for the New Millennium*, Vol. 2. Tübingen: Gunter Narr, pp. 555–63.

Banks, David (2002). 'Systemic Functional Linguistics and the *théories de l'énonciation*: *Face à face* or *tête à tête* ?', *Anglophonia*, 12, 171–82.

Banks, David (2003). 'The evolution of grammatical metaphor in scientific writing', in Anne-Marie Simon-Vandenbergen, Miriam Taverniers and Louise Ravelli (eds),

Grammatical Metaphor: Views from Systemic Functional Linguistics. Amsterdam: John Benjamins, pp. 127–47.

Banks, David (2004). 'Anglophone systemicists and French enunciativists: shall the twain never meet?' *Language Sciences*, 26, 391–410.

Banks, David (2005). *Introduction à la linguistique systémique fonctionnelle de l'anglais*. Paris: L'Harmattan.

Banks, David (2008a). *The Development of Scientific Writing: Linguistic Features and Historical Context*. London: Equinox.

Banks, David (2008b). 'The significance of thematic structure in the scientific journal article, 1700–1980', in Nina Nørgard (ed.), *Systemic Functional Linguistics in Use*. Odense Working Papers in Language and Communications, no. 29. <http://www.sdu.dk/~/media/Files/Om_SDU/Instittuter/ISK/Forkningspublikationer/OWPLC/Nr29/David%>

Banks, David (2008c). 'Some implications of thematic structure in the scientific journal article, 1700–1980', *RANAM, Recherches Anglaises et Nord Américaines*, 41, 9–23.

Banks, David (2009a). 'Starting science in the vernacular: Notes on some early issues of the Philosophical Transactions and the Journal des Sçavans, 1665–1700', *ASp, la revue du GERAS*, 55, 5–22.

Banks, David (2009b). 'Creating a specialized discourse: the case of the *Philosophical Transactions*', *ASp, la revue du GERAS*, 56, 29–44.

Banks, David (2010a). 'Transitivity and thematic structure in some early issues of the *Philosophical Transactions*', *ASp, la revue du GERAS*, 58, 57–71.

Banks, David (2010b). 'The beginnings of vernacular scientific discourse: genres and linguistic features in some early issues of the *Journal des Sçavans* and the *Philosophical Transactions*', *E-rea*, 8:1. <http://erea.reviews.org/1334>

Banks, David (2011). 'The place of diachronic studies in LSP', *Moderne Sprachen*, 55:2, 177–89.

Banks, David (2012a). 'The implications of genre related choices in early issues of the *Journal des Sçavans* and the *Philosophical Transactions*', in Stephania M. Maci and Michele Sala (eds), *Genre Variation in Academic Communication: Emerging Disciplinary Trends*. Bergamo: CELSB Libreria Universitaria, pp. 85–104. <http://dinamico.unibg.it/cerlis/page.aspx?p=259>

Banks, David (2012b). 'Thematic structure in eighteenth century astronomical texts: A study of a small sample of articles from the *Corpus of English Texts on Astronomy*', in Isabel Moskowich and Begoña Crespo (eds): *Astronomy 'Playne and Simple': The Writing of Science Between 1700 and 1900*. Amsterdam: John Benjamins, pp. 221–38.

Banks, David (2012c). 'Diachronic ESP: at the interface of linguistics and cultural studies', *ASp, la revue du GERAS*, 61, 55–70.

Banks, David (2013a). 'Les formes et fonctions de la modalité dans le *Journal des Sçavans* et les *Philosophical Transactions* à la fin du 17ème siècle', in David Banks (ed.), *La Modalité, le mode et le texte spécialisé*. Paris: L'Harmattan, pp. 17–32.

Banks, David (2013b). 'The use of grammatical metaphor in French political tracts', in Gerard O'Grady, Tom Bartlett and Lise Fontaine (eds), *Choice in Language: Applications in Text Analysis.* Sheffield: Equinox, pp. 111–24.

Banks, David (2013c). 'Les origins épistolaires de l'article scientifique', in David Banks, (ed.), *Le Texte épistolaire du XVIIe siècle à nos jours: Aspects linguistiques.* Paris : L'Harmattan, pp. 37–51.

Banks, David (2015). 'Thematic structure and progression in some late seventeenth century French texts', in Sonja Starc, Carys Jones and Arianna Maiorani (eds), *Meaning Making in Text: Multimodal and Multilingual Functional Perspectives.* Sheffield: Equinox, pp. 7–30.

Banks, David (2016). 'On the (non)necessity of the hybrid category Behavioural process', in Donna R. Miller and Paul Bayley (eds), *Hybridity in Systemic Functional Linguistics: Grammar, Text and Discursive Context.* Sheffield: Equinox, pp. 21–40.

Barber, C. L.(1962). 'Some measurable characteristics of modern scientific prose', in F. Behre (ed.), *Contributions to English Syntax and Philology.* Stockholm: Almqvist and Wiksell, pp. 21–43.

Barber, Charles (1997). *Early Modern English.* Edinburgh: Edinburgh University Press. (First published in 1976.)

Barnes, Sherman B. (1936). 'The editing of early learned journals', *Osiris*, 1, 155–72.

Bazerman, Charles (1988). *Shaping Written Knowledge: The Genre and Activity of the Experimental Article in Science.* Madison: University of Wisconsin Press.

Biagioli, Mario (1996). 'Etiquette, interdependence, and sociability in seventeenth century science', *Critical Inquiry*, 22:2, 193–238.

Biber, Douglas, Stig Johansson, Geoffrey Leach, Susan Conrad and Edward Finegan (1999). *Longman Grammar of Spoken and Written English.* Harlow: Pearson Education.

Birn, Raymond (1965). 'Le Journal des Savants sous l'ancien régime', *Journal des Savants*, janvier–mars, 15–35.

Bluhm, R. K. (1958). 'Remarks on the Royal Society's finances 1660–1768', *Notes and Records of the Royal Society of London*, 13:2, 82–103.

Bluhm, R. K. (1960). 'Henry Oldenburg, F.R.S. (c.1615–1677)', in Harold Hartley (ed.), *The Royal Society: Its Origins and Founders.* London: The Royal Society, pp. 47–56.

Boyle, Robert (2003 [1661]). *The Sceptical Chymist.* Mineola, NY: Dover.

Brading, Katherine (2012). 'Newton's law-constitutive approach to bodies: a response to Descartes', in Andrew Janiak and Eric Schliesser (eds). *Interpreting Newton: Critical Essays.* Cambridge: Cambridge University Press.

Butler, Christopher S. (2003a). *Structure and Function: A Guide to Three Major Structural-Functional Theories. Part 1. Approaches to the Simplex Clause.* Amsterdam: John Benjamins.

Butler, Christopher S. (2003b). *Structure and Function. A Guide to Three Major Structural-Functional Theories. Part 2. From Clause to Discourse and Beyond.* Amsterdam: John Benjamins.

Caffarel, Alice (2006). *A Systemic Functional Grammar of French: From Grammar to Discourse.* London: Continuum.

Camusat, Denis François (2011 [1734]). *Histoire critique des journaux.* Charleston, SC: Nabu Press [facsimile of 1734 edition].

Chomsky, Noam (1957). *Syntactic Structures.* The Hague: Mouton.

Chomsky, Noam (1965). *Aspects of the Theory of Syntax.* Cambridge, MA: M.I.T. Press.

Clark, George (1956). *The Later Stuarts 1660–1714*, 2nd edn. Oxford: Oxford University Press.

Coates, Jennifer (1983). *The Semantics of the Modal Auxiliaries.* London: Croom Helm.

Cocheris, Hippolyte (1860). *Histoire du Journal des Savants depuis sa foundation jusqu'à nos jours*. Paris: A. Durand.

Crosland, Maurice (2005). 'Relationships between the Royal Society and the Académie des Sciences in the late eighteenth century', *Notes and Records of the Royal Society*, 59:1, 25–34.

Culioli, Antoine (1990). *Pour une linguistique de l'énonciation. Tome 1. Opérations et représentations.* Gap : Ophrys.

Culioli, Antoine (1999a). *Pour une linguistique de l'énonciation. Tome 2. Formalisation et opérations de repérage.* Gap: Ophrys.

Culioli, Antoine (1999b). *Pour une linguistique de l'énonciation. Tome 3. Domaine notionnel.* Gap : Ophrys.

Daremberg, Charles (1859). 'Journal des Savans (1665–1859)', *Journal des Débats Politiques et Littéraires*, 20 avril 1859, p. 23.

Dear, Peter (1985). '*Totius in Verbum*: rhetoric and authority in the early Royal Society', *Isis*, 76, 1245–61.

Dear, Peter (2005). 'What is the History of Science the history of? Early modern roots of the ideology of modern science', *Isis*, 96:3, 390–406.

Debus, Allen G. (1970). *Science and Education in the Seventeenth Century: The Webster-Ward Debate.* London: Macdonald.

Dupuy, Micheline (1994). *Henriette de France, Reine d'Angleterre.* Paris : Perrin.

Eggins, Suzanne (1994). *An Introduction to Systemic Functional Linguistics.* London: Pinter.

Evelyn, John (1906). *The Diary of John Evelyn*, ed. Austin Dobson, Vol. 2. London: Macmillan and Co.

Fara, Patricia (2002). *Newton: The Making of Genius.* London: Picador.

Farrington, Benjamin (1951). *Francis Bacon: Philosopher of Industrial Science.* London: Lawrence and Wishart. (First published 1949.)

Firbas, Jan (1992). *Functional Sentence Perspective in Written and Spoken Communication.* Cambridge: Cambridge University Press.

Foucault, Michel (1969). *L'Archéologie du savoir.* Paris: Gallimard.

Gascoigne, Robert Mortimer (1985). *A Historical Catalogue of Scientific Periodicals, 1665–1900: With a Survey of Their Development.* New York: Garland.

Gignoux, C.-J. (1941). *Monsieur Colbert*. Paris: Bernard Grasset.

Gotti, Maurizio (1996). *Robert Boyle and the Language of Science*. Milano: Guerini.

Gotti, Maurizio (2006). 'Disseminating early modern science: specialized news discourse in the *Philosophical Transactions*', in Nicholas Brownlees (ed.), *News Discourse in Early Modern Britain*. Bern: Peter Lang, pp. 41–70.

Gribbin, John (2005). *The Fellowship: The Story of a Revolution*. London: Allen Lane.

Gross, Alan G. (1996). *The Rhetoric of Science*, 2nd edn. Cambridge, MA: Havard University Press.

Gross, Alan G., Joseph E. Harman and Michael Reidy (2002). *Communicating Science: The Scientific Article from the 17th Century to the Present*. Oxford: Oxford University Press.

Hahn, Roger (1971). *The Anatomy of a Scientific Institution: The Paris Academy of Sciences, 1666–1803*. Berkeley: University of California Press.

Hall, A. Rupert (1962). *The Scientific Revolution 1500–1800. The Formation of the Modern Scientific Attitude*. 2nd edn. Boston: Beacon Press.

Hall, Marie Boas (1975). 'The Royal Society's role in the diffusion of information in the seventeenth century (1)', *Notes and Records of the Royal Society of London*, 29:2, 173–92.

Hall, Marie Boas (1994). *The Scientific Renaissance 1450–1630*, New York, Dover. (First published 1962.)

Hall, Marie Boas (2002). *Henry Oldenburg: Shaping the Royal Society*. Oxford: Oxford University Press.

Halliday, M. A. K. (1978). *Language as Social Semiotic: The Social Interpretation of Language Meaning*. London: Arnold.

Halliday, M. A. K. (1988). 'On the language of physical science', in M. Ghadessy (ed.), *Registers of Written English: Situational Factors and Linguistic Features*. London: Pinter, pp. 162–78. [Reprinted in Halliday and Martin (1993), pp. 54–68; and Halliday (2004), pp. 140–58.]

Halliday, M. A. K.(1994). 'The construction of knowledge and value in the grammar of scientific discourse, with reference to Charles Darwin's *The Origin of Species*', in Malcolm Coulthard (ed.), *Advances in Written Text Analysis*. London: Routledge, pp. 136–56. [Reprinted in Halliday and Martin (1993), pp. 86–105.]

Halliday, M. A. K. (1998). 'Things and relations: Regrammaticising experience as technical knowledge', in J. R. Martin and Robert Veel (eds), *Reading Science: Critical and Functional Perspectives on Discourses of Science*. London: Routledge, pp. 185–235. [Reprinted in Halliday (2004), pp. 49–101.]

Halliday, M. A. K. (ed. Jonathan Webster) (2004). *The Language of Science*. London: Continuum.

Halliday, M. A. K. (revised by Christian M. I. M. Matthiessen) (2014). *Halliday's Introduction to Functional Grammar*, 4th edn. London: Routledge.

Halliday, M. A. K. and J. R. Martin (1993). *Writing Science: Literacy and Discursive Power*. London: Falmer Press.

Halliday, M. A. K and Christian M. I. M. Matthiessen (1999). *Construing Experience through Meaning: A Language-based Approach to Cognition*. London: Cassell.

Henry, John (2002a). *The Scientific Revolution and the Origins of Modern Science*, 2nd edn. Basingstoke: Palgrave.

Henry, John (2002b). *Knowledge Is Power: Francis Bacon and the Method of Science*. Cambridge: Icon Books.

Hill, Christopher (1969). *The Century of Revolution 1603–1714*. London: Sphere Books. (First published 1961.)

Hirschfield, John Milton (1981). *The Académie Royale des Sciences, 1666–1683*. New York: Arno Press.

Huddleston, Rodney D. (1971). *The Sentence in Written English: A Syntactic Study Based on an Analysis of Scientific Texts*. Cambridge: Cambridge University Press.

Hunter, Michael (1982). *The Royal Society and Its Fellows 1660–1700: The Morphology of an Early Scientific Institution*. Chalfont St Giles: The British Society for the History of Science.

Hunter, Michael (2009). *Boyle: Between God and Science*. New Haven: Yale University Press.

Hyland, Ken (1998). *Hedging in Scientific Research Articles*. Amsterdam: Benjamins.

Johns, Adrian (2000). 'Miscellaneous methods: authors, societies and journals in early modern England', *British Journal for the History of Science*, 33:2, 159–86.

Jones, Richard Foster (1982). *Ancient and Moderns: A Study of the Rise of the Scientific Movement in Seventeenth Century England*. New York: Dover. (First published 1961.)

Kishlansky, Mark (1996). *A Monarchy Transformed: Britain 1603–1714*: London: Penguin.

Knowles, Gerry (1979). *A Cultural History of the English Language*. London: Arnold.

Kronick, David A. (1962). *A History of Scientific and Technical Periodicals: The Origins and Development of the Scientific and Technological Press 1665–1790*. New York: Scarecrow Press.

Kronick, David A. (1990). 'Notes on the printing history of the early *Philosophical Transactions*', *Libraries and Culture*, 25:2, 243–68.

Kronick, David A. (1991). *Scientific and Technical Periodicals of the Seventeenth and Eighteenth Centuries: A Guide*. Metuchen, NJ: Scarecrow Press.

Larreya, Paul (1984). *Le Possible et le nécessaire: Modalités et auxiliaries modaux en anglais britannique*. Paris: Nathan.

Le Ru, Véronique (2005). *Voltaire newtonien: Le combat d'un philosophe pour la science*. Paris : Vuibert/ADAPT.

Licoppe, Christian (1994). 'The crystallization of a new narrative form in experimental reports (1660–1690). The experimental evidence as a transaction between philosophical knowledge and aristocratic power', *Science in Context*, 7:2, 205–44.

Licoppe, Christian (1996). *La Formation de la pratique scientifique: Le discours de l'expérience en France et en Angleterre (1630–1820)*. Paris: La Découverte.

Longnon, Jean (1965). 'Le troisième centenaire du Journal des Savants', *Journal des Savants*, janvier–mars, 7–14.

Lyons, Henry (1944). *The Royal Society 1660–1940: A History of Its Administration under Its Charters*. Cambridge: Cambridge University Press.

Martin, J. R. (1992). *English Text: System and Structure*. Amsterdam: John Benjamins.

Martin, J. R. and David Rose (2008). *Genre Relations: Mapping Culture*. London: Equinox.

Martinet, André (1985). *Syntaxe générale*. Paris: Armand Colin.

McClellan, James E., III (2001). 'The *Mémoires* of the *Académie Royale des Sciences*, 1699–1790: a statistical overview', in Robert Halleux, James McClellan, Daniela Berariu and Geneviève Xhayet (eds), *Les Publications de l'Académie Royale des Sciences de Paris (1666–1793)*, Vol. 2. Turnhout: Brepols, pp. 7–36.

McKie, Douglas (1948). 'The arrest and imprisonment of Henry Oldenburg', *Notes and Record of the Royal Society of London*, 6:1, 28–47.

McKie, Douglas (1960). 'The origins and foundation of the Royal Society of London', in Harold Hartley (ed.), *The Royal Society and Its Founders*. London: The Royal Society, pp. 1–37.

Merton, R. K. (1938). 'Science, technology and society in seventeenth century England', *Osiris*, 4, 360–32.

Moessner, Lilo (2007). 'News filtering processes in the *Philosophical Transactions*', in Andreas H. Jucker (ed.), *Early Modern English News Discourse*. Amsterdam: John Benjamins, pp. 205–21.

Morgan, Betty Trebelle (1928). *Histoire du Journal des Sçavans depuis 1665 jusqu'en 1701*. Paris: Presses Universitaires de France.

Morgan, John (2009). 'Science, England's "interest" and universal monarchy: the making of Thomas Sprat's *History of the Royal Society*', *History of Science*, 47, 27–54.

Moskowich, Isabel and Begoña Crespo (eds) (2012). *Astronomy 'Playne and Simple': The Writing of Science between 1700 and 1900*. Amsterdam: John Benjamins.

Mulligan, Lotte (1973). 'Civil war, politics, religion and the Royal Society', *Past & Present*, 59, 92–116.

Newton, Isaac (1952 [1730]). *Opticks, or a Treatise of the Reflections, Refractions, Inflections and Colours of Light*. New York: Dover.

O'Donnell, Mick, Michele Zappavigna and Casey Whitelaw (2008). 'A survey of process type classification over difficult cases', in Carys Jones and Eija Ventola (eds), *New Developments in the Study of Ideational Meaning: From Language to Multimodality*. London: Continuum, pp. 47–64.

Palmer, Frank (1974). *The English Verb*. Harlow: Longman.

Palmer, Frank (1986). *Mood and Modality*. Cambridge: Cambridge University Press.

Palmer, Frank (2003). 'Modality in English: theoretical descriptive and typological issues', in Roberta Facchinetti, Manfred Krug and Frank Palmer (eds), *Modality in Contemporary English*. Berlin: Mouton de Gruyter, pp. 1–17.

Paris, Gaston (1903). 'Le *Journal des Savants*'. *Journal des Savants*, janvier, 5–34.

Perkins, Michael R. (1983). *Modal Expressions in English*. London: Pinter.

Quinton, Anthony (1980). *Francis Bacon*. Oxford: Oxford University Press.

Ravelli, L. J. (1988). 'Grammatical metaphor: an initial analysis', in E. H. Steiner and R. Veltman (eds), *Pragmatics, Discourse and Text: Some Systemically-inspired Approaches*. London: Pinter.

Riegel, Martin, Jean-Christophe Pellat and René Rioul (2009). *Grammaire méthodique du français*, 2nd edn. Paris: Presses Universitaires de France.

Rowlett, Paul (2007). *The Syntax of French*. Cambridge: Cambridge University Press.

Salager-Meyer, Françoise (1994). 'Hedges and textual communicative function in medical English written discourse', *English for Specific Purposes*, 13:2, 149–70.

Salager-Meyer, Françoise (1995). 'I Think That Perhaps You Should': a study of hedges in scientific discourse', *Journal of TESOL-France*, 2:2, 127–44.

Salomon-Bayet, Claire (2008). *L'Institution de la science et l'expérience du vivant*, 2nd edn. Paris: Flammarion.

Savory, Theodore H. (1953). *The Language of Science: Its Growth, Character and Usage*. London: André Deutsch.

Sprat, Thomas (2003 [1667]). *History of the Royal Society of London for the Improving of Natural Knowledge*. Whitefish, MT: Kessinger (facsimile of the 1667 edition. London: J. Martyn).

Stimson, Dorothy (1968). *Amateurs and Scientists: A History of the Royal Society*. New York: Henry Schuman.

Swales, John (1985). *Episodes in ESP*. Oxford: Pergamon.

Taavitsainen, Irma and Päivi Pahta (eds). *Medical Writing in Early Modern English*. Cambridge: Cambridge University Press.

Tarone, Elaine, Sharon Dwyer, Susan Gillette and Vincent Icke (1981). 'On the use of the passive in two astrophysics journal papers', *ESP Journal*, 1:2, 121–39. [Reprinted in Swales (1985), pp. 191–205.]

Tarone, Elaine, Sharon Dwyer, Susan Gillette and Vincent Icke (1998). 'On the use of passive and active voice in astrophysics journal papers: with extensions to other languages and other fields', *English for Specific Purposes*, 17:1, 113–32.

Taverniers, Miriam (2003). 'Grammatical metaphor in SFL: a historiography of the introduction and initial study of the concept', in Anne-Marie Simon-Vandenbergen, Miriam Taverniers and Louise Ravelli (eds), *Grammatical Metaphor: Views from Systemic Functional Linguistics*. Amsterdam: John Benjamins, pp. 5–34.

Thompson, Geoff (2004). *Introducing Functional Grammar*, 2nd edn. London: Arnold.

Turner, G. W. (1972). 'The passive construction in English scientific writing', *Journal of the Australasian Universities Language and Literature Association (AUMLA)*, 18, 181–97.

Valle, Ellen (1999). 'A collective intelligence: the life sciences in the Royal Society as a scientific discourse community, 1665–1995'. Turku: Anglicana Turkuensia.

van Valin, Robert D., Jr. (2001). *An Introduction to Syntax*. Cambridge: Cambridge University Press.

Ventola, Eija (1996). 'Packing and unpacking of information in academic texts', in Eija Ventola and Anna Mauranen (eds), *Academic Writing: Intercultural and Textual Issues*. Amsterdam: John Benjamins, pp. 153–94.

Vittu, Jean-Pierre (2001). 'Qu'est-ce qu'un article au *Journal des savants* de 1665–1714?' *Revue Française d'Histoire du Livre*, 112/113, 129–48.

Vittu, Jean-Pierre (2002a). 'La formation d'une institution scientifique : le *Journal des Savants* de 1665 à 1714. Premier article: D'une entreprise privée à une semi-institution', *Journal des Savants*, janvier–juin, 179–203.

Vittu, Jean-Pierre (2002b). 'La formation d'une institution scientifique : le *Journal des Savants* de 1665 à 1714. Second article : L'instrument central de la République des Lettres', *Journal des Savants*, juillet–décembre, 347–77.

Vittu, Jean-Pierre (2005). 'Du *Journal des Savants aux Mémoires pour l'histoire des sciences et des beaux-arts*: l'esquisse d'un système européen des périodiques savants', *XVIIe siècle*, 228, 527–45.

Weber, Max (1930). *The Protestant Ethic and the Spirit of Capitalism*, trans. Talcott Parsons. London: George Allen and Unwin.

Author index

Subject index

www.ingramcontent.com/pod-product-compliance
Lightning Source LLC
LaVergne TN
LVHW010444080826
844660LV00026B/1215

* 9 7 8 1 7 8 1 7 9 8 3 0 0 *